Indigenous (In)Justice

INDIGENOUS (IN)JUSTICE

HUMAN RIGHTS LAW AND BEDOUIN ARABS
IN THE NAQAB/NEGEV

Edited by
Ahmad Amara, Ismael Abu-Saad,
and Oren Yiftachel

International Human Rights Clinic
Human Rights Program Series
Harvard Law School

DISTRIBUTED BY HARVARD UNIVERSITY PRESS

The International Human Rights Clinic at Harvard Law School's Human Rights Program publishes a "Human Rights Practice Series" of books with Harvard University Press. Books in this series are designed to further interdisciplinary scholarship and practical understanding of leading human rights issues.

International Human Rights Clinic
Human Rights Program
Harvard Law School
6 Everett Street
Third Floor
Cambridge, MA 02138
United States of America

hrp@law.harvard.edu
http://www.hup.harvard.edu

ISBN: 978-0-9796395-6-2

Library of Congress Cataloging-in-Publication Data

Indigenous (in)justice : human rights law and Bedouin Arabs in the Naqab/Negev / edited by Ahmad Amara, Ismael Abu-Saad, and Oren Yiftachel.
    p. cm.
Includes bibliographical references.
ISBN 978-0-9796395-6-2
1. Bedouins--Legal status, laws, etc.--Israel. 2. Land tenure--Law and legislation--Israel. 3. Bedouins--Israel--Negev--Economic conditions. I. Amara, Ahmad. II. Abu-Saad, Ismael, 1958- III. Yiftachel, Oren, 1956- IV. Title: Indigenous injustice.
KMK2107.M56I53 2012
342.569408'73--dc23   2012002716

Printed by Signature Book Printing, http://www.sbpbooks.com

CONTENTS

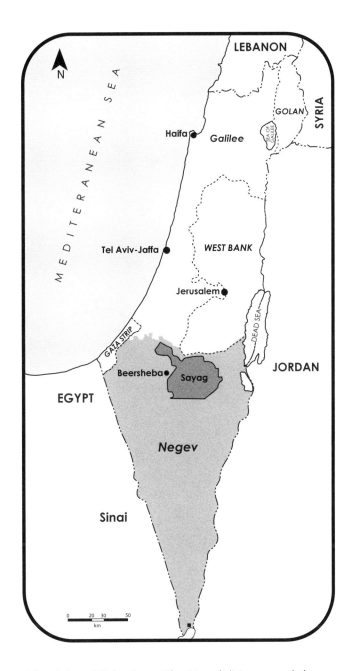

Map I: Israel Palestine – The Naqab/Negev and the
Sayag (Siyag) Area

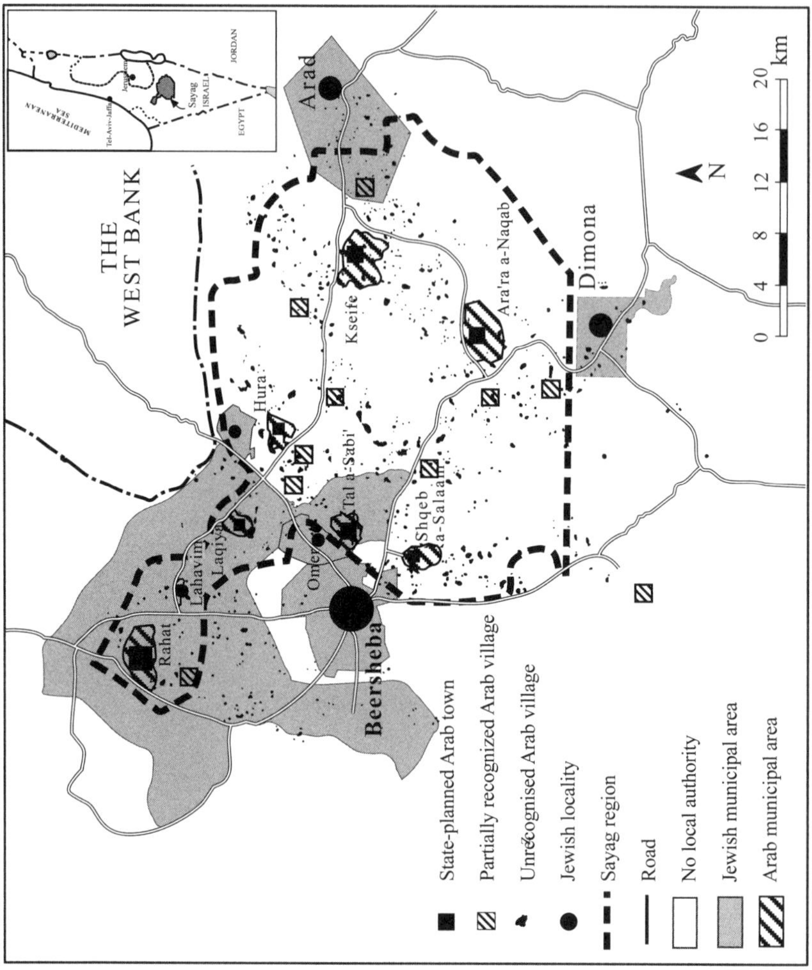
THE WEST BANK
Arad
Dimona
Beersheba
Rahat
Lahavim
Laqiya
Omer
Hura
Kseife
Tal a-Sabi'
Shqeb a-Salaam
Ara'ra a-Naqab
N
0 4 8 12 16 20 km
MEDITERRANEAN SEA
Tel-Aviv-Jaffa
Jerusalem
Sayag
ISRAEL
EGYPT
JORDAN
State-planned Arab town
Partially recognized Arab village
Unrecognised Arab village
Jewish locality
Sayag region
Road
No local authority
Jewish municipal area
Arab municipal area

Source: Based on Ministry of Interior data and aerial photograph analysis.

Map II: Bedouin Arab Settlements in the Sayag (Siyag) Area

Acknowledgments

The production of a book is always a team effort. Here, too, a number of individuals and institutions deserve special gratitude for their contributions, which helped this book see the light of day.

The students of the International Human Rights Clinic at Harvard Law School formed the backbone of this volume. *Indigenous (In)Justice* is the fruition of a project on the human rights of the Naqab (Negev) Bedouin Arabs that the Clinic started in 2007. The students did a great deal of work in this regard, including undertaking voluminous amounts of research, conducting brainstorming sessions on the Naqab and field trips to the region, and authoring various drafts. The students include Karen Botrous, Evan Engstrom, Shannon Erwin, Noga Firstenberg, Hedayat Heikal, Paul Hughes, Hebah Ismail, Maggie Morgan, Scott Paltrowitz, Sofia Panjwani, Deborah Popowski, Chris Rogers, Dinesha Samararatne, Daniel Saver, Hannah Simpson, Elizabeth Summers, Teale Toweill, Marissa Vahlsing, and Preeti Verma. Special thanks are due to Cosette Creamer and Zinaida Miller, both co-authors of chapters in the volume, for the intensive work that they did throughout the Clinic's efforts and the volume's publication process. Their efforts, comments, and ideas were invaluable.

The staff of the Regional Council for the Unrecognized Villages (RCUV) was essential in making the Clinic's field trips possible. Special thanks go to the chairpersons of the RCUV, Hussein al-Rafaya'a and Ibrahim al-Waqili; to the director, Atwa Abu-Freih; and to Yeela Livnat-Raanan, Sleiman Abu-Obayed, and Ali Abu-Sbayeh. We extend our great thanks to the residents of the unrecognized villages in the Naqab who trusted the Clinic's team and shared their stories.

This volume also benefited from discussions and ideas from a number of individuals. Tyler Giannini was particularly helpful during the fieldwork phase, as well as throughout the writing and publication processes. His insights and comments on the chapters' final drafts were invaluable to the current form of the volume. Similarly, Mindy Roseman's comments on earlier drafts of the chapters helped refine the ideas discussed. The initial ideas and suggestions of James Cavallaro, as well as his positive energy, made our work on the volume easier. Needless to say, each author bears responsibility for the content and accuracy of his or her contribution.

We are grateful to the Robert H. Arnow Center for Bedouin Studies and Development at Ben-Gurion University of the Negev, particularly the Center's director, Suleiman Abu-Bader, for providing funding for the publication of this volume. Their generous grant permitted thorough editing and layout, both essential for the book's quality.

We are also grateful to the journal *HAGAR Studies in Culture, Polity and Identities* for granting us permission to reuse some materials previously published in the journal's special issue on the Naqab Bedouins (vol. 6, no. 2, 2008).

We immensely appreciate the work of those who shepherded us throughout the publication process—most of all, our unflagging and meticulous copyeditor, Morgan Stoffregen. We also thank Catlin Rockman for doing an excellent job on the layout; Suzy Ashhab for designing the cover; Rani Mandelbaum and Roni Livnon for preparing the maps; and Mary Ann Lane of Harvard University Press and Cara Solomon, Communications Coordinator at the Harvard Human Rights Program, for shepherding the book through the process.

Last but not least, we are grateful to our families, who showed their support and understanding along the way by listening to us share our frustrations and dilemmas, and by tolerating our long working nights. To all of them, we are most thankful.

As editors, we have found this project immensely rewarding because of the insights provided by the authors. But beyond pure scholarship, we dedicate this book to the tens of thousands of indigenous Bedouins whose suffering continues in the Naqab to this very day. We therefore hope that the volume contributes to the understanding and resolution of one of the most pressing human rights issues plaguing Palestinian-Jewish relations in Israel—namely, indigenous injustice.

Ahmad Amara, Ismael Abu-Saad, and Oren Yiftachel
September 2012
New York and Beersheba

Introduction

Ismael Abu-Saad and Ahmad Amara

Then the bulldozers arrived at dawn on July 27, accompanied by more than 1,000 armed police officers carrying out a court order. They tore down about 40 unlicensed concrete-block homes, shacks and other structures and uprooted hundreds of trees. Within hours, the villagers and volunteers put up flimsy tents and a few shacks, for shelter from the scorching sun and to stake the Bedouins' claim to the land. In a test of wills, the Israelis have already been back to destroy the structures three more times.

(Kershner, 2010)

The *New York Times* reported this story about the demolition of the Palestinian Bedouin Arab village of Al-Araqib in the Naqab (Negev),[1] southern Israel, on August 25, 2010. Less than a year later, in April 2011, the village had been demolished and rebuilt 21 times. According to Israel's police spokesman, "the homes had been 'illegally built' and were destroyed in line with a court ruling issued 11 years ago" (*BBC News*, 2010). The intensity of the demolitions and the entrenched positions of the Israeli government and the Palestinian Bedouin Arabs over the village's existence made Al-Araqib a symbol of the long-standing land dispute between Naqab Bedouin Arab citizens[2] and the Israeli government. The village's frequent demolitions have brought the Bedouin land issue back into the public eye both within and beyond Israel. Yet the origins of this issue, in particular its historical background and legal aspects, are largely absent from the contemporary public and scholarly debates. In Israel, for example, the media often presents the Bedouin land issue in a manner that portrays Bedouins as lawbreakers who encroach on the state's lands (see, e.g., Kabha, 2008). Through an in-depth domestic, comparative, and international legal analysis, this edited volume explores the Naqab Bedouin Arab question and analyzes its origins within broad historical and political contexts. The "Bedouin question," in this context, is used to refer to the historical and current cultural, social, and political affairs of this community. At the center of the Bedouin question lies a prolonged dispute over land rights and a history of expulsion, displacement, land dispossession, forced urbanization, and a housing crisis of tens of Bedouin villages deemed "illegal" by the State of Israel.

Since both the British and the Israelis have developed a strong legalistic culture in Palestine, the law is an essential prism for understanding the Bedouin question and, more broadly, British and Israeli policies in Palestine.[3] Some of the laws relevant to the Bedouin question date back to 1858, thus creating a legal continuum that extends from the late Ottoman Empire's laws and legal reform in 1858 to the British Mandate land laws (1917–1948) to Israeli law (after 1948). *Indigenous (In)Justice* critically evaluates Israeli authorities' use of law regarding the Bedouin question and examines previous use of the same laws by the Ottoman and British rules. Furthermore, due to the commonalities that the Bedouin Arab question shares with other indigenous groups around the world, this volume also provides an international and comparative legal perspective in an attempt to highlight common legal practices and gaps that currently exist in various contexts and, at the same time, highlight the special circumstances of each situation.

The Bedouins share many common characteristics with indigenous groups in other countries. At hand, the Bedouins are a case of a tribal society that lived for centuries as a nomadic and semi-nomadic society. They were subjected to a process of "modernization" under a colonial regime and, later, treatment as a native minority in a modern settler nation-state (Yiftachel, 2003; see also Zureik, 1979). This process involved the regulation of Bedouin life through formal state law, the formalization of property, censuses, sedentarization, planning, the undermining of customs, and more. Such practices, according to

James Scott, are part of the modern state's attempt to simplify its classic functions of "taxation, conscription and prevention of rebellion" (Scott, 1998:3). Further, Scott argues, the state aims to "rationaliz[e] and standardiz[e] what was a social hieroglyph into a legible and administratively more convenient format" so that the state's capacity for large-scale social reengineering is increased (Scott, 1998:3, 11–52). The chapters in this volume draw on and discuss several of these modernization practices, including land tenure formalization, cadastral surveys, and interactions between state law and customary law—all of which seek, in part, to record and monitor Bedouin life.

The Naqab Bedouins are part of the broader indigenous Arab people of Palestine, and this indigenous status is central to the analytical framework of this volume. For this volume, the working definition of this terminology and framework starts with José Martinez-Cobo (1986), the Special Rapporteur of the Sub-Commission on Prevention of Discrimination and Protection of Minorities, and his landmark Study on the Problem of Discrimination against Indigenous Populations:

> [Indigenous peoples are] communities, peoples and nations . . . which, having a historical continuity with pre-invasion and pre-colonial societies that developed on their territories, consider themselves distinct from other sectors of the societies now prevailing in those territories, or parts of them. They form at present non-dominant sectors of society and are determined to preserve, develop and transmit to future generations their ancestral territories, and their ethnic identity, as the basis of their continued existence as peoples, in accordance with their own cultural patterns, social institutions and legal systems. (quoted in United Nations Department of Economic and Social Affairs 2009:4)

In addition, according to Asbjørn Eide, indigenous peoples "are, as a group, in an inferior position in the country, in political and economic aspects" (1988:28). The International Labour Organization's Convention 169 on Indigenous and Tribal Peoples (ILO 169), specifies in article 1(1)(b) that indigenous peoples are

> peoples in independent countries who are regarded as indigenous on account of their descent from the populations which inhabited the country, or a geographical region to which the country belongs, at the time of conquest or colonisation or the establishment of present State boundaries and who, irrespective of their legal status, retain some or all of their own social, economic, cultural and political institutions.

Since there is no formal legal definition of indigenous peoples that successfully captures their diversity worldwide, self-identification as indigenous is a central criterion of the designation (Hirtz, 2003). This criterion is well-enshrined in article 1(1) of ILO 169, which states that "[s]elf-identification as indigenous or tribal shall be regarded as a fundamental criterion for determining the groups to which the provisions of this Convention apply."[4]

The world's indigenous peoples are bound by a common experience of having been "discovered" and subjected to colonial expansion into their territories, which has led to the destruction of entire social, cultural, and economic orders, as well as the loss of land and resources. Settler states have often violated the most basic rights of indigenous peoples and have subjected them to oppressive laws and policies designed to serve the interests of the colonial-settler society and culture. This has commonly led to indigenous peoples' ongoing political, social, and economic marginalization. Too often, the legacy of these policies has been poverty, low educational levels, high infant mortality, and high unemployment rates (Coates, 2004).

Throughout the world, indigenous peoples face the challenge of protecting their cultural practices and their remaining lands. Sometimes, their struggle for the protection of their basic rights is made immeasurably more difficult due to the general public's ignorance of their history, culture, and contemporary lives. Indigenous peoples' claims to territory and cultural autonomy are based mainly on the fact that indigenous peoples predated the creation of the nation-states that now rule over them. As one can imagine, states are quite sensitive to such claims, which essentially serve to question the legitimacy of a state's establishment (Whitt, 2009).

Indigenous peoples are generally marginalized and regarded as second-class citizens within the nation-state.[5] Whereas their suffering is frequently felt most acutely at the beginning of a state's establishment—when a state's claim over indigenous peoples' territory often leads to major land loss—ongoing governmental policies of marginalization, land dispossession, and usurpation of indigenous peoples' traditional cultural and political forms help ensure that this inferior status continues. Land and resources are two central elements needed for indigenous peoples to sustain not only their traditional economic livelihood but their cultural continuity, which is intricately tied to their territories. As Rodolfo Stavenhagen explains:

> For most indigenous peoples, survival is the major challenge in a world that has systematically denied them the right to existence as such. Historically linked to the land as the source of their main livelihood, they have long struggled to gain and keep access to this precious resource that is also the essential element of their identity as distinct cultures and societies. Land rights are the major issue faced by native peoples around the world and are at the center of numerous conflicts involving indigenous communities, particularly as a result of globalization. (2006:208–209)

In most cases, settler states have considered the demands of indigenous communities to be threatening and at odds with national policies and interests. Thus, most colonial-settler states, both individually and collectively through bodies such as the United Nations (UN), have rejected the demands of indigenous peoples for recognition of their rights to land, cultural autonomy, and self-government (Abu-Saad and Champagne, 2006; Champagne and Abu-Saad, 2003). However, indigenous communities' demands for recognition of their land rights have been traditionally designed not to threaten the existence of the nation-state but rather to reassert the basic rights cherished and required by indigenous peoples to ensure their survival.

These demands have also sought to redefine indigenous peoples' relationship with the state. For example, indigenous peoples have desired a democratization of relations with the nation-state that concretely incorporates respect for their cultural, territorial, political, and economic rights and uniqueness, and that acknowledges the historical injustices committed against them. Such indigenous rights often have not been congruent with the history and beliefs surrounding the formation of most contemporary nation-states. As a result, there has been a clash between indigenous and non-pluralistic settler-state narratives, worldviews, land claims, governing traditions, and visions for the future (Abu-Saad and Champagne, 2006; Champagne and Abu-Saad, 2003). In most cases, relations between nation-states and indigenous peoples have maintained their colonial nature and thus require sustained critical attention from both human rights scholars and indigenous peoples themselves. Oren Yiftachel's epilogue in this volume suggests several theoretical frameworks—particularly the "colonial lens"—for reexamining such relationships in general, and the relationship between Israeli authorities and indigenous Bedouin Arabs in particular.

The Palestinian Bedouin Arabs in the Naqab desert have experienced ongoing displacement, political conflict, cultural disruption, and dispossession since the establishment of the State of Israel in 1948. *Indigenous (In)Justice* is, to the best of our knowledge, the first scholarly collection of legal and human rights essays to systematically analyze their predicament. The chapters situate the particular questions of the

Naqab Bedouin case within key international debates, including the scope and application of the UN Declaration on the Rights of Indigenous Peoples, the territorial dispossession of indigenous peoples, and the indivisibility and interrelationship of economic, social, cultural, civil, and political rights.

The idea for this volume was conceived in Harvard Law School's International Human Rights Clinic in 2007, and, over the course of the next several years, Clinic staff and students laid the book's groundwork. The Clinic's research team began in the tent of Bir-Hadaj, where it lived for about ten days, and in numerous other Bedouin villages, where it conducted dozens of extensive qualitative interviews. Thereafter, the Clinic undertook several research missions to the Naqab, in which the team met with activists, academics, governmental officials (including an acting minister), and local Bedouin Arab residents. As part of its work, the Clinic submitted a position paper to and appeared before the Goldberg Commission.

The Clinic's work on Bedouin land and housing rights issues highlighted the need for a deep examination of the "Bedouin question" from different legal perspectives. Thus, *Indigenous (In)Justice* explores the history, land conflicts, and contemporary conditions of the Naqab Bedouin Arabs from an indigenous rights perspective, drawing on both international law and the experiences of indigenous peoples from Australia, Canada, and the United States. The analyses in the book's chapters enrich existing human rights and academic discourses by highlighting the nature of the relationship that defines the interaction between indigenous peoples and their states, as well as the legal structures that can lead to the domination of indigenous peoples and the violation of their basic human rights.

The volume is divided into three sections and includes an expanded epilogue. Each section includes chapters that explore different dimensions of the complex, multilayered issue of Naqab Bedouin Arab rights—though the chapters' arguments invariably interact with one another. The first section sets the stage for the following two sections by outlining the specificities of the Bedouin experience in Israel and its legal dimensions. The second section provides the international legal framework on indigenous peoples' rights, social and economic rights, and women's rights, and demonstrates the interrelationships between these sets of rights. The third section draws on the experiences of indigenous peoples in Australia, Canada, and the United States, in addition to exploring the shortcomings of state law and individual human rights law in meeting indigenous peoples' needs. The epilogue takes the current state of scholarship on the Bedouin question and suggests several prisms that scholars can use to better understand the Bedouin case.

In chapter one, Ismael Abu-Saad and Cosette Creamer provide a historical overview of the experience of the Bedouin Arab community, starting with the Ottoman rule in Palestine and ending with the present day. They offer an in-depth description and analysis of the Israeli government's efforts to transform the Bedouins from land-based pastoralists into urbanized wage-laborers detached from their land. They examine the evolution of Israeli policies toward the Naqab Bedouin Arabs, which culminated in a plan of forced urbanization, and discuss the settler-colonial vision inherent in the conceptualization and implementation of the urban model. Abu-Saad and Creamer also discuss the Bedouins' response to Israeli government policies and their resistance to the urbanization program.

Chapter two, by Ahmad Amara and Zinaida Miller, illuminates the legal complexities around planning and land aspects of the Bedouin question. This chapter discusses the regulatory framework utilized in the reconstruction of space in Israel in general since 1948, and in the Bedouin Arab space in the Naqab in particular. The authors analyze the legal, institutional, and planning mechanisms that have functioned both to systematically dispossess Palestinians of their lands and to nationalize such lands to make them available for use by the Jewish population. Amara and Miller outline the legal processes leading to land expropriation, nationalization, skewed ethnic allocation, land development, and forced urbanization, paying special attention to the Israeli judiciary, legislation (both new and old), the complex web of state institutions that implement policy, and patterns of Bedouin response. The chapter locates the Bedouin case within the broader case of Palestinian land dispossession within Israel by the Israeli government.

Noa Kram, in chapter three, explores the legal history of land disputes between the State of Israel and the Naqab Bedouin Arabs. This chapter brings to the surface the roots of the contradictions between the state's legal arguments—which are based on Ottoman, British, and Israeli legislation and court rulings—and the Bedouin Arabs' indigenous legal mechanisms for determining land use and ownership rights. Kram challenges the lack of acknowledgment of indigenous Bedouin practices of land ownership within the conventional legal and academic Israeli discourse. She furthermore argues that the conflict over land reflects power imbalances between the Israeli legal apparatus and the Bedouins' oral practices.

In the second section, chapter four by Rodolfo Stavenhagen (former UN Special Rapporteur on the Rights of Indigenous Peoples) and Ahmad Amara analyzes the development of the specialized field of international law that protects the rights of indigenous peoples and discusses the applicability of this legal regime to the situation of the Naqab Bedouin Arabs. The authors describe relevant legal advancements achieved by the International Labour Organization (through ILO 169) and the UN (through the Declaration on the Rights of Indigenous Peoples). They argue that these legal developments were possible, in part, due to the critical role played by indigenous groups worldwide. Stavenhagen and Amara also explore regional developments related to indigenous peoples' rights and apply this analysis to the Naqab Bedouins, mindful of the similarities and differences between the various cases. Finally, the authors highlight the legal provisions of the UN Declaration that ought to apply to the Bedouins as an indigenous people within the State of Israel; such provisions mainly relate to traditional territory, housing, and cultural practices.

In chapter five, Rashida Manjoo, the UN Special Rapporteur on Violence against Women, addresses the systemic and structural factors that affect indigenous women's right of access to adequate housing, with a particular focus on the impact of gender-based discrimination and violence against women. Manjoo argues that the situation of indigenous Naqab Bedouin women in the villages with no "legal status"—known as "unrecognized villages"—is in violation of Israel's international legal obligations. She outlines how this situation affects Bedouin women's right to adequate housing, education, and health, and creates an environment conducive to violence against them. Manjoo further claims that Israel's policy of forced eviction and forced urbanization of Bedouin women directly contravenes its obligations to ensure that its citizens have the freedom to choose their residence. Following Bedouin women's relocation, the resulting living spaces disregard the women's economic, social, cultural, and spatial needs, leading to a more restricted and, in some cases, more violent life.

The book's third section enriches our understanding of the Bedouin question by drawing on the comparative experiences of other indigenous peoples and legal systems. In chapter six, John Sheehan explores Bedouins' claims for recognition of their property rights as indigenous peoples, drawing on the Australian experience of Aboriginal property rights. Sheehan critiques Israel's reliance on a patchwork body of multifarious laws and legal regimes reaching back to Ottoman times, which it has used to justify the denial of Bedouin land claims. Instead, he argues, the significant advances in common-law native title jurisprudence—as demonstrated by Australia's watershed *Mabo* decision and subsequent cases of the Australian High Court—represent a coherent body of respected case law that can and should inform Israeli jurisprudence in the area of Bedouin property.

In chapter seven, Duane Champagne distinguishes between indigenous rights, citizens' rights, and human rights, and discusses their application to the case of the Naqab Bedouins. He argues against equating indigenous rights issues with citizens' rights and human rights issues, with which nation-states in the international community have been engaged. Champagne explores Bedouin claims to land, cultural continuity, and other indigenous rights within the context of the Israeli state, and makes comparisons with the struggles of indigenous peoples in other settler states (e.g., Canada and the United States). He suggests redefining the relationship between the State of Israel and Bedouin Arab citizens through the realization of both citizens' and indigenous rights. As is the case for most other settler states, the Israeli state lacks institutional mechanisms for acknowledging or including Bedouin indigenous rights perspectives, which prevents it from achieving a consensual form of citizenship, human rights, or nationality that can fairly achieve the goals of establishing the rights of indigenous peoples as citizens.

Oren Yiftachel's epilogue reflects on the book's chapters and on past literature on the Bedouin question to provide a research roadmap for the future. This chapter, which provides a broad historical-geographical overview of the Bedouin issue, brings to the fore the dialectical relationships and theoretical arguments concerning the Bedouin question. Yiftachel summarizes the state of scholarship on this issue and provides a critique of its scope, aims, and methods. He suggests a more comprehensive approach, rarely used in the literature, in which the plight of Bedouins in Israel is analyzed through an internal colonial lens. He focuses on three critical aspects of the colonial framework: settler society, indigeneity, and "gray space." These angles, Yiftachel argues, provide a sound framework within which policy, territory, economy, and politics affecting the Bedouins in Israel can be analyzed and credibly explained.

While the volume offers, as noted by Yiftachel, several new angles for the study of Bedouin society, it does not exhaust the many dimensions of this complex topic. Nor is this volume free from its own theoretical or analytical shortcomings. However, we hope that it will be the beginning of a revised scholarship in this field that can better address and scrutinize the Bedouin Arab question. We also hope that it will lead to more than scholarship by bringing about positive change in the state of affairs in the Naqab, which, based on the daily realities in the region, does not seem to suggest a promising future.

Indeed, in September 2011 the Israeli government approved the Prawer-Amidror Plan, which devises new strategies for Bedouin settlement and planning in the Naqab.[6] These strategies entail minimal recognition of hitherto "unrecognized" villages and a slightly improved compensation rate for land that remains in possession of Bedouin claimants; however, the report cancels any proposed land compensation for those claimants who were removed from their land. The Prawer-Amidror Plan also approves the future removal of up to 40,000 Bedouins from their villages to townships and newly recognized villages. The plan, which was formulated in secrecy, has been rejected by most Bedouins. It appears to continue the governmental line of circumventing Bedouin land ownership and possession, and is likely to further intensify the conflict between the state and its indigenous citizens.

In addition, the government's approval of the Prawer-Amidror Plan has highlighted again the profound marginality of Bedouins in Israeli society. As the plan was being drafted, Israel was undergoing an unprecedented wave of social protest, during which hundreds of thousands took to the streets in major cities, including Beersheba, chanting, "the people demand social justice." In response, the government speedily appointed the Trachtenberg Committee to respond to the protests, and it adopted a series of recommendations to alleviate social injustices. The Trachtenberg Committee operated with notable openness and transparency, with a process that included broad public participation and live broadcasts of its meetings. In stark contrast, at precisely the same time, the government developed in secrecy and approved the much more problematic Prawer-Amidror Plan, which virtually ignores the long injustices conferred on the Bedouins.[7]

In light of this ongoing discrepancy, this book offers scholars and students of Bedouin Arab society in the Naqab new paths to investigate an important core of the Bedouin predicament—the Bedouins' history and status as an indigenous group within a settler society. Such research, as illustrated in the pages that follow, has the potential not only to show the legacy of troubled history but to offer directions for renewing society in such a manner that Naqab Bedouins are fully recognized as equal citizens holding their own identity and place, and that their historical injustices are duly acknowledged. In this way, the book hopes to chart a path toward indigenous justice.

REFERENCES

Abu-Saad, I., and Champagne, D. (eds.). (2006). *Indigenous Education and Empowerment: International Perspectives*. Walnut Creek, CA: AltaMira Press.

BBC News. (2010). "Israel police raze 'illegal' Bedouin village in Negev." July 27. http://www.bbc.co.uk/news/world-middle-east-10777040 (accessed September 14, 2011).

Center for Public Management and Policy. (2007). *The Burden on the Judiciary: Comparative Analysis of 17 Countries; Summary Report*. (Hebrew).

Champagne, D., and Abu-Saad, I. (eds.). (2003). *The Future of Indigenous Peoples: Strategies for Survival and Development*. Los Angeles: American Indian Studies Center, UCLA.

Coates, K. (2004). *A Global History of Indigenous Peoples: Struggle and Survival*. Basingstoke, Hampshire: Palgrave Macmillan.

Committee for Socio-Economic Change. (2011). "Public Participation." http://hidavrut.gov.il (accessed November 17, 2011).

Cook, J. (2002). "Israel's Vietnam." *Al-Ahram Weekly Online* 598:8–14.

Dinero, S. (2004). "New Identity/identities formulation in post-no-madic community: The case of Bedouin of the Negev." *Negev National Identities* 6(3):261–275.

Eide, A. (1988). "Internal conflicts under international law." In K. Rupesinghe (ed.), *Ethnic Conflict and Human Rights* (pp. 23–33). Tokyo: United Nations University; Oslo: Norwegian University Press.

Hirtz, F. (2003). "It takes modern means to be traditional: On recognizing indigenous cultural communities in the Philippines." *Development and Change* 34(5):887–914.

Israeli Courts. (n.d.). "Annual statistical reports." http://www.court.gov.il/heb/home.htm (accessed September 14, 2011) (Hebrew).

Kabha, M. (2008). "The Hebrew online media's treatment of Arab citizens in the Negev." *HAGAR Studies in Culture, Polity and Identities* 8(2):159–172.

Kershner, I. (2010). "A test of wills over a patch of desert." *New York Times*, August 25. http://www.nytimes.com/2010/08/26/world/middleeast/26israel.html (accessed September 14, 2011).

Likhovski, A. (2006) *Law and Identity in Mandate Palestine.* Chapel Hill: University of North Carolina Press.

Martinez-Cobo, J. (1986). Study of the problem of discrimination against indigenous populations, Sub-Commission on the Prevention of Discrimination and the Protection of Minorities, U.N. Doc. E/CN.4/Sub.2/1986/7/Add.4.

Marx, E. (1967). *Bedouin of the Negev.* Manchester: Manchester University Press.

Negev Coexistence Forum for Civil Equality. (2011). "The Prawer Plan." http://www.dukium.org/heb/?page_id=8182 (accessed November 17, 2011) (Hebrew).

Scott, J. C. (1998). *Seeing Like A State: How Certain Schemes to Improve the Human Condition Have Failed.* New Haven, CT: Yale University Press.

United Nations Department of Economic and Social Affairs. (2009). *State of the World's Indigenous Peoples.* New York: United Nations.

Stavenhagen, R. (2006). "Indigenous peoples: Land, territory, autonomy, and self-determination." In P. Rosset, R. Patel, and M. Courville (eds.), *Promised Land: Competing Visions of Agrarian Reform* (pp. 208–217). Oakland, CA: Food First Books.

Whitt, L. (2009). *Science, Colonialism, and Indigenous Peoples: The Cultural Politics of Law and Knowledge*. New York: Cambridge University Press.

Yiftachel, O. (2003). "Bedouin-Arabs and the Israeli settler state: Land policies and indigenous resistance." In D. Champagne and I. Abu-Saad (eds.), *The Future of Indigenous Peoples: Strategies for Survival and Development* (pp. 21–47). Los Angeles: American Indian Studies Center, UCLA.

Zureik, E. (1979). *The Palestinians in Israel: A Study in Internal Colonialism*. London: Routledge & K. Paul.

NOTES

1. The Naqab ("Negev" in Hebrew) desert is the area that lies in the southern part of Israel/Palestine and extends along the great rift from the Dead Sea to Aqaba, and whose western side consists of the official border between Egypt and Israel. The Naqab constitutes 12.5 million dunams, about 60% of Israel's 20.7 million dunams. These 12.5 million dunams are equal to about 3,100 square acres. See Marx (1967:1–7).

2. The Naqab Bedouin Arabs are part of the Palestinian people. They were autonomous semi-nomadic tribes in southern Palestine for centuries. During the conflict years of 1947–1949, the vast majority of Naqab Bedouins were driven out by Israeli forces or fled to the Gaza Strip, the Sinai Peninsula, and Jordan. Those who remained in the Naqab became Israeli citizens. In this volume, we primarily refer to this population as "Bedouin Arabs." However, due to length and repetition considerations, we use "Arab" and "Bedouin" interchangeably throughout the first three chapters. In the rest of the book, each author uses his or her own terminology.

3. For example, during the British Mandate, the British established a major judicial complex, which included about one hundred different courts. The number of lawyers in Palestine increased from 113 in 1922 to more than 1,000 in 1948, due to the increasing Jewish immigrants and to the opening of law schools and legal courses. In addition, the number of cases in state courts (excluding tribal and religious courts) increased from 43,087 cases in 1922 to 140,369 cases in 1934—at a rate much faster than that of actual population growth. The migration to Palestine of educated European Jews familiar with legalistic and bureaucratic systems helped further the legalistic culture in Palestine. See Likhovski (2006:26, 28, 106–123). With regard to Israel's legalistic culture, see, for example,

a comparative study between Israel and seventeen European countries, Australia, and New Zealand, where Israel showed the highest legal activity per person: 184.15 occurrences per person in Israel compared to an average of 89.56 per person in the other countries (Center for Public Management and Policy, 2007:18). For more on the Israeli judicial structure, see Israeli Courts (n.d.).

4. Convention concerning Indigenous and Tribal Peoples in Independent Countries, C169 I.L.O. (1989).

5. The following quote from Avigdor Lieberman, an Israeli parliamentary member and current minister of foreign affairs, who immigrated to Israel from the former Soviet Union in 1978, typifies the way in which indigenous peoples—regardless of their formal legal status—are not considered full citizens, particularly when it comes to their land rights and claims. In response to the Naqab Bedouins resisting removal from their traditional lands, he said:

> We must stop [the Bedouins'] illegal invasion of state land by all means possible. The Bedouin have no regard for our laws; in the process we are losing the last resources of state lands. One of my main missions is to return the power of the [Israel] Land Authority in dealing with the non-Jewish threat to our lands. (quoted in Cook, 2002:2)

6. To view the text of the Prawer-Amidror Report, see Negev Coexistence Forum for Civil Equality (2011). The government adopted the Prawer Plan through Government Resolution No. 3707 on September 11, 2011. The full text of the resolution can be viewed at http://www.pmo.gov.il/PMO/Secretarial/Decisions/2011/09/des3707.htm (Hebrew).

7. For the Trachtenberg Committee Report and the venues for public participation, see Committee for Socio-Economic Change (2011).

Abstract

This chapter describes the socio-political changes that the Naqab (Negev) Bedouin Arabs have experienced over the past half century, the means through which they have displayed their resistance to governmental efforts to simultaneously marginalize and assimilate them, and their current living conditions. It argues that state efforts to "modernize" indigenous peoples and integrate them within state structures are often carried out through displacement, land expropriation, and forced urbanization, resulting in severe disruptions of traditional cultural lifestyles. In the context of the Naqab, this dynamic of forced urbanization has been further complicated by the backdrop of the broader Israeli-Palestinian conflict. Similar to other indigenous communities in modern states, however, the Naqab Bedouin Arabs have developed local forms of resistance to the methods of control and assimilation employed by the Israeli state.

CHAPTER 1

Socio-Political Upheaval and Current Conditions of the Naqab Bedouin Arabs

Ismael Abu-Saad and Cosette Creamer

Introduction

The state of Israel discriminates against me negatively, it deprives and neglects me, consigns me to the economic, social and political margins. . . . The state doesn't show an interest in what I think or feel, or in what I am willing or able to contribute. . . . To my great regret, the Israeli Jews still have not internalized the significance of the far-reaching consequences of the brutal fact that the Palestinian Arabs within the borders of the state, and beyond, are the indigenous inhabitants of this land, and as such, their rights in this place are not subject to denial or appeal. The indigenous Palestinians of this land were not engaged as the temporary custodians of the land for hundreds of years until the Jews would return to it and push them aside.

(Zeidani, 2005:89–90)

Over the past half century, with the formation of nation-states and the encroachment of modernization, Bedouin life throughout the Middle East has changed to varying degrees. This change has been particularly dramatic for the Bedouin Arabs living in the Naqab (Negev) Desert in southern Israel. They are among the indigenous Palestinian Arabs who remained on their lands after the 1948 conflict (Al-Nakba)[1] and who today form a part of the Arab minority in Israel. They have inhabited the Naqab Desert for many generations and were subject at various times to Ottoman rule, the British Mandate government, and after 1948 the State of Israel. Traditionally, the Naqab Bedouins were organized into nomadic or semi-nomadic tribes whose livelihood was based on animal husbandry and seasonal agriculture. They were widely dispersed throughout the Naqab in order to meet the needs of their herds. Extended family and tribal groupings lived in proximity, and some household members would migrate seasonally to seek out pasture for the herds and then return to their home base to tend their fields. Prior to 1948, 90% of the Bedouin population in the Naqab lived as subsistence farmers, while 10% earned their living from raising livestock. In fact, over 2 million dunams (494,200 acres) of the 12.6 million dunams of land used by the Bedouins were cultivated, primarily in the north and northwestern areas of the Naqab.[2] Today the Bedouins of the region struggle to retain possession of—much less cultivate—386,000 dunams of land.[3]

Because of their traditional semi-nomadic and pastoral lifestyles, Bedouin communities have been often marginalized and viewed as incompatible with the machinery and planning objectives of modern states. In fact, indigenous peoples around the world who are living in modern states are confronted with assimilation efforts by those states, particularly forced urbanization. These efforts to "modernize" indigenous peoples and integrate them within state structures are often carried out through displacement and land expropriation, resulting in severe disruptions of traditional cultural lifestyles. In the context of the Naqab, this dynamic of forced urbanization has been further complicated by the backdrop of the broader Israeli-Palestinian conflict. Similar to other indigenous communities in modern states, however, the Naqab Bedouins have developed local forms of resistance to the methods of control and assimilation employed by the Israeli state. This chapter explores the socio-political upheaval experienced by the Naqab Bedouin Arabs, the means through which they have displayed their resistance to governmental efforts that have attempted to simultaneously marginalize and assimilate them, and their current living conditions.

Bedouin Arabs under the Ottoman Empire and British Mandate

Bedouin Arab tribes have lived in Palestine since at least the fifth century. They largely controlled the Naqab region during the Ottoman period from the sixteenth to nineteenth centuries, during which time they enjoyed relative autonomy, freedom of movement, and use of land. Each Bedouin tribe spread throughout the territory where it grazed its flocks, sometimes covering hundreds of square miles, which the tribe as a whole controlled. The extent of the controlled territory depended on the power of each tribe, which inevitably led to territorial tribal feuds. Each tribe selected its own sheikh, but under Ottoman rule, the Turkish authorities had to confirm their selection.

The Ottoman Empire occupied the region in 1519 and initially administered it through Turkish rulers in Jerusalem and Gaza. The Turkish rulers largely ignored the tribal in-fighting until the 1870s, when the Ottoman government began holding tribal sheikhs personally responsible for the outcomes of such feuds. The Ottomans also set the boundaries of tribal territories, and these boundaries remained relatively static until after the 1948 conflict. The two largest tribal confederations—the Tarabīn and the Tiāha—acquired the most fertile territory in the northern regions of the Naqab, while the 'Azāzmah were located in the arid mountains of the central area and the tribes of the Gubarāt and Hanāgrah confederations were pushed to the coast (al-'Ārif, 1934:31; Marx, 1967).

In 1900, the Ottoman government built the town of Beersheba, where it established an administrative center in order to better control the Bedouin tribes and to strengthen its presence while engaging in negotiations over the border with Egypt. In an implicit recognition of Bedouin land ownership, the Ottomans purchased land from the 'Azāzmah tribe in order to build the city of Beersheba. During this period, the Turks also sought to build a separate judicial system for the Bedouins, so as to further administrative objectives, such as tax collection. The creation of this administrative center—in addition to the fixing of tribal land boundaries and the introduction of wage labor into the Naqab economy—effectively began a process of "sedentariza-tion," which continued during the British Mandate period (Musham, 1959:549).

Great Britain controlled the Naqab region between 1917 and 1948—under a League of Nations Mandate from 1922—during which time British authorities intervened very little in the daily activities of the Bedouin Arabs. Like the Ottomans before them, the British were not particularly interested in developing the Naqab region (Swirksi, 2008:25–45). Still, under British rule, the value of land rose in some areas of the Naqab, as farming increased and tribal sheikhs (primarily though not exclusively) bought and consolidated land on which they employed tribesmen as sharecroppers. The total number of Bedouins in the region during this period ranged from 65,000 to 100,000, with tribes recognizing each other's lands (Abu-Saad, 2008a).[4] With respect to agriculture, the 1942 Survey of Palestine reported that the entire northern area of the Naqab was either "cultivated" or "cultivated in patches," indicating the agricultural use that the Bedouin Arabs had made of almost all the land during this period (Maddrell, 1990:5).

Overall, the British brought a semblance of Western law and admin-istration to the region and created the first formal Western schools for the Bedouins (Abu-Saad, 1991:235). Sedentarization increased during the British Mandate period, as the British military authorities employed some Bedouins, and the Bedouins also intensified their involvement in land cultivation. The Mandate authorities commenced a process of land title settlement in Palestine and enacted a number of land laws, including the 1928 Land (Settlement of Title) Ordinance. This ordinance required residents to register land claims, while promising those who held land under traditional Arab law that their land rights would not be affected (Yiftachel, 2000:9). However, for the most part, the Bedouin Arabs did not register their land holdings, particularly given that there were few challenges to their land rights at the time. In addition, the process of land settlement undertaken by the British Mandate focused more on the northern areas of Palestine than on the southern regions.

Zionist Policy in the Pre-Israeli State Period

The Zionist movement was a colonial venture that began in Europe in the late 1800s with the goal of establishing a Jewish state in Palestine. It was based on the premise that Palestine was a territory that belonged exclusively to the Jewish people due to their presence on the land during biblical times. The Zionist colonial project portrayed Palestine as a "land without a people, for a people without a land" (see Masalha, 1997).

Early Zionists viewed the Palestinian Arabs as a non-European, inferior "other" (Masalha, 1997). For these Zionists, the overwhelming number of Palestinian Arabs in the future Jewish state represented a significant obstacle to their quest to establish a sovereign state of their own. A prominent Zionist leader at the time, Israel Zangwill, wrote in 1920:

> If Lord Shaftesbury was literally inexact in describing Palestine as a country without a people, he was essentially correct, for there is no Arab people living in intimate fusion with the country, utilizing its resources and stamping it with characteristic impress; there is at best an Arab encampment. (quoted in Masalha, 1997:62)

Such pronouncements by leading Zionists promoted the notion of an empty territory—empty, as Masalha explains, not in the sense of actual absence of inhabitants, but rather of a "civilizational barrenness." This notion of empty territory was then used to justify Zionist colonization and the delegitimization of the native population as a people belonging to that particular place (Masalha, 1997; Prior, 1999).

Making this fictional depiction of the country a reality required considerable effort from Zionist leaders, as at the time of the First Zionist Congress in 1897, the Palestinian Arabs, who constituted 95% of the population, owned and cultivated most of the country's arable land. In contrast, Jews made up only 5% of the population and owned 1% of the land (Prior, 1999:190). In 1930, Britain's High Commissioner for Palestine, John Chancellor, recommended the total suspension of Jewish immigration and land purchases to protect Arab agriculture, as all the arable land—then in possession of the indigenous Palestinians—could not be sold to Jews without creating a class of landless Arab cultivators (Masalha, 1992; Quigley, 1990:19). This was also true of the Naqab Desert in southern Palestine, which was inhabited and extensively cultivated by Bedouin Arabs, despite the popular Zionist imagery of the Jewish immigrants "making the desert bloom." By the mid-1940s, the Naqab's Bedouin Arab population was estimated at 65,000 to 95,000, organized into 95 semi-nomadic tribes (Falah, 1989; Marx, 1967; Yiftachel, 2003), while the Jewish population in the Naqab consisted of 475 persons, living in four settlements (Prior, 1999).

Given extensive Arab presence in Palestine and the need to maintain European and international support for the Zionist project, the leaders of the Zionist movement publicly claimed that the rights of the indigenous inhabitants of Palestine would be protected and upheld. At the same time, they strove to achieve a Jewish majority by promoting Jewish immigration to Palestine and sought to bring about the removal or transfer of Palestinian Arabs from the territory of the future Zionist state.

This Zionist ideology of transforming the people, the land, and the character of Palestine into a Jewish state has played, and continues to play, a defining role in shaping Israeli policies and institutions. One of the last remaining frontiers to be settled, according to the Zionist ideology, is the Naqab Desert in southern Israel, which makes up 60%

of the total land area of Israel but contains only 8% of its population (Yiftachel, 2006). The Bedouins continue to represent an anathema to the Zionist colonization project.

The 1948 Arab-Israeli Conflict and the Creation of the State of Israel

The events immediately prior to, during, and after the 1948 Arab-Israeli conflict resulted in the exodus or expulsion of over 80% of the Palestinian Arab population in Israeli-held territory. This included the expulsion of roughly 80%–85% of the Naqab Bedouin Arab population to the surrounding territories or countries (the West Bank, Gaza Strip, Jordan, and Egypt), which reduced their numbers to approximately 11,000 (Falah, 1985a:37).[5] Of the original ninety-five Bedouin tribes inhabiting the Naqab, only nineteen remained in sufficient numbers to receive official recognition from the new Israeli government.

The 1947 United Nations decision to partition Palestine into two states (Jewish and Arab) had left large sections of the Naqab outside the boundaries of the future Jewish state, including Beersheba and surrounding lands. As a result, Zionist leadership interested in the region made substantial efforts during the 1948 conflict to conquer this area (Swirksi, 2008:26). The Israeli army eventually succeeded, but the government initially had difficulty obtaining international recognition of its possession of the Naqab. It was not until the 1956 war that Israel's sovereignty over the region was recognized internationally.[6]

During and following the 1948 conflict, Israeli authorities imposed military government on areas of the country with large indigenous populations. The military government served, first and foremost, as a tool for consolidating control over the Palestinian Arab minority, evidenced by the fact that its regulations were not enforced against the Jewish community. While inconsistent with democratic principles, this one-sided enforcement of military rule was fully consistent with furthering the Zionist aim of creating a Jewish state and increasing Jewish (while decreasing Arab) control over the land. To this end, the regulations of the military government typified traditional imperialist attitudes, giving state authorities extensive and extremely rigorous powers. Enforcement of these regulations resulted in the near complete loss of individual freedoms and property rights, and impinged on virtually every aspect of life, from control over freedoms (e.g., freedom of speech, movement, means of transportation, and the press) to the expropriation of property (Jiryis, 1976:17).

Using these expanded powers, the Israeli authorities took control of most of the land in the Naqab and deprived Bedouin Arabs of the freedom to migrate seasonally with their herds and cultivate their lands. Twelve of the remaining nineteen Naqab Bedouin tribes were removed from their lands, and the entire population was confined to a specially designated Restricted Area in the northeastern Naqab. This area, known for its low fertility, represented only 10% of the territory that the Bedouin Arabs had controlled prior to 1948 (Falah, 1989). Due to the military regulations imposed on them, the Bedouins could not return to or cultivate their lands; they were isolated from the Palestinian Arab population in other parts of Israel; and they needed special permits to leave their designated sections of the Restricted Area to look for jobs, education, markets, grazing, and the like (Marx, 1967). These restrictions represented a process of coerced and accelerated sedentarization, which all but ended their traditional way of life.

During the military government's tenure, authorities also took great care to prevent Bedouins' migration out of the Restricted Area. Bedouin men who were given permits to work in the Jewish sector were not allowed to bring their families with them, thus ensuring their return to the Restricted Area. Even within the Restricted Area, a Bedouin of one tribe could not visit the area of another tribe without the permission of the military governor (Marx, 1967).

The Israeli authority's record during this period was one of intimidation and violence, in which collective punishment against the Naqab Bedouins was common. Ghazi Falah (1985a) documented several massacres, as well as cases of expulsion of Bedouins up until 1959, eleven years after the establishment of the state. Jiryis maintained that "[m]ore than any other group, the Naqab Bedouin suffered the full and unrestrained harshness of military rule" (1976:122). As one Bedouin sheikh stated:

> [T]he land expropriation and the forced expulsions without compensation or the right to return . . . brought the Bedouin to a situation which [was] difficult both psychologically and materially, and to a lack of security unlike anything they had previously known. (cited in Lustick, 1980:13)

After transferring the Naqab Bedouins to the Restricted Area, the Israeli planning authorities largely neglected them for the next twenty years. No settlement, agricultural, or industrial plans were prepared for this region, and, as a result, dozens of "spontaneous" Bedouin Arab settlements emerged. The seven tribes that originally lived in the Restricted Area settled on their own lands, while those that had been transferred to the Restricted Area by the government settled in the areas in which they had been placed. These settlements were characterized by tin shacks, cabins, and tents because the building of permanent structures (e.g., stone or concrete structures) was prohibited in the Restricted Area. State planning authorities refused to recognize what they viewed as "irregular" or "spontaneous" settlements and, as a consequence, denied these settlements basic infrastructure and services, such as electricity, running water, and roads (Abu-Saad, 2000; Marx, 2000; Yiftachel, 2006).

Displacement and Forced Urbanization: Government-Planned Towns

Policy Goals

During the 1948 conflict and its aftermath, the Palestinian Arab population in the Naqab and throughout the country was reduced to a minority, and thus major Zionist policy objectives were achieved. This in itself freed up extensive tracts of land corresponding to the Zionist policy of "land redemption," a process expanded during the military government by removing many of the remaining Palestinians from their lands and concentrating them in closed areas, further reducing their land base. In the Naqab, the Israeli government enacted a number of laws and military regulations to enable the state to confiscate land previously owned or used by the Bedouins and ultimately to register this land as state property. The Bedouin Arabs, confined to the Restricted Area while these laws took effect, were effectively unable to contest the state's registration of their lands.

The 1953 Land Acquisition (Validation of Acts and Compensation) Law retroactively endorsed expropriations undertaken directly after the 1948 conflict. It provided the Israeli state with the right to register previously confiscated land in its name if various conditions were met, including that the owner was not in possession of the property on April 1, 1952. Under this law, much of the Bedouin land outside the Restricted Area was registered as state land, usually without the knowledge of its Bedouin owners. The land was then transferred to the Development Authority, a body established in 1952 to administer Palestinian refugee lands and make them available to the state's settlement bodies for its development plans (Yiftachel, 2000:11).

The 1965 Planning and Construction Law created a hierarchy of planning bodies that drew up master plans at the national, district, and local levels. These planning authorities did not acknowledge the existence of populated Bedouin villages in the Restricted Area on the original master plans and thus zoned their land as agricultural or military areas, rather than residential. Through this zoning process, these Bedouin villages were rendered "illegal" and thus denied provision of governmental services and infrastructure, including roads, electricity, and running water (Abu-Saad, 2008a:5). In addition, their unrecognized status under this zoning law rendered it impossible for these villages to apply for or receive permits to build. Thus, all structures—even those existing prior to 1965 or even 1948—in these "unrecognized villages" were deemed illegal by the state and subject to demolition. The same law also allowed for confiscation of land for public purposes, which led to more state confiscation of Bedouin land in the Naqab, including land that the state later used to build government-planned Bedouin towns (Yiftachel, 2006).

This program was an extreme expression of the common indigenous experience of having colonizers appropriate entire indigenous territories and then "gift back" small pockets/reservations of land to the dispossessed indigenous communities (Smith, 1999). The core rationale for the program of urban settlements for the Bedouin Arabs in the Naqab was based on the ideological nature of spatial planning in Israel. Dispersion of the Jewish population throughout the land continued to be one of Israel's major national planning goals. The Bedouins' widely dispersed settlement and extensive land use even within the Restricted Area, not to mention their land ownership claims, represented an obstacle to the ongoing Zionist conquest and development of "frontier" desert areas (Gradus and Stern, 1985; Kimmerling, 1982). Thus, the governmental plan to remove the Bedouin population from the land and settle them in higher density towns was designed to further decrease the extent of their claim on the land and to stem their "spontaneous" settlement activities (Law-Yone, 2003; Shamir, 1996). These considerations took priority over concerns about how gravely the high density urban model disrupted the Bedouins' traditional way of life socially, culturally, and economically.

By the late 1960s, the rapidly developing Israeli economy required growing numbers of workers. As such, the unskilled Bedouin workforce, who would no longer have the land resources to maintain their traditional livelihood in urban-style towns, could participate as low-wage workers in the industrial and economic development of the Jewish towns in the Naqab. As Moshe Dayan stated during his term as minister of agriculture in 1963:

> We should transform the Bedouins into an urban proletariat—in industry, services, construction and agriculture. Eighty-eight percent of the Israeli population are not farmers; let the Bedouins be like them. Indeed, this will be a radical move, which means that the Bedouin would not live on his land with his herds, but would become an urban person who comes home in the afternoon and puts his slippers on. His children would be accustomed to a father who wears trousers, does not carry a *shabaria* [the traditional Bedouin knife] and does not search for head lice in public. The children would go to school with their hair properly combed. This would be a revolution, but it may be fixed within two generations. Without coercion but with governmental direction . . . this phenomenon of the Bedouins will disappear. (*Haaretz*, 1963)

The government-expressed rationale for this policy has been multifaceted and often cast in the benevolent light of desiring to "modernize" the Bedouins and enable more efficient provision of services. This rationale is belied by the selection of an explicitly urban and highly concentrated settlement model, which represents the destruction of the Bedouins' traditional lifestyle. If the goals of the government were in actuality only to modernize and provide Bedouins with services more efficiently, both aims could have been achieved by planning small agricultural villages or cooperatives with a land base (such as the Jewish *moshavim* and *kibbutzim*) for the Bedouins. This would have coincided with Bedouin demands for their own development and would not have required the extreme alienation from their land and traditional lifestyle that urbanization entailed. In fact, there were strong cultural factors that made urban settlements unattractive to the indigenous Bedouin Arabs.[7]

Policy in Practice

As part of its forced urbanization goals, in March 1962 the Israeli government set up a committee tasked with examining and recommending proposals for residential development in the Naqab, including proposals for concentrating the Bedouin population. It recommended establishing permanent settlements—or townships—in a very small area of the Restricted Area consisting of only 7,600 dunams (Swirski and Hasson, 2006:13). In 1965, the Supreme Bedouin Committee approved three sites in the Restricted Area where permanent settlements could be established for the Bedouins—outside of Beersheba, outside of Shoval, and at Kseife, near Tel Almalih (Tel Malhata). The government agreed to cover development costs, but residents were required to "finance housing construction, with the help of a mortgage amounting to 70% of the basic cost of building a dwelling unit" (Swirski and Hasson, 2006:13–14).

In 1968, the Housing Ministry launched the first town, Tal a-Sabi', by building forty-nine small houses (70 square meters) on 400-square-meter lots of land (Lewando-Hundt, 1979). Each Bedouin family was to receive a renewable forty-nine-year lease for the lot, for which it was expected to sign away all claims to land owned in the past. The houses were built in a linear pattern, extending out on both sides of a central commercial area, consisting of a few shops, a school, and a clinic (Gradus and Stern, 1985; Marx, 2000). The small houses were unsuitable for large families with an average of eight to nine children, and the high density of the town itself conflicted with the Bedouins' traditionally widely dispersed settlements.

The predominant Bedouin response was refusal to move to Tal a-Sabi'. The land was being offered for lease for only forty-nine years and not for real purchase of full ownership. The state retained the right to enter the property at any time and for any purpose, and the Bedouins were denied the right to oppose any changes in the size or boundaries of the plot occupied. In effect, the contract lacked the requirements of security of tenure (Falah, 1983:314). Due to the failure of this settlement, the Israeli governmental planners who initiated a second settlement, Rahat, in the early 1970s, made a limited effort to take some Bedouin lifestyle and cultural factors into account, while still maintaining an urban model and advancing the aim of reducing the land occupied by the Bedouins. In this second town, Bedouin tribes or extended families were placed in different sections of the town according to their traditional relations, territorial distribution, and willingness to move. Each street and lane was identified with an extended family, and its households were concentrated on adjacent lots (Falah, 1983; Gradus and Stern, 1985; Marx, 2000). Furthermore, instead of providing small lots with small two-room houses, as was done in Tal a-Sabi', the Ministry of Housing allowed people to purchase or lease a "large" vacant lot (500–800 square meters) for each household within an extended family. The Bedouins were then free

Table 1. Government-Planned Towns in the Naqab: Year of Establishment and Population of Bedouins

Town	Founded*	Population (2008)†
Tal a-Sabi'	1968	14,600
Rahat	1972	43,900
Ara'ra a-Naqab	1981	13,500
Kseife	1982	11,200
Shqeb a-Salaam	1984	7,100
Hura	1989	11,800
Laqiya	1990	9,700

* Marx (2000).
† Israel Central Bureau of Statistics (2008: table 3).

to build their houses according to their own budgetary resources and household and social needs. The planning model used in Rahat was extended to new neighborhoods that were added to Tal a-Sabi', as well as to the additional five planned Bedouin towns that were established during the 1980s and 1990s (see table 1).

Over time, the Bedouin families that had been rendered landless by the removal from their traditional lands and relocation to the Restricted Area, as well as those that had been landless before 1948 and those that were affected by a new wave of displacements in the 1980s, moved to the planned urban settlements. For the Bedouins without land, moving to the towns was preferable to their ambiguous temporary status on lands classified as "state land" or, according to Bedouin law, land belonging to another family or tribe. This process moved slowly, as social or economic infrastructure and employment opportunities were lacking in the towns (Marx, 2000:113). These economic conditions increased reluctance to become completely urbanized. Doing so would entail giving up animal husbandry, which provided the Bedouins with a safety net supporting their participation in the labor market, particularly since they tended to hold the most vulnerable positions in this market.

Furthermore, aside from the provision of basic services (water, electricity, telephone service, schools, and clinics), the government-planned towns lacked essential urban characteristics. In his 2002 report, the state comptroller reported that none of the Bedouin towns had a completed sewage system, even though they had been in existence for many years and thousands of families had already paid for this essential system (State Comptroller, 2002:109). In four of the seven towns (Tal a-Sabi', Ara'ra a-Naqab, Hura, and Laqiya), the sewage system was not operational at all. Unlike their neighboring urban settlements in the Jewish sector, these government-planned towns also lacked intra- and inter-city public transportation, banks, public libraries, public parking lots, and recreational and cultural centers.

The one exception was the largest town, Rahat, of over 43,000 inhabitants, which had one bank, one post office, and a cultural center. Public transportation services commenced in Rahat in May 2009 (Abu-Saad, 2003; Lithwick, 2000).

Local Government in the Planned Bedouin Towns

The seven Bedouin towns in the Naqab are among the most recent government-established towns in Israel, with the local governing body of the oldest (Rahat) having been established in 1980 and of the most recent (Hura and Laqiya) in 1990. All of their local councils were headed by non-resident Jewish mayors appointed by the Ministry of the Interior for many years, as the Bedouins were considered incapable of governing themselves in their new urban context (Abu-Saad, 2008b; Swirski and Hasson, 2006; Yiftachel, 2006). It has been the Ministry of the Interior's standard procedure to appoint a council of professionals for an initial period (e.g., until the next nationally scheduled local council elections, every four or five years) in all newly established towns in order to facilitate their initial development. One of the first appointed mayors to head the Bedouin town of Laqiya had previously worked for the military administration of Palestinians in the occupied West Bank, which raises the question of just what type of "professional" skills the Interior Ministry deemed essential to establishing and developing a Bedouin town. Furthermore, the "initial period" of an appointed council for the Bedouin towns stretched for over ten years in all cases, until the Bedouin inhabitants of the towns themselves challenged it in the Israeli Supreme Court, which ordered the Ministry to allow the Bedouin towns to hold local elections. The first elections for local authorities in Rahat and Tal a-Sabi' were held in 1988 and 1992, respectively, while elections in the remaining five Bedouin local authorities were held in 2000, again only after the involvement of the Supreme Court.

Despite the formal apparatus of locally elected government, self-governance or autonomy in the Bedouin towns is limited for a number of reasons. First, their access to and control over land is so circumscribed that they barely have enough to meet the needs of natural population growth by replicating the same high-density urban model, and thus they cannot begin to consider other development or land-use options. While the populations of the townships constitute 16% of the population of the Beersheba subdistrict, their jurisdiction covers only 0.5% (60 square kilometers) of the subdistrict area (12,945 square kilometers). As Shlomo Swirski and Yael Hasson have explained:

> These facts are particularly striking when Bedouin localities are compared with Jewish ones: Dimona, whose population is smaller than Rahat's (33,700 and 34,100 residents, respectively, in 2003), has an area of jurisdiction of 30.6 sq. km.—3.5 times that of Rahat (8.85 sq. km). Omer, whose population is around half of that of its Bedouin neighbor, Tel Sheva, has an area of jurisdiction which is 2.7 times that of Tel Sheva. (2006:58)

Second, the budgets of the government-planned towns are the lowest in the entire country (Swirski and Hasson, 2006:51). One of the main reasons for this is that the low socio-economic status of the Bedouins living in the towns, together with the lack of local economic activities, translates into a very low income from property and local business taxes. Extra budgetary support from the government, despite oft-voiced official concern for improving the conditions and attractiveness of the towns, has been insufficient, and these town budgets remain the lowest in the country. Furthermore, governmental authorities have done nothing to address the clear need for large-scale investment in educational and economic infrastructures or to generate local places of employment, even though a detailed development plan for the seven towns, created through a joint Bedouin-university initiative, was submitted to the government (Abu-Saad and Lithwick,

2000). Such investment would generate a higher level of self-funding and could thus be translated into greater capacity for independent indigenous development. The national government's lack of support for any such initiatives, however, suggests that it prefers the status quo of urbanized Bedouins who remain impoverished and dependent.

Education, health, and social welfare services in the Bedouin towns are supplied by and controlled through national governmental channels and, as with other governmental provisions, receive minimal and often insufficient funding given the scope of needs (Abu-Saad, 2008b; Abu-Saad, Lithwick, and Abu-Saad, 2004; Golan-Agnon, 2006). Many small (and even competing) non-governmental organizations dealing with a wide array of issues have sprouted up in the Bedouin towns in the past two decades in response to the lack of services. However, in most cases, both their organizational missions and their funding sources are determined by members of the Jewish Israeli majority, which has tended to thwart their ability to develop indigenous models of service provision and support in the urban context.

Regional Non-Integration

At the same time that the governmental urbanization policy was actively being pursued to "modernize" the Bedouins so that they could be integrated into the Israeli labor market and society, the government-planned towns were being excluded from the broader development plans for the region. In several key regional plans, for both the Naqab and the Beersheba metropolitan area (including the 1972 District Plan, the 1991 "Naqab Front" strategy, the 1995 Beersheba Metropolitan Development Plan, and the 1998 renewed District Plan), the areas of Bedouin towns and unrecognized villages were either left blank, as if nonexistent, or designated for public use, such as sewage plants, recreational forests, or industrial zones (Yiftachel, 2000,

2006). Important new infrastructure developments, such as the new Trans-Israel Highway, recently improved railway facilities, and even inter-city bus services have taken virtually no account of the Bedouin towns and their needs. The systematic underdevelopment of the government-planned Bedouin towns is evident from the official governmental document ranking local and regional authorities in Israel according to a socio-economic index, which places the Bedouin localities at the bottom of the list (see table 2).

While the urbanization of the Naqab Bedouins suited the policy goal of reducing their de facto use of and control over land resources, no real attempt has been made by the state to integrate the new Bedouin towns into the national infrastructure in a viable and meaningful sense. They were not given sufficient resources for independent development because Israeli governmental policy toward the indigenous Palestinian minority has consistently aimed at maintaining their dependence on the Jewish economic and power structures in order to maximize the state's control over them (Abu-Saad, 2008b, 2010; Lus-

Table 2. Socio-Economic Ranking of Local and Regional Localities in the Naqab

Local Authorities	Rank*
Tal a-Sabi'	1
Kseife	2
Ara'ra a-Naqab	3
Shqeb a-Salaam	4
Rahat	6
Hura	8
Laqiya	9
Regional Authorities	Rank
Abu Basma	1

* The number 1 denotes the *lowest* ranking among the 197 local authorities and the 54 regional authorities in Israel.

Source: Israel Central Bureau of Statistics (2009).

tick, 1980). As such, the towns that the Israeli government planned for the Bedouins bear less resemblance to urban centers of economic, educational, service, and social activity than to the typical colonial model of reservations, except with urban-style density, built to facilitate the transfer of land use and control to the dominant Jewish majority. For Naqab Bedouin Arabs who wanted to establish permanent homes and receive basic services, the only legal alternative was to move into the government-planned urban settlements. However, this represented a traumatic cultural, as well as economic, decision. Thus, over four decades after the initiation of the urban resettlement program, only half of Bedouins live in the government-planned towns. The remainder live in "unrecognized villages."

Unrecognized and Newly Recognized Villages

A little under half of the Bedouin Arab population—around 84,000 people—live in localities or towns that are unrecognized by the Israeli state. An unrecognized village can be home to between 60 and 600 families (500–5,000 people) that typically live in tents or makeshift wooden or metal shacks (Regional Council of Unrecognized Villages, 2000). These villages do not appear on official Israeli maps and lack official road signs. Due to Bedouin Arab resistance to the urbanization program, the Israeli government has undertaken numerous efforts to pressure the inhabitants of unrecognized localities to move to the government-planned towns (Abu-Saad, 2005). The unrecognized villages are denied services such as paved roads, public transportation, electricity, running water, garbage disposal, telephone service, community health facilities, and, in many cases, schools. The residents of the unrecognized villages are acutely aware of the discriminatory governmental policies toward them. A resident of the unrecognized village of Tarabin al Sana (located next to the Jewish town of Omer) described the situation:

> Look how we live. We live like animals in the mud. Then walk through that gate into Omer and see how nicely they live there. Our kids have to get up at 6:15 to be bussed to school in one of the recognized townships. Next door the kids of Omer walk out the door at 7:50 a.m. to be at the local school at 8:00 a.m. But they still want to get rid of us. Why can't we become residents of Omer? I'm an Israeli citizen, I have been living in this village all my life, this is my home, why can't I keep living here? (Human Rights Watch, 2008:22)

Bedouin Arabs in the unrecognized villages are also denied permits to build any sort of permanent housing. All forms of housing are considered illegal and subject to heavy fines and demolition (Abu-Saad, 2005, 2008b; Falah, 1989; Maddrell, 1990; Shamir, 1996; *Statistical Yearbook of the Negev Bedouin*, 1999). Governmental demolition activities escalated between 2006 and 2010, and, in a new development, entire villages have been destroyed. For example, on June 25, 2007, all dwellings in the village of Um Al-Hiran were demolished, leaving 150 people homeless. All of their possessions were confiscated, including medicine, children's books, school materials, and food. The village of Twail Abu Jarwal, which had around 100 residents, was demolished for the first time in 2006. The residents responded by rebuilding their homes, and governmental forces destroyed their village over thirty times between then and 2010 (Regional Council of Unrecognized Villages, 2010).

In terms of government, the unrecognized villages are denied their own officially recognized representative authorities or local councils. Consequently, they are denied two clear rights: a local authority to provide them with basic services and the right to elect local representatives. The majority of residents of the unrecognized villages live in areas devoid of any municipal authority. Even those who do live in an area under a municipal authority, such as those villages within the jurisdiction of Jewish regional councils like Bnei Shimon and Ramat

Hanegev, do not receive public services from these bodies and are not eligible to participate in their elections.

This situation remained largely static until 2000, when the government decided to grant "recognition" (full recognition for some, but partial recognition for the majority) to ten villages (see table 3).[8] Although recognition would appear to fulfill much of what the Bedouin population has claimed and demanded over the decades, the process has been fraught with difficulties. The main concerns include the seemingly arbitrary selection of the area to be recognized and the absence of effective local participation in the planning of these newly "recognized" villages. The process involves the demarcation of a limited area within a contested site as officially "recognized"; this newly demarcated boundary of the relevant zoning plan is referred to as the "blue line" (International Human Rights Clinic, 2008). Those Bedouins who live outside these new borders generally have refused to move within them, and others have voiced concern that the territory is insufficient for future natural expansion. Moreover, some of the land within the new borders is subject to outstanding land ownership claims.[9]

Table 3. List of Unrecognized Villages Undergoing Governmental Recognition Process

Name	Population (2005)
Elgren (El-Said)	3,900
Im Bateen	3,500
Im Metnan (Abu Krenat)	4,050
Kaser El Ser	2,900
Tlaa' Rshaid (Moladah)	3,200
Abu Tlool (Elshahabi)	4,000
Alfora'a	3,900
Amra (Tarabeen)	1,000
Beir Haddaj	4,700
Drejat	1,050

Source: The Arab Center for Alternative Planning, http://www.ac-ap.org.

In September 2003, the Ministry of the Interior established the Abu Basma Regional Council as the local authority of the newly recognized villages; the council began operating in early 2004. Despite its ostensible role as representative of several Bedouin villages, it is headed by a Jewish mayor who operates from the council offices in Beersheba. The most recent strategy of the Israeli government has been to emphasize the inability of the Bedouin population to succeed in formal legal settings and thus the need to turn to alternative measures. However, as an alternative, the Abu Basma Regional Council is a "representative" body for a population that feels absent from its operations. The representatives themselves, although formally the "representatives" of the newly recognized villages, were appointed by the government (Human Rights Watch, 2008).

Administrative Mechanisms Governing the Unrecognized Villages

Historically, Bedouins in general, and the residents of the unrecognized villages in particular, have been governed by a number of administrative structures and units set up especially for the Bedouin Arabs. These include most notably the Green Patrol, the Bedouin Education Authority, and the Bedouin Advancement Authority, all of which are directed by Israeli Jewish appointees (Abu-Saad, 2001, 2008b; Swirski and Hasson, 2006; Yiftachel, 2006). The creation of the Abu Basma Regional Council represents a continuation of the Israeli government's "special" and segregated treatment of issues affecting the Bedouins. While it has involved official governmental recognition of villages that were previously unrecognized and subject to demolition, it has also involved abdicating substantial land claims in exchange for official recognition and planning. In addition to its responsibility for the newly recognized villages, the council is tasked with the provision of education and welfare services to the unrecognized villages. The initial concept was to create a "transitional" council to prepare the way for a more representative entity, but a 2009 law undermined the hope that the council might in fact prove representative. In a demonstration of the close relationship between the council and the Israeli government, a law passed in December 2009 permitted the government to postpone elections to the council until the Ministry of the Interior "deems the local Bedouin ready to run their own affairs" (Cook, 2009). The Ministerial Committee on the Non-Jewish Sector announced a "comprehensive development plan for the Abu Basma Regional Council" in 2005, proposing a three-year plan to develop services and infrastructure. However, relatively little of the promised NIS 470 million was transferred to the council (Human Rights Watch, 2008). An additional three administrative bodies for the Bedouins, described briefly below, are still functioning either independently of or as a part of the Abu Basma Regional Council.

The Green Patrol

The Green Patrol was established by the Israeli government in 1976 as a paramilitary unit to pressure Bedouin Arabs to move into urban settlements. Officially, the Green Patrol is located in the Ministry of Environmental Affairs, but it operates through a committee of directors-general with representatives of the Israeli military, the Jewish National Fund, the Ministry of Agriculture, the Ministry of Defense, the Ministry of the Interior, the Ministry of Construction and Housing, and the Israel Land Administration (ILA), most of which also contribute to its funding (Swirski and Hasson, 2006; Tabibian-Mizrahi, 2004).

The Green Patrol's official mandate is to preserve nature and oversee state lands. In practice, this organization acts to police, harass, and evict Bedouin Arabs living outside the urban settlements (Abu-Saad, 2000, 2008b; Swirski and Hasson, 2006; Yiftachel, 2006). It operates to both prevent the Bedouins from "creating facts" on land occupied by them but not officially designated Bedouin settlements, and to reduce the number of Bedouin flocks considered as "dangerously overgrazing" according to the 1950 Black Goat Law (Falah, 1985b:365). In response, Naqab Bedouins have filed numerous reports of harassment against the Green Patrol (what they call the "Black Patrol") for their tactics, which include destroying Bedouin Arab dwellings, crops, and trees; intimidation by shooting into the air; beatings; and killing livestock (Swirski, 2008:40).

The Bedouin Education Authority

In the absence of local municipal bodies for the unrecognized villages that would normally provide education services, these services were provided through the Bedouin Education Authority (BEA), established by the Ministry of Education in 1981. The BEA was responsible for the building, maintenance, and renovation of the sixteen schools and seventy kindergartens and for bussing 12,000 schoolchildren to these schools and kindergartens, as well as to the high schools in the planned towns (there are no high schools in the unrecognized villages).

Rather than developing educational services within the unrecognized villages, the BEA worked primarily to control the community, awarding services on a discretionary basis as part of the politics of patronage, so that these services were provided not as a right but as a favor dispensed to those who were loyal. This patronage overrode even the planning regulations and resulted in the provision of services in an ineffective and irrational manner (Abu-Saad, 2001, 2003, 2008b; Human Rights Watch, 2001).

From its inception, the BEA was run by Jewish directors who worked for the benefit of a close network of clients. The patronizing and control-oriented approach of the BEA is exemplified by its former director, Moshe Shohat, who characterized the Bedouin community members organizing to improve their school services as "blood-thirsty

Bedouins who commit polygamy, have 30 children and continue to expand their illegal settlements, taking over state land" (Lazaroff, 2002). When Shohat was questioned about providing indoor plumbing in Bedouin Arab schools, he responded, "In their culture they take care of their needs outdoors. They don't even know how to flush a toilet" (Berman, 2001). In response to the public Bedouin outcry, the Ministry of Education initially condemned Shohat's remarks, but refused to remove him. This led, on September 23, 2001, to the filing of a petition in the Supreme Court to have Shohat removed and to have the Ministry of Education issue a public bid for his replacement among Bedouin Arab citizens in the Naqab.[10] The Ministry of Education then informed the Court on March 25, 2002, that it intended to dismiss Shohat as a result of financial irregularities in his management of the BEA; one year later, in March 2003, Shohat was dismissed. At the Supreme Court hearing in May 2004, the Attorney General's Office notified the Court that the state intended to dissolve the BEA by January 2005 and that the newly planned Abu Basma Regional Council would provide all educational services to children living in both the newly recognized Bedouin Arab towns (under Abu Basma's jurisdiction) and the remaining unrecognized villages (Adalah, 2004). Thus the BEA often served as a means of control over the community rather than to provide educational services in a manner respectful of and responsive to their needs and concerns. This approach continued even after the establishment of the Abu Basma Regional Council, as its Education Department is headed by a Jewish director, perpetuating the BEA's control-oriented approach to providing these services.

The Bedouin Advancement Authority

The Bedouin Advancement Authority (BAA), established in 1984, controlled the planning and policy development and implementation for the Bedouin Arab community in the Naqab until recently. All state funding for Bedouin Arab communities, including the development budgets of the recognized Bedouin towns, came through the BAA office rather than directly from the various state ministries, as has been the practice with all other localities (including other Palestinian Arab localities) in Israel. Administratively, the BAA was a subunit of the ILA, which indicates an agenda behind the benevolent name— namely, nationalizing Bedouin land and concentrating Bedouins in the townships. The BAA received a large budget to settle land claims of the Bedouin Arab community through the payment of very low compensation, but generally the money reverted back to the central government unused (Abu-Saad, 2008b; Swirski and Hasson, 2006). In addition to land resources, the BAA had absolute control over provision of access to water for the Naqab Bedouin Arabs in unrecognized villages. Since these villages are not connected to the national water system, their inhabitants are given access to water in designated central locations at very high prices, from which they must transport the water to their homes in containers. The BAA operated a highly restrictive water policy, using this as another means to encourage people to leave their land and move to the seven government-sanctioned towns. The BAA also had a monopoly on all planning for the Bedouin Arab community. Thus, it was responsible for opening new neighborhoods in the original seven government-planned towns and establishing new towns. In short, no development could occur for any Naqab Bedouin Arab community, recognized or unrecognized, if not sanctioned and carried out by the BAA (Swirski and Hasson, 2006).

In July 2007, the government issued a resolution to establish a new "special" body that would replace the BAA, called the "Bedouin Authority." This new body has assumed all responsibility over land and housing issues related to the Bedouin community (Abu-Saad, 2008b).

Organized Community Resistance

In 1997, Bedouin Arabs living in the unrecognized villages formed their own council, the Regional Council for the Unrecognized Villages (RCUV), as a grassroots community movement (Abu-Saad, 2008b; Yiftachel, 2006). The RCUV drew up and submitted its own plans for regional development to the Ministry of the Interior. However, the Ministry did not accept the RCUV's proposed plan for more appropriate rural settlement models and has remained intent on continuing with the same unsuccessful urban model with only superficial improvements, even though it faces serious and organized resistance from the Bedouin Arab community. The first level of resistance is that people *en masse* are refusing to move to the planned towns, despite the many coercive measures used against them. In addition, they are expanding their dwellings to meet the needs of their natural population growth, as well as building small businesses and other community structures (e.g., mosques and soccer fields). Many have begun building more permanent structures (e.g., cinderblock and stone houses rather than tin shanties) and their response to house demolitions is to rebuild rather than relocate. The more recent governmental plans for "recognizing" additional villages have not lessened this community resistance, since these plans entail resettling the village inhabitants in high-density urban locations around government-constructed service centers. Most of the community has steadfastly refused to cooperate with the "urbanizing" plans and has continued to insist on an agricultural-based development model (Abu-Saad, 2008b).

At a second level of resistance, various local Bedouin Arab community organizations, along with nationwide organizations representing the indigenous Palestinian minority, have begun launching proactive legal action. They have exploited cracks in the Israeli legal structure to oppose the discriminatory practices driven by Judaization policies that contradict the tenets of law and governmental responsibilities to its citizens (Yiftachel, 2006). For example, during the 1990s, the government's responsibility to provide compulsory education to all children aged three to sixteen was used in successful appeals to the Israeli Supreme Court to obtain permission to build preschools and supply (generator-powered) electricity to elementary schools in the unrecognized villages. At the same time, the Supreme Court denied appeals to build high schools in the unrecognized villages. In addition, a lawsuit brought against the Ministry of Health to have public mother-and-child health-care clinics was successful and resulted in the opening of such clinics in some of the unrecognized villages (Adalah, 2009).

More recently, the Supreme Court ruled that the planners of the new regional Beersheba Metropolitan Plan must make an official commitment to include Bedouin Arab concerns, opinions, and representation in the planning process (though there is considerable skepticism in the Bedouin Arab community as to how this will be done, and what will be done, since their request for agricultural villages was denied and they were told they had to "be more realistic") (Yiftachel, 2006). In addition, the decision to expand the municipal boundaries of the Jewish town of Omer by annexing the land owned and occupied by Bedouin Arabs in several adjoining unrecognized villages was challenged in the Supreme Court, so that the expansion was nearly totally cancelled (Yiftachel, 2006). Since 2000, however, there have also been a number of failed efforts to use the legal route, with, for example, the denial of appeals to provide a point for drinking water in an unrecognized village and to provide electricity to cancer patients and others with life-threatening illnesses in unrecognized villages (Abu-Saad, 2008b; Yiftachel, 2006).

The third level of resistance was the formation of several alliances of local and national non-governmental organizations, such as the Forum Together for Equality and Growth, the Negev Coexistence Forum for Civil Equality, and the Recognition Forum. These alliances coordinate a range of self-help and non-profit programs for community empowerment, education, and legal representation (Yiftachel, 2006). The local resistance has led to an increasing interest and involvement of international organizations on Bedouin human rights, including Human Rights Watch, the International Human Rights Clinic of Harvard Law School, and the Habitat International Coalition.

Governmental Response to Community Resistance

The sustained Bedouin community resistance has led to several Israeli government initiatives. One was the Barak government's decision in November 2000 to set up centers to provide services for residents of the unrecognized villages in conjunction with a declaration calling for a "comprehensive, all-inclusive multi-year master plan to be drawn up for the establishment of the settlements for the Negev Bedouin." This was purportedly to be carried out with representatives of the Bedouin population and to take account of the various tribes' needs and desires. Although the RCUV viewed these developments in a positive light, it refused the request of the Barak government to drop Bedouin land claims in the wake of the decision (Swirski and Hasson, 2006:64–66).

In late 2003, the Israeli government passed a series of three resolutions with regard to the Bedouin population and the Naqab. Resolution 881 ratified the earlier Barak government decision to recognize seven unrecognized villages.[11] At the same meeting, the Sharon government instituted a multiyear plan to address the Bedouin population. The six-year NIS 1.1 billion plan endorsed the previous plans for recognition of seven unrecognized villages but primarily focused on changes in law enforcement as a method to address the governmental plans and the Bedouins in the Naqab (Abu-Ras, 2006; Swirski and Hasson, 2006:59, 81). Three months later, follow-up resolutions outlined specific steps for implementing the earlier plans.[12]

Implementation of the legislation focused on the creation of a coordinated administration under the authority of the Israeli police force for the enforcement of land laws, including the management of such bodies as the Green Patrol and the Ministry of Internal Security. Additional enforcement units in the police force and Attorney General's Office were established by the same legislation (Swirski, 2007:25).

When requested by the Sharon government to accept the decision as a final settlement—precisely the request made by the Barak government several years earlier—the RCUV refused. As one report describes it, the RCUV viewed the Sharon Plan as "a declaration of war" against its community, since a large portion of the funds targeted for the Bedouins was to be utilized for law enforcement rather than development or improvement of rural areas in which the majority of the Bedouins live. Since ILA budget allocations have been skewed consistently away from the line item for "planning and development in the minorities sector" (Swirski and Hasson, 2006:69, 72), the reservation of further funds for "law enforcement"—meaning eviction and house demolitions—rather than development of Bedouin areas revealed the government's priorities regarding the Bedouins.

Thus, the government's response to the Naqab Bedouins' continued resistance to urbanization policies has been to increase the role of Green Patrol and other paramilitary measures, in some cases directly focusing on harassment of the leaders of the Bedouin Arab resistance (Cook, 2003).[13] These measures perhaps foreshadow a fallback to the days immediately before and after the 1948 conflict, when the military acted with full power and took measures to "empty" the land for Jewish settlement.

Current Living Conditions of the Naqab Bedouin Arabs

Health Status and Social Services

Health indicators for the Naqab Bedouin Arab community indicate that this population suffers from problems endemic in both developing and developed societies. Though the infant mortality rate among the Naqab Bedouins (13.7 per 1,000) is lower than that in most developing countries, it is over four times higher than the infant mortality rate among Israeli Jews (3.1 per 1,000). Half (50%) of Naqab Bedouin Arabs are under the age of thirteen (Israel Central Bureau of Statistics, 2007). Overcrowding in Bedouin Arab households is common, where families numbering seven or more constitute 40%–45% of households, as compared to 1%–10% of households in Israeli Jewish settlements (Israel Central Bureau of Statistics, 1999). These conditions are associated with higher rates of illness, hospitalization, and mortality for infectious diseases among Bedouin Arab children than Jewish children (Abu-Saad et al., 2001).

Chronic diseases, such as ischemic heart disease, acute myocardial infarction, cerebrovascular disease, and diabetes, rare among the Bedouin Arabs until the 1970s, are increasing rapidly (Tamir et al., 2007). A study conducted in 1985 found that urbanized Bedouin Arab men were significantly more likely than traditional Bedouin Arab men to be obese and overweight, indicating that urbanization and the associated changes in lifestyle were altering the pattern of cardiovascular risk factors in this population (Fraser et al., 1990). Recent studies on diabetes among urbanized Israeli Jews and Bedouin Arabs in the Naqab indicate that the disease is approximately twice as prevalent among Bedouin Arabs than among Jews (Abu-Saad et al., 2001). Research also indicates that the management of chronic diseases is poorer among Bedouin Arabs than among Jews (Cohen et al., 2005; Tamir et al., 2007).

The seven government-planned towns for the Naqab Bedouins continue to have much lower levels of health services and poorer quality of such services than other towns throughout the region, despite the community's greater health needs (Abu-Saad et al., 2004). There are insufficient social service professionals and few recreational facilities in the towns, in spite of major problems of youth violence and crime, as well as an urgent need for childcare facilities. The number of social workers, for example, is about one-quarter to one-fifth of those in comparable Jewish towns. These services are essential for the building of a healthy, secure community. The shortage of Bedouin Arab professionals in these fields poses a major obstacle to ensuring the delivery of high-quality services. The obvious lesson is that investment in training more Bedouin Arab professionals is of the highest priority.

There were no health clinics in the unrecognized villages until 1994, and today there are only twelve primary health clinics and eight family care clinics serving all of the unrecognized villages, with limited hours and overcrowded conditions.[14] Bedouin Arabs living in the unrecognized villages are at much higher risk for infectious and many other diseases because of the living conditions imposed on them by governmental policies (e.g., lack of community curative and preventative health clinics, running water, mains electricity, sewage systems, and paved roads) (Almi, 2003, 2006; Gottlieb, 2006). Bedouins from unrecognized villages are less likely than those from the planned towns to be aware of health services; they are more likely to complain about the distance from health-care facilities and to argue that services are not provided when needed, that they are too expensive, and that language barriers affect their ability to obtain them (Al-Krenawi, 2004:46–47). Ambulances must be ordered for complicated treatment that cannot be administered at the basic facilities in the unrecognized villages, and these ambulances refuse to enter the villages. Instead, patients must be taken from the village to the main road, lengthening the transportation time for those in need of critical treatment.[15]

The average Bedouin woman has 7.2 children, yet women in the unrecognized villages do not receive specialized treatment at most clinics because doctors are general practitioners.[16] It is therefore not surprising that 80% of women in the unrecognized villages go without care (Gottlieb, 2008). Infant mortality rates in the unrecognized villages are three times the local average in the Naqab and about twice as high as the average for the Palestinian Arab population (Gottlieb, 2005). Special tests for women (such as pregnancy monitoring, antenatal diabetes detection, and ultrasounds) are almost completely unavailable at primary care clinics (Physicians for Human Rights–Israel, 2009). Moreover, physicians are usually male, and women "cannot speak about intimate issues" with them,[17] both because of gender differences and because half the physicians and administrative assistants do not speak Arabic (Physicians for Human Rights–Israel, 2009:22).

As of 2004, there was one mental health center servicing all Bedouin villages, recognized and unrecognized, and a maximum of two psychologists who spoke Arabic in the Naqab (Al-Krenawi, 2004:65). Mental health services have been provided free of charge only to schoolchildren in need of special education or classified as "at risk."[18] Parents have hesitated to send their daughters to receive these services because of the "stigma" that adversely "affects their chances of getting married in the future."[19] A recent survey found that 66% of the women surveyed in recognized villages were aware of the availability of mental health services, as opposed to 39% of women surveyed in the unrecognized villages (Al-Krenawi, 2004:50).

Educational Services

The Israeli public school system has functioned to maintain the effective cultural, socio-economic, and political subordination of its Palestinian Arab citizens through the imposition of aims, goals, staffing, and curriculum to which the students cannot relate, as well as the substandard and discriminatory provision of educational resources, programs, and services (Abu-Saad, 2008c; Tarrow, 2008). Together, these result in a markedly poorer level of educational achievement and rates of students qualified to enter higher education. As with every other aspect of the education system in Israel, these inequitable outcomes are a matter not of chance but of policy.

As figure 1 indicates, the percentage of Naqab Bedouin Arab children who drop out before graduating from high school has been decreasing; however, they still have the highest dropout rates in the country. In 2008, 27% dropped out, compared to 22% and 16% in the broader minority Palestinian Arab sector and the Jewish sector, respectively (Israel Ministry of Education and Culture, 2006, 2009).

To compound the problem of high dropout rates in Naqab Bedouin Arab schools, the success rates of the children who do stay in school and complete the twelfth grade have been very low, even compared with other Arab students in Israel, as figure 2 demonstrates. In the 2007–2008 academic year, only 27% of Naqab Bedouin Arab high school students passed the matriculation exams (a basic requirement for continuing on to higher education), compared with 32% in the broader Arab sector and 51% in the Jewish sector (Israel Ministry of Education and Culture, 2009). Furthermore, as figure 3 shows, an even lower percentage of Bedouin Arab students have matriculated at a level that qualifies them to apply to the university (16% in 2005; see Israel Ministry of Education and Culture, 2006).

Among the barriers to the full realization of the right to education within the Bedouin community have been the predominance of culturally irrelevant textbooks and curriculum and the lack of qualified teachers. The national curriculum has tended to emphasize Jewish history and values while generally disregarding the Bedouin Arab narrative, thereby alienating Bedouin students (Tarrow, 2008:148, 150, 154). With respect to teachers, a 1998 Investigatory Committee on the Bedouin Educational System in the Negev presented a report to the minister of education recommending an increase in human resources in Bedouin educational institutions. Specifically, the report

Figure 1. Dropout Rates in Age Cohort of 17-Year-Olds among Bedouins, Arabs, and Jews, 1990–2008

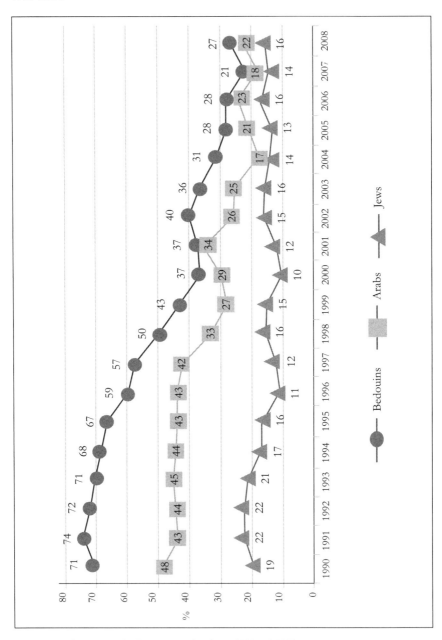

Source: Israel Ministry of Education and Culture (2006, 2009).

Figure 2. Percentage of Students from Age Cohort of 17-Year-Olds Who Pass the Matriculation Exam among Bedouins, Arabs, and Jews, 1990–2008

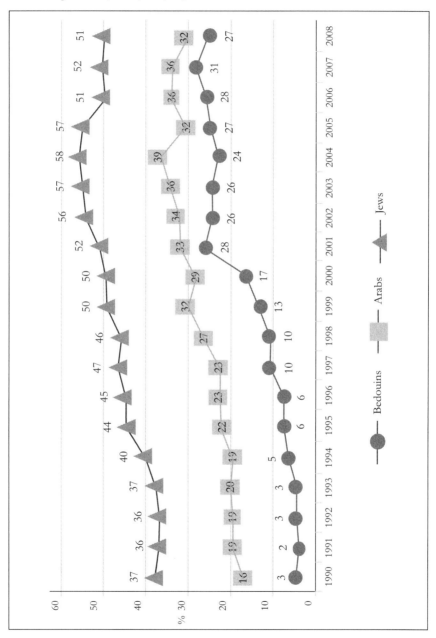

Source: Israel Ministry of Education and Culture (2006, 2009).

Figure 3. Rate of Matriculation Certificates Meeting Minimal Requirements for Admission to University among Bedouins, Arabs, and Jews, 2001–2005

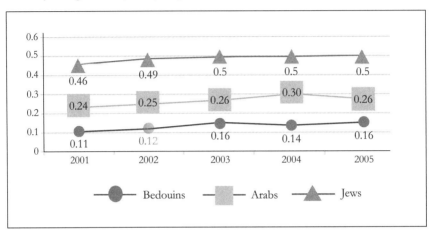

Source: Israel Ministry of Education and Culture (2006).

encouraged the government to train and hire more qualified teachers. As of 2006, the Abu Basma Regional Council established two teacher-training facilities in the Naqab; nevertheless, a large number of Arab teachers from the north must still be employed. The shortage of qualified teachers has been linked to the relatively low quality of education in Bedouin schools (Tarrow, 2008:147–148).

Lastly, the lack of access to schools in Bedouin communities severely restricts Bedouin children from receiving adequate education. One study found that 75% of the inhabitants of unrecognized villages live more than one kilometer away from an elementary school and that 63% live more than five kilometers away (Abu-Bader and Gottlieb, 2008:129). While recent building programs have increased the amount of educational infrastructure in Bedouin communities, the increased capacity also reflects an increase in population and therefore does not greatly mitigate the general shortage of schools and libraries. Additionally, education is economically inaccessible to many Bedouins, especially higher education (Tarrow, 2008:148, 155).

The Naqab Bedouins in the Context of the Global Indigenous Struggle

Indigenous peoples around the world have survived concerted efforts to exterminate, isolate, and assimilate them. Ironically, efforts to assimilate them through urbanization has created a new generation of indigenous peoples with the unique skills, capabilities, and inside knowledge required to better carry on the struggle for survival as indigenous communities, as well as to better use the systems, structures, and resources of mainstream society for their peoples' development. They have faced many coercive pressures and attacks on the cultural, social, economic, and political foundations of their societies and yet have survived. They have experienced the breakdown of traditional social structures, but in many cases have responded by adapting and rebuilding new social structures—particularly in urban areas (Abu-Saad, 2008b). Thus, despite the many negative aspects of the government-planned urbanization of the Naqab Bedouins in Israel, if the story of indigenous survival worldwide is any indication, they too will survive, with their identity and connectedness to their history, heritage, and land. In the years that have passed since Israel's establishment, there has been little or no change in its land policies, despite the state's lack of success in completely removing the indigenous presence from the land. The indigenous Palestinian Bedouins have almost no rights to "state lands," despite their "formal" status as Israeli citizens, because "state lands" are in actuality "Jewish lands," as the next chapter elaborates. Because of this, Palestinian Bedouins are effectively reduced to the illegitimate and dehumanized status of "the non-Jewish threat." After more than half a century as citizens of Israel, they remain illegal invaders and a threat to the vision of Zionism.

The resistance of the Palestinian Arab minority in Israel, however, has steadily evolved over the past fifty years. Within the past decade, indigenous Palestinian human rights organizations have emerged throughout the country, and they are beginning to develop channels of resistance, using the legal and civil mechanisms of Israeli society with some measure of success (Abu-Saad, 2008b). The Naqab Bedouins, who, even in the face of great adversity, have shown the tenacity typical of the Palestinian people to withstand efforts to remove them from their land, have also begun to organize their resistance through the development of their own (albeit unrecognized by the government) regional council.

The government's response to this resistance, particularly under the leadership of Prime Ministers Sharon, Olmert, and Netanyahu, has been to intensify the use of coercive measures to achieve its goals. However, the ongoing and increasingly conflict-ridden deadlock between the Israeli government and the Naqab Bedouin Arabs will endure for as long as the state is unwilling to relinquish its colonial goals of Judaizing and de-Arabizing the land and to listen to indigenous voices, representing the interests of all of its citizens equally.

In addition to the question of how indigenous peoples will adapt and respond to the changes imposed on them by mainstream society, we must ask how mainstream society will adapt and respond to the reality of indigenous peoples' persistent survival and their place in modern nation-states. Indigenous peoples will continue the struggle to preserve their cultures and their rights. The way in which nation-states respond to these struggles will serve as a litmus test for their "democratic" accountability, tolerance, and universality.

Indigenous peoples worldwide have shown a readiness to negotiate with nation-states to create more multicultural and democratic societies. Although their urbanization has been detrimental on some levels, on other levels it has empowered them with new skills for carrying on the resistance. New heights of pan-indigenous cooperation at the national, regional, and international levels have also been empowering and may serve to facilitate more successful negotiations between indigenous communities and nation-states, creating more equitable, productive, consensual, and democratic relationships (Champagne and Abu-Saad, 2003b).

The experience of indigenous peoples worldwide holds an important lesson for the Bedouin Arab case in the Naqab. Successive plans and policies, ranging from extermination to separation to assimilation, have treated indigenous peoples as a "problem" to be solved according to settler society interests. Virtually all of these plans have resulted in failure at an extremely high social cost to indigenous societies, as well as a high moral and social cost to mainstream societies. These failed policies have in many cases eventually led to violent confrontation and to growing demands from indigenous communities for self-determination. They have also created incrementally expanding recognition by mainstream societies that indigenous "problems" cannot be solved unless indigenous peoples play a major and meaningful role in the development of the solutions, which should address past injustices committed against them.

REFERENCES

Abu-Bader, S., and Gottlieb, D. (2008). "Education, employment and poverty among Bedouin Arabs in southern Israel." *HAGAR Studies in Culture, Polity and Identities* 8(2):121–136.

Abu Hussein, H., and McKay, F. (2003). *Access Denied: Palestinian Land Rights in Israel*. London: Zed Books.

Abu-Ras, T. (2006). "Land disputes in Israel: The case of the Bedouin of the Naqab." *Adalah's Newsletter* 24:1–9.

Abu-Saad, I. (1991). "Towards an understanding of minority education in Israel: The case of the Bedouin Arabs of the Negev." *Comparative Education* 27(2):235–242.

———. (2000). "Land issues and Bedouin urbanization." *Karkah* 50:159–169 (Hebrew).

———. (2001). "Education as a tool for control vs. development among indigenous peoples: The case of Bedouin Arabs in Israel." *HAGAR International Social Science Review* 2(2):241–259.

———. (2003). "Israeli 'development' and education policies and their impact on the Negev Palestinian Bedouin." *Holy Land Studies* 2(1):5–32.

———. (2005). "Forced sedentarisation, land rights and indigenous resistance: The Palestinian Bedouin in the Negev." In N. Masalha (ed.), *Catastrophe Remembered: Palestine, Israel and the Internal Refugees* (pp. 113–142). London: Zed Books.

———. (2008a). "Introduction: State rule and indigenous resistance among Al Naqab Bedouin Arabs." *HAGAR Studies in Culture, Polity and Identities* 8(2):3–24.

———. (2008b). "Spatial transformation and indigenous resistance: The urbanization of the Palestinian Bedouin in southern Israel." *American Behavioral Scientist* 51:1713–1754.

———. (2008c). "Present absentees: The Arab school curriculum in Israel as a tool for de-educating indigenous Palestinians," *Holy Land Studies* 7(1):17–43.

———. (2010). *Arabs of the Neqab: Past, Present and Future Challenges.* Beersheba: The Center for Bedouin Studies and Development and the Negev Center for Regional Development, Ben-Gurion University of the Negev.

Abu-Saad, I., and Lithwick, H. (2000). *A Way Ahead: A Development Plan for the Bedouin Towns in the Negev.* Beersheba: The Center for Bedouin Studies and Development and the Negev Center for Regional Development, Ben-Gurion University of the Negev.

Abu-Saad, I., Lithwick, H., and Abu-Saad, K. (2004). *A Preliminary Evaluation of the Negev Bedouin Experience of Urbanization: Findings of the Urban Household Survey.* Beersheba: The Center for Bedouin Studies and Development and the Negev Center for Regional Development, Ben-Gurion University of the Negev.

Abu-Saad, K., Weitzman, S., Abu-Rabiah, Y., Abu-Shareb, H., and Fraser, D. (2001). "Rapid lifestyle, diet and health change among urban Bedouin Arabs of southern Israel." *Food, Nutrition and Agriculture* 28:45–54.

Adalah. (2004). "News update: In response to Adalah's petition, Attorney General notifies Supreme Court that the Bedouin Education Authority will be dismantled by January 2005." May 9. http://www.adalah.org (accessed November 17, 2011).

———. (2009). "News update: Adalah petitions Supreme Court against health ministry demanding re-opening of mother and child clinics in three Arab Bedouin unrecognized villages in the Naqab." December 16. http://www.adalah.org/eng/pressreleases/pr.php?file=09_12_16 (accessed May 30, 2012).

al-'Ārif, 'Ā . (1943). *The History of Beersheba and its Tribes*. Jerusalem: Bait al-Maqdis (Arabic).

Al-Krenawi, A. (2004). *Awareness and Utilization of Social, Health/Mental Health Services Among Bedouin-Arab Women, Differentiated by Type of Residence and Type of Marriage*. Beersheba: The Center for Bedouin Studies and Development, Ben-Gurion University of the Negev.

Almi, O. (2003). "No man's land: Health in the unrecognized villages in the Negev." Physicians for Human Rights–Israel. http://www.phr.org.il (accessed November 17, 2011).

———. (2006). "Water discipline: Water, the state and the unrecognized villages in the Negev." Physicians for Human Rights–Israel. http://www.phr.org.il (accessed November 17, 2011).

Arab Association for Human Rights. (1999). "Article 26: Factsheet No. 3: The Arab Bedouin of the Negev." Nazareth, Israel: HRA. http://www.arabhra.org (accessed November 17, 2011).

Arenstein, Z. (1978). "A case for the Bedouin." *Jerusalem Post*, May 31.

Berman, R. (2001). "Bedouin probe seen as 'farce.'" *The Jewish Week*, August 17.

Champagne, D., and Abu-Saad, I. (eds.). (2003a). *The Future of Indigenous Peoples: Strategies for Survival and Development*. Los Angeles: American Indian Studies Center, UCLA.

———. (2003b). "Concluding remarks and conference declaration." In D. Champagne and I. Abu-Saad (eds.), *The Future of Indigenous Peoples: Strategies for Survival and Development* (pp. 249–257). Los Angeles: American Indian Studies Center, UCLA

Cohen, A. D., Gefen, K., Ozer, A., Bagola, N., Milrad, V., Cohen, L., Abu-Hammad, T., Abu-Rabia, Y., Hazanov, I., and Vardy, D. A. (2005). "Diabetes control in the Bedouin population in southern Israel." *Medical Science Monitor* 11(8):376–380.

Cook, J. (2003). "Bedouin in the Negev face new 'transfer.'" The Middle East Research and Information Project (MERIP). http://www.merip.org (accessed November 17, 2011).

———. (2009). "Bedouins in Israel denied elections." *The National*, December 7.

Falah, G. (1983). "The development of the 'planned Bedouin settlement' in Israel 1964–1982: Evaluation and characteristics." *Geoforum* 14(3):311–323.

———. (1985a). "How Israel controls the Bedouin." *Journal of Palestine Studies* 14(2):35–51.

———. (1985b). "The spatial pattern of Bedouin sedentarization in Israel." *GeoJournal* 11(4):361–368.

———. (1989). "Israel state policy towards Bedouin sedentarization in the Negev." *Journal of Palestine Studies* 18(2):71–90.

Fraser, D., Weitzman, S., Blondheim, S., Shany, S., and Abou-Rbiah, Y. (1990). "The prevalence of cardiovascular risk factors among male Bedouins: A population in transition." *European Journal of Epidemiology* 6(3):273–278.

Golan-Agnon, D. (2006). "Separate but not equal: Discrimination against Palestinian Arab students in Israel." *American Behavioral Scientist* 49(8):1075–1084.

Goldberg Commission. (2008). Final report of the Commission to Propose a Policy for Arranging Bedouin Settlement in the Negev. December 11. http://www.moch.gov.il/spokesman/pages/doverlistitem.aspx?listid=5b390c93-15b2-4841-87e3-abf31c1af63d&webid=fe384cf7-21cd-49eb-8bbb-71ed64f47de0&itemid=42 (accessed November 17, 2011) (Hebrew).

Gottlieb, N. (2005). "Accessibility and utilization of antenatal care among the Arab Bedouin of the unrecognized villages of the Negev Desert." Physicians for Human Rights–Israel. http://www.phr.org.il (accessed November 17, 2011).

———. (2006). "On the path to health: Access to antenatal care in the unrecognized villages of the Negev." Physicians for Human Rights–Israel. http://www.phr.org.il (accessed November 17, 2011).

———. (2008). "Gender and health in the unrecognized villages of the Negev." Physicians for Human Rights–Israel. http://www.phr.org.il (accessed November 17, 2011).

Gradus, Y., and Stern, E. (1985). "From preconceived to responsive planning: Cases of settlement design in arid environments." In Y. Gradus (ed.), *Desert Development: Man and Technology in Sparselands* (pp. 41–59). Dordrecht, Netherlands: Reidel.

Haaretz. (1963). July 31 (Hebrew).

Human Rights Watch. (2001). *Second Class: Discrimination Against Palestinian Arab Children in Israel's Schools*. New York: Human Rights Watch.

———. (2008). *Off the Map: Land and Housing Rights Violations in Israel's Unrecognized Bedouin Villages*. New York: Human Rights Watch.

International Human Rights Clinic, Harvard Law School. (2008). *International and Comparative Studies in Land and Property Claims: The Case of the Bedouin of the Negev in Israel: Submission to the Public Committee for Arranging the Settlement of Bedouin in the Negev*. Beersheba: International Human Rights Clinic.

Israel Central Bureau of Statistics. (1999). *Israel Statistical Abstract 50*. Jerusalem: Central Bureau of Statistics.

———. (2007). *Israel Statistical Abstract 58*. Jerusalem: Central Bureau of Statistics.

———. (2008). *Israel Statistical Abstract 59*. Jerusalem: Central Bureau of Statistics.

———. (2009). "Characterization and classification of local authorities by the socio-economic level of the population." http://www.cbs.gov.il (accessed November 17, 2011).

Israel Ministry of Education and Culture. (2006). *Matriculation Examination Data for 2005*. Jerusalem: Ministry of Education and Culture.

———. (2009). *Matriculation Examination Data for 2008*. Jerusalem: Ministry of Education and Culture.

Jiryis, S. (1976). *The Arabs in Israel*. New York: Monthly Review Press.

Kimmerling, B. (1982). "Settlers without frontiers." *The Jerusalem Quarterly* 24:114–128.

Law-Yone, H. (2003). "From sedentarization to urbanization: State policy towards Bedouin society in Israel." In D. Champagne and I. Abu-Saad (eds.), *The Future of Indigenous Peoples: Strategies for Survival and Development* (pp. 175–183). Los Angeles: American Indian Studies Center, UCLA.

Lazaroff, T. (2002). "A roller-coaster year." *Jerusalem Post*, March 8.

Lewando-Hundt, G. (1979). "Tel Sheva: A planned Bedouin village." In A. Shmueli and Y. Gradus (eds.), *The Land of the Negev* (pp. 662–672). Jerusalem: Defense Ministry Press (Hebrew).

Lithwick, H. (2000). *An Urban Development Strategy for the Negev's Bedouin Community*. Beersheba: Center for Bedouin Studies and Development and the Negev Center for Regional Development, Ben-Gurion University of the Negev.

Lustick, I. (1980). *Arabs in the Jewish State: Israel's Control of a National Minority*. Austin, TX: University of Texas.

Maddrell, P. (1990). *The Bedouin of the Negev*. Report No. 81. London: Minority Rights Group.

Marx, E. (1967). *Bedouin of the Negev*. New York: Praeger.

———. (2000). "Land and work: Negev Bedouin struggle with Israel bureaucracies." *Nomadic Peoples* 4(2):106–120.

Masalha, N. 1992. *Expulsion of the Palestinians: The Concept of "Transfer" in Zionist Thought, 1882–1948*. Washington, D.C.: Institute for Palestine Studies.

———. 1997. *A Land Without a People: Israel, Transfer and the Palestinians*. London: Faber and Faber.

Musham, H. V. (1959). "The sedentarization of the Bedouins in Israel." *International Social Science Journal* 11(4):539–549.

Physicians for Human Rights–Israel. (2009). "The bare minimum: Health services in the unrecognized villages in the Negev." http://www.phr.org.il/default.asp?PageID=157&ItemID=340 (accessed November 17, 2011).

Prior, M. (1999). *Zionism and the State of Israel: A Moral Inquiry*. London: Routledge.

Quigley, J. (1990). *Palestine and Israel: A Challenge to Justice*. Durham, NC: Duke University Press.

Regional Council of Unrecognized Villages. (2000). *Characteristics of the Arab Bedouin Unrecognized Villages in the Negev*. Beersheba: RCUV (Hebrew).

———. (2010). *Records*. Beersheba: RCUV (Hebrew).

Shamir, R. (1996). "Suspended in space: Bedouins under the law of Israel." *Law and Society Review* 30(2):231–257.

Smith, L. T. (1999). *Decolonizing Methodologies: Research and Indigenous Peoples*. London: Zed Books.

State Comptroller. (2002). *State Comptroller Report 52b*. Jerusalem: Office of the State Comptroller (Hebrew).

Statistical Yearbook of the Negev Bedouin. (1999). Beersheba: The Center for Bedouin Studies and Development and the Negev Center for Regional Development, Ben-Gurion University of the Negev.

Swirski, S. (2007). *Current Plans for Developing the Negev: A Critical Perspective*. Tel Aviv: Adva Center.

———. (2008). "Transparent citizens: Israel government policy toward the Negev Bedouins." *HAGAR Studies in Culture, Polity and Identities* 8(2):25–45.

Swirski, S., and Hasson, Y. (2006). "Invisible citizens: Israel government policy toward the Negev Bedouin." Tel Aviv, Adva Center. http://www.adva.org/UPLOADED/NegevEnglishFull.pdf (accessed November 17 2011).

Tabibian-Mizrahi, M. (2004). *Trespassing on Land and Buildings*. Jerusalem: Knesset Research and Information Center (Hebrew).

Tamir, O., Peleg, R., Dreiher, J., Abu-Hammad, T., Abu Rabia, Y., Abu Rashid, M., Eisenberg, A., Silbersky, D., Kazanovich, A., Khalil, E., Vardy, D., and Shvartzman, P. (2007). "Cardiovascular risk factors in the Bedouin population: Management and compliance." *The Israeli Medical Association Journal* 9(9):652–655.

Tarrow, N. (2008). "Human rights and education: The case of the Negev Bedouins." *HAGAR Studies in Culture, Polity and Identities* 8(2):137–158.

Yiftachel, O. (2000). *Lands, Planning and Inequality: The Distribution of Space between Jews and Arabs in Israel: A Position Paper.* Tel Aviv: Adva Center (Hebrew).

———. (2003). "Bedouin-Arabs and the Israeli settler state: Land policies and indigenous resistance." In D. Champagne and I. Abu-Saad (eds.), *The Future of Indigenous Peoples: Strategies for Survival and Development* (pp. 21–47). Los Angeles: American Indian Studies Center, UCLA.

———. (2006). *Ethnocracy: Land and Identity Politics in Israel/Palestine.* Philadelphia: University of Pennsylvania Press.

Zeidani, S. (2005). "The Palestinian Arab predicament in Israel." In Y. Reiter (ed.), *Dilemmas in Arab-Jewish Relations in Israel* (pp. 89–96). Tel Aviv: Schocken (Hebrew).

NOTES

1. *Al-Nakba* means "the Catastrophe" and is the word Palestinians use to describe their dispossession and displacement in 1948.

2. A dunam is an Ottoman measuring unit equivalent to 1,000 square meters. Four dunams equal one acre. Arenstein (1978) noted that the Bedouins worked between one and two million dunams before Israel was created. According to Abu Hussein and McKay (2003:127), approximately two million dunams were estimated to be in the possession of the Bedouins before 1948. See also Arab Association for Human Rights (1999); Maddrell (1990:5).

3. The residents of the unrecognized villages currently hold 180,000 dunams of land, or 1.3% of the total area of the Naqab (Goldberg Commission, 2008:16).

4. Marx (1967:10) estimates 55,000–65,000 Bedouins during this time.

5. According to the Goldberg Commission Report (2008), the number was 12,740 in 1951. Senior Zionist statesman Chaim Weitzman declared this Palestinian exodus "a miraculous simplification of Israel's tasks" (cited in Lustick, 1980:28).

6. Great Britain had expressed interest in maintaining control over the region, and proposals were put forth to transfer the Naqab to the Palestinian Arab state or Hashemite Kingdom. After 1948, both Jordan

and Egypt also claimed sovereignty over the Naqab or alternatively demanded a corridor through the region (Swirski, 2008:26).

7. Law-Yone has explained it thus:

    Hierarchies of space based on tribal social structure were replaced by repetitive lots of uniform size, shape and orientation. Gradations of proximity, enclosure and openness of the desert were replaced by the spatial logic of European urban form. New and strange definitions of private and public spheres were grafted onto a society that had its norms, which were no longer considered valid. (2003: 181)

8. In 2000, the government of Israel announced the recognition of six Bedouin villages and indicated that it would consider three additional villages for future recognition. In addition to those initially designated nine villages, the state has also been pursuing a recognition process for three additional villages (Israel Government Resolution No. 2562 [47/ Arab], November 30, 2000 (Hebrew)).

9. Interview with Dudu Cohen, Head of the Planning Unit for the Abu Basma Regional Council, Beersheba, December 2, 2009; interview with Hussein Al-Rafaya'a, Chairperson of the RCUV, Beersheba, October 21, 2007; International Human Rights Clinic (2008).

10. Supreme Court 7383/01, *Megel el-Hawashleh et al. v. Minister of Education et al.*, May 3, 2004.

11. Resolution 881 (Arab/15), September 25, 2003, cited in Swirski (2007:25).

12. Resolution 2886, December 12, 2003; Resolution 2959, December 23, 2003.

13. Committee on Economic, Social and Cultural Rights, Concluding Observations: Israel, U.N. Doc. E/C.12/1/Add.90 (2003).

14. Interview with Wasim Abbas, Director of Health Programs in the Unrecognized Villages, Physicians for Human Rights–Israel, and Dr. Monsour of the Wadi Anni'am Health Clinic, Wadi Anni'am, Israel, December 24, 2009.

15. Ibid.

16. Ibid.

17. Ibid.

18. Interview with Suaad Abuobeid, Mental Education Unit, Abu Basma Regional Council, Beersheba, December 24, 2009.

19. Ibid.

Abstract

This chapter analyzes the regulatory framework utilized in the reconstruction of space in Israel, particularly Bedouin space in the Naqab, since 1948. The analysis focuses on the legal, institutional, and planning mechanisms that have functioned to systematically nationalize land and Judaize space in Israel's southern region. The chapter outlines a process of land expropriation, nationalization, skewed ethnic allocation, and land development, paying special attention to Israeli legislation, the complex web of state institutions that implement policy, and patterns of Bedouin response. The chapter is informed by theories of settler societies, ethnocratic nationalism, and Bedouin indigeneity, and is based on scholarly literature, legal documentation, court cases, and field interviews with Bedouin citizens of the Naqab. It argues that Israeli land policy and planning, governed by the goal of Judaization, has utilized a range of legal and extralegal instruments to render Bedouin claims to recognition and equity invisible by limiting Bedouins' land resources while attempting to urbanize and modernize them.

CHAPTER 2

Unsettling Settlements:
Law, Land, and Planning in the Naqab

Ahmad Amara and Zinaida Miller

Introduction

The contemporary situation of the Bedouin Arabs of the Naqab[1] is a product of multiple historical, political, and legal factors, among the most significant being the reorganization of political life around ethno-national objectives after 1948, the interests of the state in organizing and controlling both territory and population, and conceptions of modernization and development. Historical legacies of the Ottoman and British systems, in combination with the peculiarities of Israeli ethnocracy, resulted in a system that formally includes Bedouin Arabs as citizens and yet paints them as outside the national collective and as enemies of "progress"—concepts defined in the Israeli state lexicon as both "modern" and "Jewish."

Comprehending the position of Bedouin citizens of the Israeli state requires an examination of the politics, historical narratives, and legal techniques that have structured the State of Israel. In the pre-state 1930s, dominant sectors within both the immigrant Jewish settler community and the native Arab population of Palestine perceived the

The authors are grateful to Geremy Forman, Alexandre Kedar, Cosette Creamer, Aziza Ahmed, and Ylana Miller for their invaluable comments. This chapter is based in part on interviews conducted in Beersheba, Rahat, Hura, Laqiya, and several unrecognized villages in the Naqab. Interviews were sponsored by Harvard Law School's International Human Rights Clinic and coordinated with the Regional Council for the Unrecognized Villages.

conflict between them as a zero-sum game in which any gains by one party meant an equal loss to the other. As Kimmerling has pointed out, the "central resources in the conflict were land and people—both tangible, measurable and easily quantifiable" (2001:44; see also Shafir, 1989). In the post-1948 world, however, the newborn Israeli state was formulated as an ethnocratic regime, a "distinct regime type established to enhance the expansion and control of a dominant ethno-nation in multiethnic territories" (Yiftachel, 2003:24; see also Yiftachel, 2006). As Yiftachel describes, ethnocracies constitute a subset of settler societies that seek the ongoing expansion of the dominant population's settlement and that promote a "frontier ethos" to consolidate the nationalist ideology of the dominant population. They typically combine formal democracy (regular elections with representation for all citizens) with various systems for facilitating land seizure and marginalizing indigenous populations. In such regimes, ethnicity rather than citizenship forms the basis for power and resource distribution (Yiftachel, 2006).

Today, the Bedouin inhabitants of the Naqab live primarily in "unrecognized villages" (visible to any visitor yet obscured in the eyes of the state) and Bedouin-only townships. While the Bedouins are citizens of the Israeli state, they have been subject to an ongoing state project of "modernization," urbanization, dispossession, and marginalization. The Naqab region has been designated a "frontier" for further Judaization; as a result, many of the resident Bedouins have been reconstructed not just as poor and primitive but as criminals and trespassers. Although a variety of human rights concerns have been raised by Bedouins and their advocates, much of the conflict between the state and its indigenous citizens can be traced to questions of land possession. While the state seeks continually to strengthen its control of the Naqab, many Bedouin Arabs continue to claim rights over land that they have possessed, cultivated, or grazed for centuries. Some Bedouin citizens maintain "illegal" residence on a portion of their claimed lands despite harsh living conditions and brutal state practices. The state continues a long-standing nationalization project, accomplished mainly through processes of forced urbanization, discriminatory planning policies, occasional criminalization of Bedouin "trespassers," and asymmetric court battles.

Although the story of land dispossession and demographic struggle is one shared with the larger Palestinian population of Israel, the history of the Naqab Bedouin Arabs has its own mechanics, policy discourses, and legal techniques. This chapter elucidates the contemporary and historical situation of the Naqab Bedouins in several ways. First, it deploys a descriptive, or mapping, exercise that aims to demonstrate the historical evolution of the Israeli legal system and its interpretation of the rules of predecessor systems to consistently privilege governmental claims over Bedouin claims. Second, it demonstrates the ways in which the rigidity of the Israeli court system regarding Bedouin claims has been both repeatedly reinforced and ostensibly mitigated by the creation of special governmental bodies to address the conditions of Bedouin life in the Naqab. These governmental committees have been employed to settle land disputes in ways that avoid implication of Israeli wrongdoing in 1948, to make increasingly unlikely any possible reinterpretation of Ottoman or British land laws, and to help institutionalize the continuing processes of urbanization and modernization. Third, the chapter highlights the ways in which Israel's planning system has helped construct the invisibility and vulnerability of Bedouin citizens, often by creating the background conditions against which Bedouin claims must be litigated.

The chapter thus argues that three major modes of state action form the contours of the Bedouin situation: (1) legislation that (in the early years of the state) expropriated Bedouin land or (in later years) restricted Bedouin land claims and contributed to creating "unrecognized villages" that were denied public services and infrastructure; (2) court decisions that reinterpreted Ottoman, British, and Israeli law to make Bedouin victories in land claims cases nearly impossible; and (3) administrative committees that bureaucratized and depoliticized Bedouin claims by making them technical matters to be resolved through compensatory formulas.

Finally, this chapter reveals the few places in which Bedouin citizens have experienced the possibility of some victories—whether through specialized committees or by using Israeli laws or international norms to make claims on the state for social services (particularly health and education) or village recognition—and suggests some possible costs or tradeoffs involved with these strategies. The history, institutional development, discourse, and legal decisions of the State of Israel make clear that the deck has been stacked against the Bedouin citizenry. However, the inherent tensions of the ethnocratic system, between formal rights accorded with citizenship and institutionalized ethnic discrimination, offer at least the possibility for some contestation.

The Bedouin Case through the Israeli Legal Lens

The establishment of the State of Israel and the institutionalization of aspects of Zionist ideology, particularly in terms of the "redemption" of the land of Israel from non-Jews, has resulted in inevitable and unresolved conflicts between the state and the indigenous Bedouin Arabs (among others). State policies have both reflected and institutionalized a concept of "nationalization as Judaization" and thus of land (in a complex relationship to population) as a crucial terrain for struggle and control. The process of land seizure and the attempts to consolidate state control of the Naqab have relied heavily on the law. The Israeli state's commitment to the formality of law has resulted in a complicated system of legal regulation often formulated to achieve the state's political objectives.

This section begins by providing a brief historical background against which Bedouin dispossession has taken place,[2] including the continuity of powerful pre-state Zionist organizations and their restrictive policies after 1948. It then outlines the main legislative tools employed since 1948 to expropriate land in Israel, particularly in the Naqab. Despite the specificity of the Bedouin case, the situation faced by the Bedouin Arabs of the Naqab falls within a broader set of modes of dispossession developed by the Israeli state to ensure control of the majority of Israel's territory by the state. After discussing these modes of dispossession, the section describes the land claims filed in the early 1970s by the Bedouin community and outlines the state's subsequent reactions to these claims.

Background

In 1948, the newborn State of Israel covered 20.6 million dunams of land,[3] constituting 78% of Mandatory Palestine. Of this area, however, only 8.5% of the land was officially owned by Jewish individuals and organizations. Added to the land and property inherited by the state from the British Mandate (under the 1951 State Property Law[4]), the total under state or Jewish ownership was still only 13.5% (Kedar, 2001:946).[5] As a result, an early priority of the state was the transfer of Arab land to state and Jewish control. In the early 1950s, those Bedouins who remained in Israel (approximately 11,000 people out of a pre-war population of about 90,000) were forcibly transferred by the Israeli army to the Restricted Area of the Naqab.[6] Through legislation depriving Palestinian refugees and "absentees" of their pre-1948 land holdings (as well as through judicial and administrative procedures described below), the Israeli state eventually came to control 93% of the country's land, administered by the Israel Land Administration (ILA). The remaining 7% of the land is under private ownership, almost equally divided between Jews and Arabs (Kedar, 2001:947). In addition to state seizure of land from Palestinian Arabs, the land regime made state land available and accessible almost exclusively to "the Jewish people" collectively, whether in Israel or abroad. Palestinian citizens, by contrast, have been blocked from leasing or acquiring rights to about 80% of state and public land (Yiftachel, 2006:143).

Organizational control

Although the legislation discussed below constituted the greatest force of expropriation in the early years of the state, certain administrative bodies that continued the objectives of the pre-1948 Zionist movement contributed heavily to the development of the land system. Three organizations in particular played (and continue to play) a crucial role in the allocation and control of land in Israel: the Jewish National Fund (JNF), the Jewish Agency, and the ILA.

Originally established in 1901 to acquire land in Palestine for "the purpose of settling Jews on such lands and properties,"[7] the JNF was granted special privileges under Israeli law after the establishment of the state, including facilitating land transfers from the state to the JNF, and considerable power in designing Israeli land policy. Following the purchase of two million dunams from the state in the early 1950s, the JNF became the largest agricultural landowner in Israel—and one that acted for the benefit of Jews alone (Holzman-Gazit, 2002; Yiftachel, 2006:139).[8]

The Jewish Agency was created in 1929 by the World Zionist Organization to facilitate immigration of Jews to Palestine in order to secure a Jewish majority and, after 1948, to strengthen the Jewish character of the state. Since 1960, the Jewish Agency has been involved in managing and leasing state land from the ILA to establish settlements designated exclusively for Jews. Non-Jews are excluded by virtue of the Jewish Agency mission itself, which is to serve the Jewish community exclusively.[9]

The third organization operating in Israel to maintain the ethnocratic land regime is the ILA. Established by the Israel Land Administration Law in 1960 and mandated to administer land owned by the state, the Development Authority, and the JNF, the ILA administers the 19,508,000 dunams (4,820,500 acres) of state and public land.[10] The law also allocates 50% of the ILA Council's seats to the JNF, thereby delegating significant power to the JNF in the area of Israeli land policy.[11] In compliance with the JNF's mission, the ILA cannot sell land; rather, it can lease land to the public, to the JNF, or to the Jewish Agency (for up to ninety-eight years), but must maintain land ownership on behalf of the Jewish people.[12] Under the 1961 Memorandum and Articles of Association of the JNF, the ILA is empowered to administer all JNF-owned lands. Due to the centrality of land to the Bedouins, the ILA has played a particularly significant role in Bedouin life, having been the "senior partner" in all governmental committees addressing Bedouin land and housing matters. Since 1986, the ILA has acted as the central Bedouin affairs governmental institution through the Bedouin Advancement Authority (BAA). The BAA was established to resolve Bedouin land claims through negotiation with Bedouin claimants and their resettlement in government-planned townships, although over the years it acquired more power with regard to the Bedouin community in both the townships and the unrecognized villages.

Expropriation through legislation

As a result of the state's interest in transferring control of territory to either Jewish public or state control, legislation passed soon after the establishment of the state was aimed at achieving mass land expropriation. The two main instruments employed were the 1950 Absentee Property Law (Transfer of Property Law) and the 1953 Land Acquisition (Validation of Acts and Compensation) Law.[13]

The Absentee Property Law effectively gave the state control over the land of Palestinian refugees (about 75% of the pre-1948 Palestinian Arab population) by defining those who were outside the borders of the State of Israel between November 29, 1947, and September 1, 1948, as "absentee owners" (art. 1) and thus subject to state land expropriation. The state appropriated between 4.2 and 6.6 million dunams under this law.[14]

Passed three years later, the Land Acquisition Law retroactively endorsed expropriations undertaken directly after the 1948 War, and laid the ground for further expropriation. It determined that land which had been controlled by the state since 1948 with no legal basis could be registered as state land if the land met the following three conditions: (1) it was not in possession of a third party in April 1952; (2) it was used or allocated by the state between May 14, 1948, and April 1, 1952, for development, settlement, or security purposes; and (3) it was still needed for such purposes. Land meeting the three conditions was transferred to the Development Authority, a body established in 1950 to administer the property of the Palestinian refugees and other property confiscated under the Land Acquisition Law.[15] The Development Authority populated Palestinian refugees' houses mainly with immigrant Jewish families and made land available to state authorities for developing new Jewish settlements. Under this law, much of the Bedouin land outside the Restricted Area was registered as state land, usually without the knowledge of the Bedouin owners. Of the 1.25 million dunams expropriated under the Land Acquisition Law, 137,400 dunams were expropriated from Bedouins in the Naqab (Noach: 2009b:36).

Legislation passed in the early 1950s thus established a foundation for continuing discrimination in the allocation, ownership, and use of land in Israel. Later legislation built on this foundation through planning measures, as well as continuing "justified" expropriation. For example, the 1965 Planning and Construction Law not only enabled further expropriation but eventually served both to make Bedouin Arab villages illegal by definition (by excluding them from zoning maps) and to restrict expansion of other Arab localities. The law created a hierarchy of planning bodies that drew up master plans at the national, district, and local levels. These planning authorities did not acknowledge the existence of populated Bedouin villages in the Restricted Area and zoned the land as national parks and reserves, agricultural areas, or military areas, rather than as residential. Due to this zoning process, Bedouin villages were rendered "illegal" and thus denied provision of public services and infrastructure, including roads, electricity, and running water; in addition, they were and are subject to demolition—even those villages that existed before 1965 or even before 1948 (Abu-Saad, 2008:5; Marx, 2000). The same 1965 law allowed for confiscation of land for public purposes (the government confiscated more than 60,000 dunams), leading to further state confiscation of Bedouin land in the Naqab, including land that the state used to build government-planned Bedouin townships (45,670 dunams confiscated in 1967) (Noach, 2009b:38).[16]

A further piece in the regulatory edifice was added in 1980. The Negev Land Acquisition Law (Peace Treaty with Egypt), also known as the Peace Law, was created in the context of the 1978 peace treaty with Egypt. Addressing the relocation of military bases in the Sinai, the law authorized the Israeli government to confiscate specifically designated land in the Naqab in order to build an airbase. A master plan for the northern Naqab formulated by the Planning Division of the Ministry of the Interior and published in 1976—two years prior to the peace treaty—indicates that the Israeli state specifically contemplated the construction of the airbase in areas heavily populated by Bedouin citizens (Falah, 1989:80).

Although the Peace Law implied recognition of the traditional rights of the Bedouins over their land by offering compensation for claimed lands, it also authorized the government to use force to remove owners or tenants who did not vacate the specified land within three months. The state expropriated more than 65,000 dunams of land belonging to the Bedouins of Tal al-Malah and removed approximately 7,000

Bedouins (750 families) from their land. The state then used the land to build, in addition to the Nevatim airbase, the government-planned townships of Kseife and Ara'ra a-Naqab for Bedouin families displaced from the site (Swirski and Hasson, 2006:20).[17]

Claims and counterclaims

In the early 1970s, the state declared the northern Naqab, including the Restricted Area, subject to land title settlement processes, in accordance with the 1969 Land Rights Settlement Ordinance (which had replaced the 1928 Land (Settlement of Title) Ordinance).[18] Bedouin citizens were asked to file land claims under the ordinance. By 1979, Bedouin Arabs had filed 3,220 claims to 778,856 dunams.[19] As described in detail below, Israeli authorities utilized the predecessor Ottoman and British land legislation to categorize Naqab land— including land claimed by Bedouin Arabs—as "dead land" (*mawat*). The effect of this designation was to prohibit Bedouins from acquiring rights over the land through the otherwise applicable doctrines of adverse possession or "revival" of land under articles 78 and 103 of the 1858 Ottoman Land Code (OLC). Under article 78 of the OLC, anyone who possessed and cultivated *miri* land (defined as cultivable land owned by the government) for ten years without dispute was entitled to a prescriptive deed over the land. Similarly, under article 103, anyone who cultivated *mawat* and revived it would acquire a titled deed to the land.[20]

Initiating what would become a familiar pattern of following a bureaucratic-administrative route rather than a judicial-adjudicative one, state authorities formed the 1975 Albeck Committee to address Bedouin land claims that would otherwise have been dealt with under the (relatively short) timeline of the 1969 ordinance.[21] The committee reaffirmed the state position that Bedouin land was in fact *mawat* and recommended that the government act in "good will" and go "beyond the letter of the law" (cited in Swirski and Hasson, 2006:17) to grant Bedouins some compensation for their land, on the condition that claimants give up their land claims and move to one of the government-planned townships (at the time, there were two). Concurrently, the land settlement officer (empowered by the 1969 ordinance to decide claims) was instructed by the Ministry of Justice not to proceed (Swirski and Hasson, 2006:16–19). As a result, all land claims were frozen, blocking the adjudicative option while opening the administrative path.[22] The state subsequently used the Albeck compensation scheme as a basis for future land settlement proposals over the claims. As of 2008, 380 of 3,220 land claims (12%) had been settled, covering an area of 205,670 dunams (about 18%).[23] Thousands, however, remained undecided, leaving the relevant land unregistered.

In 2003, after the publication of a new development plan for the Naqab, the Southern District Attorney's Office and the ILA began pursuing a strategy of "counterclaiming" in court against the approximately 3,000 unsettled land claims left frozen after 1975. Interpreting the reluctance of parts of the Bedouin community to pursue claims through the Albeck system as intransigence in the face of the "generous compromise" offered by the state, the government directly countered Bedouin court claims (Human Rights Watch, 2008:19). The National Strategic Plan for the Development of the Negev (Israeli Cabinet Resolution 4415), commonly referred to as "Negev 2015," included "an arrangement for the land issue to be resolved through counter-claims of ownership by the government using the courts" (Human Rights Watch, 2008:19). Although the claims themselves had been submitted more than thirty years prior, the Ministerial Committee on the Non-Jewish Sector "ordered the [ILA] to submit counter land claims" under article 43 of the Land Rights Settlement Ordinance of 1969. The ILA itself claims that the counterclaim strategy is part of a "strategy of protecting state resources . . . [and] safeguarding its land reserves for the benefit of the whole population" (Israel Land Administration, 2009:9).

By May 2008, the state had submitted about 450 counterclaims to the land officer, covering an area of 180,000 dunams. Of these counterclaims, 223 were transferred by the land officer to the Beersheba District Court in accordance with article 43 of the 1969 Land Ordinance. By May 2008, the state had won 80 counterclaim cases (62 through court rulings and 18 through out-of-court agreements), placing 50,000 dunams under state control.[24] Not a single case resulted in a decision in favor of the Bedouin claimant (Human Rights Watch, 2008:19). The counterclaim strategy had "severe implications" for the Bedouins, many of whom withdrew from (or avoided altogether) court hearings due to the high legal costs, "lack of trust in the legal system," or lack of formal documentation (Noach, 2009a:17–18). The counterclaim strategy served the interests of the Israeli government by both increasing the speed of resolution for Bedouin land claims and encouraging a perception in the Bedouin community that the Israeli court system would offer little or no opening for their claims. Finally, in conjunction with a variety of other tactics, the counterclaim measures reinforced the image of the Bedouins as illegal claimants without title to the land or appropriate "modern" evidence of ownership, easing the political ramifications of denying Bedouin land rights in one fell swoop.

Thus, a process that began with dispossession and war continued with legislative expropriation, administrative measures, and unwinnable court cases. This combination has created the appearance of a joint state edifice in which state interest in retaining territory and urbanizing the native inhabitants—in conjunction with ideological orientations and in the process of constructing a specific national identity—has resulted in a series of methods to reallocate territory from the minority population to the state. Eventually, the Bedouin inhabitants have lost their claims to land, passively resisted the system by remaining on their land and disengaging from the process, or become ensconced in an administrative system that promises resolution while retaining control over compensation and claim settlement. Central to all of these processes have been registration and land title processes and planning measures.

Land Settlement and Registration Processes

In addition to a legislative architecture built on the transfer of land to state control, the land title settlement process became an additional tool for land dispossession by the Israeli state. Despite the specific interests of the Israeli government, however, the determinations made in the post-1948 era remain intimately interconnected with the state's Ottoman and Mandate predecessors. Not only have later Israeli governmental positions attempted to dispossess Bedouin landholders due to the Bedouins' previous failure to register their land under Ottoman or British rulers, but the Israeli courts have construed Ottoman and British land law in ways that seemingly contradict both Ottoman and British interpretations. Although the predecessor doctrines were technically imported into the Israeli legal system in 1948, it was only through a series of judicial decisions that these doctrines were reinterpreted and deployed in ways designed to conform with exclusionary state policy.[25]

Bedouins traditionally controlled their own land ownership system, including lease, sale, and cultivation, according to a tribal land system that was tolerated by the authorities.[26] Their peripheral geographical location, among other factors, served to protect them from imperial or mandate bureaucracy. Further, Bedouin Arabs evaded land registration in order to avoid tax payments, to escape forced military service, and to maintain their traditional land systems. Israeli officials were later able to utilize such failure to register land during earlier eras as a justification for land seizure. The process of title registration, which began under the Ottoman Empire and continued under the Mandate, was used extensively by Israel, reflecting not only the ideological objectives of the state but a more general interest in centralization and control of territory and population through property records and population registers.

The Ottoman Empire

In 1858, the Ottoman authorities attempted to institutionalize a new land registration system by passing the OLC, which came to replace the old registration system in *sharia* courts.[27] The land categories created by the law have remained central to legal determinations of land ownership; however, the attempt to create mass land registration was not very successful. Bedouin Arabs under the Empire were uninterested in registering their land, a process that they understood—correctly— to be based on the Ottoman Empire's interest in tax revenue and military service. As a result, the majority of Bedouin land remained unregistered. By the end of the Ottoman period, only 5% of the land in Palestine had been registered, demonstrating that not only the Naqab Bedouins but most of Palestine's population had failed to register their land (Kedar, 2001:933).

The OLC codified several legal categories for land, of which two have become central to contemporary Bedouin claims: *mawat* and *miri*. *Mawat* land was defined in the OLC as uninhabited, uncultivated land, not possessed by any individual. Land was determined as *mawat* based on three possible measurements: (1) the point at which a loud voice from the nearest village, town, or inhabited place could no longer be heard; (2) half an hour's walk from the nearest inhabited place; or (3) 1.5 miles away from the inhabited place (OLC, art. 6). Crucially, under article 103, the person who first cultivated and revived *mawat* land could acquire title over it as *miri* land, a status indicating that "formal and ultimate ownership was held by the State, though a considerable degree of possession and use rights remained in the hands of the individual landholder," including the transfer of rights

(Kedar, 2001:933). Such an individual had the right to purchase it for its "*mawat* value," even if he cultivated the land without a permit from state authorities.

The British Mandate

The British Mandate government similarly attempted to institute a registration system, based both on a general interest in promoting central organization and a private property regime and on the specific requirement of fulfilling the terms of the League of Nations Palestine Mandate.[28] According to the Mandate, the British were required to "encourage, in co-operation with the Jewish Agency . . . close settlement by Jews on the land, including State lands and waste lands not required for public purposes."[29] Indeed, the first land laws to have a serious impact on Palestinian rural areas—among them the 1921 Mawat Land Ordinance—targeted state land and wastelands (Bunton, 2007:30–49). However, the Bedouins had a similar reaction to the proffered registration process under the Mandate as they had had under the Ottomans; fear of taxation, as well as an interest in protecting their customary systems, led to relatively little registration of land by the Bedouins under British rule (Swirski, 2008:29). In addition, the British land settlement process began in the northern areas of Palestine; land registration processes had not yet reached the Beersheba district when the Mandate ended in 1948. As a result, land cultivated and possessed by the Bedouin Arabs was not registered by the Mandate land department.[30]

Under the 1921 ordinance, which amended the OLC, anyone wishing to cultivate *mawat* land was required to obtain a state permit; if he failed to do so, he was considered a trespasser on the land. According to the same ordinance, anyone claiming title over *mawat* land was required to register that title with the state land authorities within a two-month period set by the ordinance—that is, by April 18, 1921.[31]

The British Mandate government, like that of the Ottomans, granted significant autonomy to Bedouin residents of the Naqab. Mandate authorities repeatedly addressed questions of title deeds and land rights in the Naqab as matters to be determined by the Bedouin tribal court established by the British, in accordance with the traditional land system. On March, 29, 1921 (two weeks prior to the statutory deadline ending the two-month window for the registration of land), Secretary of State for the Colonies Winston Churchill "reaffirmed the assurances already given at Beersheba by the High Commissioner to the Sheikhs that the special rights and customs of the Bedouin Tribes of Beersheba will not be interfered with."[32] Further, in 1930, as recorded by Chief Justice Sir Michael McDonnell, the Supreme Court of Palestine determined that

> in view of the absence of title deeds to land in the Beer-sheba area and the necessity for the production of a title deed under Article 24 of the Magistrate Law, a case such as this appears to be one of those for which the application of tribal custom under Article 45 of the Palestine Order-in-Council is specially intended. (McDonnell, 1934:458)

The Mandate's recognition of Bedouin historical land rights in the Naqab is further illustrated by the response of the Mandate authorities to a 1937 request by the Jewish Agency (headed at the time by future Israeli Prime Minister David Ben-Gurion) to allow Jews to settle on land in the Naqab. The request claimed that the Naqab land was *mawat*—in other words, state—land. In response, the Mandate authorities declared that

> [t]he cultivable land in the Beersheba sub-district is regarded as belonging to the Bedouin tribes by virtue of possession from time immemorial. . . . [I]n the past the lands have been occupied entirely as tribal land, but in recent years the practice of allotting tribal holdings has

come into existence, thus enabling sales to be made to Jewish interests. (Government of Palestine, 1937)[33]

Even in this brief excerpt, two aspects of the British relationship to Naqab land are revealed: first, the recognition of Bedouin land rights "from time immemorial" and, second, acknowledgment that the land could and should be made available through individual sales. Essentially, tribal possession was recognized, but the land was increasingly alienable—including to Jewish buyers. Whether due to their lack of interest in developing the Naqab or centralizing territorial control completely, the British authorities viewed land rights in the Naqab, even after their own 1921 Mawat Land Ordinance, to be governed primarily by local custom, and thus viewed this land as distinct from the category of *mawat* land. The absence of title deeds was regarded as an invitation to apply the law differently due to the special circumstances of the Beersheba region rather than as a method for depriving the Bedouins of their land and rights.[34]

The State of Israel

Despite the relative autonomy granted to the Bedouins under the preceding regimes, the interests of the newly established State of Israel in consolidating both state and Jewish territorial control led to increasing scrutiny of Bedouin land claims. While one version of expropriation took place through legislation in the early 1950s, a second mode of "reallocation" of land took place in the executive and judicial branches. The judicial approach involved several elements: procedural, evidentiary, and substantive. The state's interest in territorial control was closely related to the pursuit of a reinterpretation of Ottoman land law to narrow the possibility of Bedouin land control and ownership. Since *mawat* land was by definition state land, the government and the courts had a direct interest in declaring as much land as possible as *mawat*. The result was a system that dramatically narrowed the category of *miri* land while radically expanding that of *mawat* land.

Procedural and evidentiary elements redefined the ways in which Bedouin claimants could demonstrate land possession. Under the OLC, to prove that land was *miri* rather than *mawat,* and thus to gain prescriptive title by adverse possession, Bedouin claimants were required to show that they had possessed and cultivated the land for ten years without dispute (OLC, art. 78). However, additional restrictions on the type and admissibility of evidence with regard to proving adverse possession were imposed by the Israeli Supreme Court. While actual possession of land was given significant evidentiary weight during the British Mandate, its significance declined dramatically in Israeli judicial decisions, primarily during the 1950s (Kedar, 2001:974). In addition, Israeli courts required a higher standard of proof for demonstrating cultivation.[35] Under the Mandate, the cultivation requirement was determined based on the nature of the land; in some cases, fencing or plowing the land was considered sufficient. By contrast, the Israeli Supreme Court imposed a new condition of 50% cultivation, using Mandate-era aerial photos taken in 1945 by the British as proof of lack of cultivation. In addition, the Court rejected tax payment records as evidence of cultivation or to prove rights in land settlement processes (Kedar, 2001:973–984).

The substantive changes made by the Israeli government and the courts were primarily in the realm of reinterpreting the requirements for *mawat* land. The state's position on *mawat* land was largely established during the land title settlement process in the Galilee area of northern Israel in the 1950s and the 1960s; it was subsequently applied to the Naqab. The OLC had determined that the cultivation of *mawat* land—even without the authorities' permission—could be used to gain title of the land as *miri* land. This process gave significant liberty to Bedouin landholders in terms of translating their claims into title. By contrast, the Israeli Supreme Court interpreted the requirements of *mawat* in increasingly broad ways while narrowing the definition of *miri* land. In the 1961 *Badaran* case, the Court chose one formalized condition (distance) for determining *mawat* land, rather than the three (voice, walking, or distance) that the Ottoman law had allowed. The distance criterion of 1.5 miles from an inhabited settlement became the exclusive element used to determine *mawat* land.[36] This interpretation built on a 1956 case in which the Supreme Court narrowed the definition of "inhabited places," ruling that only an established city or village could be used as the baseline for the 1.5-mile requirement; the Court explicitly determined that a Bedouin encampment would not constitute a village for these purposes.[37] The OLC itself had no definition of "settlement"; while it used the terms "town" and "village" in some places, it also used the term "inhabited places" (arts. 6, 103). Thus,

> in the overwhelming majority of cases, the Supreme Court established that however long a person had possessed and cultivated a tract of land outside the immediate vicinity of a recognized town or village, ownership and possession would be attributed to the state. (Kedar, 2001:953)

Perhaps most significantly, the Court narrowed the temporal conditions for determining *mawat* land. In the *Badaran* case, Justice Zvi Berinson ruled that a settlement had to have existed "before the enactment of the 1858 OLC, which is the determining date for this matter."[38] Thus, only a settlement (defined by the Court as a village or town) that had existed since at least 1858 would constitute a legitimate point from which to measure the distance to the claimed land. This requirement was completely new; neither Ottoman nor British laws had included it. This final condition potentially rendered an extraordinary portion of the Naqab as *mawat* (and thus state) land: by 1900, forty-two years after the enactment of the OLC, Beersheba was the only city established in the region. As a result, the ILA viewed the *Badaran* decision as paving the way for the nationalization of all Naqab lands as *mawat* (state) land. In a 1964 letter to the head of the ILA, the head of the ILA Ownership and Registration Department suggested that the Naqab Bedouin land claims "be claimed (as a test case) by the state as *Mawat*, on the basis of the Supreme Court Decision in C.A. 518/61 Badaran and C.A. 274/62, Ali Suead."[39] The 1984 *Al-Hawashla* case on land rights of Bedouins in the Naqab confirmed this legal construction and made the state's test case a norm.[40]

The Court's determination in the *Al-Hawashla* case that Naqab land should be considered *mawat* (state land) unless proven to the contrary placed the burden of proof on Bedouin claimants with regard to the existence of an established settlement dating to 1858.[41] In addition, it relied on the formal requirement established under the British Mandate that anyone who had failed to register their land during the two-month registration period established in 1921 by the Mawat Land Ordinance could have no rights over the land. Although technically following British precedent, the Court was in fact relying on a requirement that the British themselves had routinely circumvented (Kedar, 2001). This decision controlled all future judicial and administrative decisions on Bedouin land claims by Israeli courts and administrative authorities, making it difficult—if not impossible—for Bedouin claimants to win a case to register their land.

The *Al-Hawashla* decision essentially endorsed the executive and legislative positions, creating a seemingly allied front among key governmental branches of the Israeli state with regard to limiting recognition both of Bedouin possession of Naqab land and of the precedents set by British courts. The decision described the indigenous population of the area as a nomadic people with no attachment to the land, thus legitimating land control by the state. As Ronen Shamir has noted:

> Nomadism becomes an essentialist ahistorical category that provides rational foundations for appropriating land on the one hand and for concentrating the Bedouins in designated planned townships on the other hand. (1996:236)

This approach made it virtually impossible for Bedouin claimants to prove their land claims before Israeli courts. Among other effects, the construction of the majority of Naqab land as state land, rather than as open for Bedouin claimants to prove as their own, paved the way for state tactics aimed at Bedouin "trespassers," including separate law enforcement techniques (such as forced eviction, house demolitions, and crop spraying).

The Bedouin Arabs of the Naqab initially faced eviction and displacement during the 1948 War and through early legislation to expropriate Arab land; subsequently, they were subjected to a complex judicial and administrative regime of procedure, evidence, and substance aimed at transferring land holdings to the state. Through the planning regime described later, Bedouin claimants were frequently constructed as illegal, being seen as defensive trespassers criminally occupying state land.

Rereading the Israeli legal argument

The dual factors of a new state attempting to consolidate control over territory and an ethnocratic regime deploying legal tactics to sustain itself were combined with a series of legal interpretations that systematically granted the Israeli government advantages in land claim cases brought by the Bedouins. In particular, the interpretation of the OLC, the procedural conditions set by Israeli courts, the evidentiary requirements, and the non-application of equity doctrine demonstrate the narrowing of Israeli law with regard to the Bedouins and the concomitant expansion of state power and control.[42]

With respect to terminology, Israeli courts have largely ignored the interchangeability of "inhabited area" with "town" or "village" in certain translations of the OLC when determining *mawat* land (art. 6). Although the 1969 Land Ordinance adopted the definition of "settlement" used in the 1928 British Land Ordinance, a definition that included a "tribal area,"[43] the Israeli Supreme Court decided not to consider Bedouin encampments as "settlements" or even "inhabited areas" in the calculation of *mawat* land.[44]

With regard to interpretive precedent, the Israeli Supreme Court chose 1858 as the definitive year for deciding the existence of a settlement for the purposes of determining whether land is *mawat*. By contrast, the Court could have interpreted the provision to mean a settlement in existence at the time of the claim, or, at the very least, it could have determined that the 1928 British Land Ordinance replaced the 1858 date as a requirement for determining a settlement.

The Israeli courts' requirement that Bedouin claimants hold official land registration disregards oral evidence and other types of unregistered documentation that article 44(b) of the 1969 Israeli Land Ordinance permits.[45] Under the ordinance, documents held by some Bedouin claimants, such as tax payments, *sanad baya'*, or *rahen*,[46] or sales contracts—coupled with oral evidence—could be considered admissible evidence for determining land claims. The ordinance thus grants courts the margin to deviate from standard evidence law and rules of admissibility. This unusual "room for maneuver" was presumably designed to allow courts to consider the particularities of the situation and the period, during which people rarely used official documents or registered their documentation. It affords the courts a flexibility that they have so far refused to utilize fully in the Naqab. The choice to formalize evidentiary requirements in this particular manner creates conditions for Bedouin failure in court.

Finally, Israeli courts have largely ignored the principle of equity in their treatment of the Bedouin land question. Article 41(a) of the 1969 Land Ordinance requires that a court, when deciding a dispute or conflict of land claims, examine land rights not only under the law but also under equity. Equity encompasses general principles of fairness; it is employed whenever the application of the formal law would lead to unfair results (Weisman, 1970:380).[47] The doctrine of equity could potentially accommodate a number of legal arguments presented by the Bedouins: the customary use of land for multiple generations, the traditional land recognition system and its acknowledgment by previous rulers (e.g., the British), and the loss of official documentation and/or existence of alternative documentation for land not necessarily registered with the state. When deciding land cases, however, the Israeli Supreme Court has not endorsed the equity argument; instead, it has relied on the formality of Ottoman and British Mandate registration laws—despite archival evidence that the British courts themselves upheld the doctrine of equity with respect to land claims as late as 1936. In that year, the Palestine Supreme Court held that "equitable rights to land exist in Palestine on the same principle as in England." Judge Richard Manning noted that the 1921 Land Courts Ordinance "directs the Court to have regard to equitable as well as legal rights to land."[48] To demand strict compliance with legal provisions and interpretations that fail to accurately reflect centuries-old land rights practices and long-term autonomous existence in the Naqab could be argued as constituting a failure of equity.

In the early years of the Israeli state, lower courts provided some favorable alternative interpretations of land rights that were subsequently reexamined and reversed by the Supreme Court. These cases included one in which a lower court ruled that the requirement for proof of land rights based only on land registration was unjust.[49] Additionally, a district court judge stated in a 1962 case that

> the purpose of the Ottoman Land Code and of the legislator was chiefly to cause the wilderness to bloom, and to settle agriculturists to cultivate the land and develop agriculture. The interpretation suggested by the State's representative [that Arab-Asuad did not qualify as a settlement] does not suit the purpose of the legislator and the aim of the statute, and appears to me to be a conservative interpretation that does not do justice.[50]

Despite such early sentiments, the "conservative interpretation" later became the norm for the Israeli authorities and courts.

De-Palestinizing and Bureaucratizing the Bedouin Arabs

Although many aspects of the expropriation and dispossession described in this chapter and accomplished through law are shared by the Palestinian people as a whole, the Bedouins are separated from the larger Palestinian population due to both historical circumstance and Israeli policies.[51] First, historically the Bedouins had a different lifestyle—characterized as semi-nomadic—from the rest of the Palestinian population of Israel. Second, the Naqab itself historically enjoyed an unusual degree of autonomy under multiple regimes due to its geographical distance from the center and its specific topographic nature. However, the distinction between the Bedouin population and the broader Palestinian Arab minority in Israel has also been constructed through exceptionalist treatment by the Israeli state, including discriminatory land and planning policies, forced urbanization, house demolitions and the denial of basic rights, and the bureaucratic differentiation of the Bedouin community through the formation of special bodies to formulate specific rules, strategies, or tactics with regard to the Bedouins.[52]

One technique that has formally separated the Bedouin population from other Israeli minorities is the creation of specific governmental bodies designed to remove Bedouin land claims from the courts and place them in specialized committees. This "pragmatic bureaucratic" tactic funnels the Bedouin population toward a system designed to "solve" the "problem" of the Bedouin Arabs (that is, their presence in unrecognized villages and their land claims in the Naqab) without recognizing their formal legal rights to the claimed land. Subject to these administrative measures, they have been treated as a "nomadic" population, understood as unattached to the land due to their lack of "modern" "spatial and temporal boundaries. Nomadism becomes a deviance that modern law cannot but attempt to correct" (Shamir, 1996:236). The Bedouin Arabs, like indigenous populations elsewhere, are classified as illegitimate claimants of land rights and as obstacles to modernization (Shamir, 1996:237). These practices of deploying the law to legitimate and justify the ethnocratic nature of the state build on the initial construction of a new post-1948 land system in Israel resting on principles of "physical seizure, nationalization, Judaization, establishment of tight central control and uneven distribution" (Yiftachel, 2006:137). These principles have been reiterated and reconstituted over time to continually reinforce the logic and practices of the state. We might therefore understand the history of Bedouin life after the establishment of the State of Israel as a narrative not just of displacement but of "illegalization"—a mode of dispossession more subtle and varied than that of purely forced relocation.

The practice of creating special committees and bodies to address the Bedouin situation has a variety of possible effects. Such committees may offer Bedouin claimants a fairer hearing than they could receive in a court system that effectively bars them from victory. Yet the move to committees and commissions rather than court hearings and adjudication also tends to turn land claims into technical issues to be addressed through precise formulas. Rather than the contestation inherent in the adversarial system, the various committees have attempted to resolve land claims through "softer" tactics and negotiations. They may offer the appearance of a neutral interest in resolving the conditions of the Bedouins, but in fact they contribute to broader state interests in the urbanization of the Bedouins and the nationalization of the Naqab.

Although effectively breaking with precedent in certain limited ways, most prominently in affirming the Bedouin narrative of displacement and negligence and in recommending the recognition of some unrecognized villages, the report of the 2008 Goldberg Commission (the most recent administrative body appointed to address the Bedouin situation) largely fails to reframe the Bedouin Arabs' situation or history as a whole. The Commission's recommendations make clear the threat to both demography and development that the Bedouin population represents to the state, while explicitly recognizing their "historical attachment" to the land and yet denying the validity of any legal claims they might have. The Commission's report states that a Bedouin victory is unlikely in an Israeli court due to procedural and precedential obstacles, ignores background causes or structural reasons for the inevitability of Bedouin defeat in Israeli courts, and suggests that an extrajudicial option presents the only possibility for "solving" the Bedouin "problem."[53] To state it differently, the Commission—like its predecessors—naturalizes the inherent prejudice of an ethnocratic regime by failing to question the "reconstitut[ion of] settlers' cultural biases and power relations into formalized rules such as property arrangements" (Yiftachel, 2006:135). In turn, administrative procedures (which offer apparent flexibility and yet generally rehearse the biases of the state) appear as the only viable option for (partial) victory.

A final consequence of the "special treatment" of the Bedouin community is division within the Palestinian minority in Israel (as well as segregation from the Israeli polity as a whole). The Bedouin Arabs of the Naqab are considered "different" enough to merit their own administrative system and policies, although the structural impediments they face are closely linked to those experienced by the Palestinian population of Israel as a whole. In certain ways, this differentiation may benefit the Bedouins—particularly in individual cases—because in fact they will likely fare better in their own bureaucracy than in the courts, where they have little or no possibility of victory. In a larger sense, however, the system of differentiation helps remove the Bedouin struggle from the larger Palestinian context, using the Bedouins' distinctiveness to depoliticize their claims because "the Bedouins, unlike the Arab population, ha[ve] not been considered a national enemy" (Shamir, 1996:238).[54]

Planning

In tandem with the land-law system, planning plays a central role in Israel's spatial policies. Planning bodies literally map the country, including or excluding settlements, controlling municipal boundaries and defining permitted types of development in each area. Since the Naqab region has long been understood as "one of Israel's prime frontiers," Jewish settlement and development are understood as crucial aspects of state policy (Yiftachel, 2006:193). As a result of Israel's various planning objectives—which include the expansion of Jewish settlement in the south—the municipalities of Bedouin townships have jurisdiction over a mere 1.9% of land in the northern Naqab region, although the Bedouins make up 25.2% of the population in the area (Human Rights Watch, 2008:29). The two "sides" of planning—increasing Jewish settlement while ignoring Bedouin villages or pressuring Bedouins to urbanize—work in tandem with a highly developed legal system and well-established land distribution system.

The 1965 Planning and Construction Law regulates land use, planning, and building issues throughout Israel. Land can be zoned by state planning authorities as residential, agricultural, public, or "other." Settlements may be developed on lands zoned as residential, where houses or other construction may be built after acquiring a permit. Since the 1970s, regional and local zoning plans have left the areas of Bedouin settlement literally "off the map" by zoning them for military or public use (e.g., as roads, reserves, or national parks) rather than as residential. Due to their "invisibility" on state zoning maps, Bedouin areas have come to be characterized by increasing rural and urban informality—communities that are expanded and consolidated while continually denied state services, or even basic recognition (Yiftachel, 2006:199–200). Such settlements are deemed illegal and are consequently subject to demolition. Thus, the legal process of claiming territory as *mawat* land constitutes a pre-condition for the "illegality" of the unrecognized villages, which are removed from public consideration due to their location on state-owned land. In parallel, "legal" residential zoning options are made available only in government-planned townships aimed at relocating the Bedouin community to urban areas.

Although the process of Judaization and concomitant Bedouin dispossession has been ongoing since the inception of the state, settlement plans have increased in the past decade, accompanied by language invoking demographic threats and the need for Jewish presence in the area. To ensure Judaization, certain settlements, though built on state and public land, are made accessible only to Jews. This limitation is frequently deployed through a system of "selection committees" that determine admission to live in communal settlements or new neighborhoods smaller than 500 households.[55] These selection committees are notoriously biased, include a senior official of the Jewish Agency or the World Zionist Organization, and routinely deny admission to Arabs, among other impoverished groups (Human Rights Watch, 2008:39). In many cases, the ILA leases land to the Jewish Agency, "which is a special status organization that promotes the interests of the Jewish nation within Israel and abroad" and which can "designate the land for the use of Jews only" (Shamir and Ziv, 2001:292). The land is then leased to "an *association* or *communal corporation* [recognized as such by state law] which, in turn, is granted autonomy to screen potential candidates for membership and residence in the association" (Shamir and Ziv, 2001:292; emphasis in original).

In 2002, the government of Israel issued a plan to establish six new Naqab settlements classified as "community settlements," a categorization that allows the state to ensure Jewish residency.[56] The plan stated that the majority of the new towns would be "jointly planned, developed, built and populated by the Jewish Agency in partnership with various government bodies at the regional and national levels" (Adalah, 2003). In 2003, the government began publicizing a new plan for thirty additional settlements in the Galilee and Naqab. Governmental officials repeatedly clarified that such settlements were intended, in part, to strengthen Jewish presence in areas with larger Bedouin populations (Hamdan, 2005:3; Human Rights Watch, 2008). Of the 136 settlements in the Naqab, there are only 15 Bedouin settlements (the townships and the newly recognized villages), although Bedouin citizens constitute 33% of the Naqab population (Israel Central Bureau of Statistics, 2010).

Two years after the plans for settlement were publicized, the Sharon government adopted the Negev 2015 development plan. This is perhaps the most comprehensive development plan yet created for the Naqab; it includes recommendations regarding population, transportation, infrastructure, health, and education, among other areas, and makes explicit reference to the Arab residents of the Naqab (Swirski, 2007).[57] A special ministry for "developing" the Naqab and the

Galilee was established in January 2005 in the wake of governmental resolutions endorsing the development of these two regions; one of its main goals has been the implementation of Negev 2015, which defines the development of the Naqab as a "national project."[58]

Shlomo Swirski argues that the full title of the plan reveals the priorities behind it: first and foremost, the state envisions the development of the Naqab as an issue of national importance, particularly since "for many Jews, the Bedouin are objects of suspicion, whose loyalty to the state is less than total; this suspicion sometimes turns into fear, as a result of the group's high fertility rate" (Swirski, 2007:8). The development aspect of the plan, mentioned in the second half of the title, appears as a secondary priority. Negev 2015 suggests incentives and plans for essentially importing ("economically productive") Israeli Jews from central Israel to the Naqab and increasing the population from 535,000 to 900,000 by 2015, as part of a plan for creating a "strong population." Although it addresses the situation of the Bedouins, the plan pointedly ignores the questions of land or village recognition so central to the Bedouin population. In addition, while the plan earmarks some (insufficient) funds for infrastructural and educational development in the recognized Bedouin townships, it includes no funding for the unrecognized villages (Swirski, 2007:14).

The Bedouin community, its villages, and its land claims are frequently interpreted and portrayed as a security issue and/or an obstacle to development: "[Bedouin] claims to ownership of vast areas was and is considered by the government as inimical to the present and future development of land resources" (Horner, 1982:165). A position paper authored by the Israeli National Security Council includes several recommendations regarding the eviction of Bedouins. Referring to the evacuation of Jewish settlements from the Gaza Strip in 2005, the Council argues that if the government was able to evacuate "8,000 citizens who were living in legal structures, it can also evacuate thousands of citizens living in illegal structures" (cited in Swirski,

2007:65).[59] In conjunction with plans for increased Jewish settlement in the Naqab as part of its development, the government allocated more resources for "law enforcement" and renewed a "counterclaim" strategy against Bedouin land claims. The counterclaim tactic has been described as a way of "protecting state resources," thus excluding the indigenous population from the allocation of state resources, depicting the Bedouins as obstacles to development, and alienating them from the legal system. Despite appearing separate from the planning sector, the counterclaim tactic in fact functions to help separate the population from the land it claims, making the land available for Jewish settlement or other purposes, such as the establishment of industrial zones.[60]

This pressure on the Bedouin community has provoked a combination of organized and unorganized resistance to state policies and planning processes, mainly utilizing strategies that take advantage of possible openings in the legal system, often with the assistance of non-governmental organizations. Alternative planning initiatives began in the mid-1990s; the Regional Council for the Unrecognized Villages (RCUV) was established by the Bedouin community in 1997 to represent the unrecognized villages. In 2000, the Israeli Supreme Court heard a petition brought by residents of the unrecognized villages against the National Planning and Construction Council over the Beersheba Metropolis Master Plan, which ignored the existence of all Bedouin unrecognized villages.[61] The petitioners originally submitted objections to the plan in 1994; in the wake of their exclusion from the plan, they petitioned the state to explain why Bedouin rural villages were ignored and why the needs of the Bedouin population should not be taken into account in the planning processes. The interim agreement reached by the parties before the Court in July 2001 included two parts: (1) the need to draw up a Beersheba metropolitan plan (a partial district master plan) that would "relate" to the Bedouin villages; and (2) the need to consider the form of rural villages in planning, examine concrete solutions while consulting the community, and take into account the RCUV's alternative plan in moving forward (Swirski and Hasson, 2006:66).

In this manner, law and planning conjoin explicitly and implicitly in the perpetuation of the ethnocratic regime to control the indigenous Bedouin Arab minority, though "territorial containment, socioeconomic deprivation, and procedural exclusions" (Yiftachel, 2003:25). Planning documents exclude, ignore, or rezone Bedouin land, thus opening the proverbial door to Jewish expansion and Bedouin urbanization. The system ensures that new Jewish settlements remain Jewish. These policies have shaped Bedouin community life in such a way that community members have the option of either moving to impoverished government-planned townships or remaining substantively invisible in unrecognized and underdeveloped villages. Essentially, planning performs both a "constructive" function (townships for Bedouins pressured by the state to urbanize, and new settlements for Jewish Israelis as part of the Judaization strategy) and a "destructive" function ("the ability to use planning tools to retard and control a population instead of improving its quality of life") (Yiftachel, 2006:202). Planning policies are integral to the larger maintenance of dispossession and transformation; while legal avenues have been used to criminalize Bedouin activity, planning creates a spatial manifestation of the separations constructed by law.

Enforcement and Resistance

As Yiftachel suggests, ethnocratic regimes unintentionally construct marginalized "inferior" ethno-classes and, ironically, may simultaneously seed the possibility for future resistance to the system by "disgruntled minorities": "These minorities often use cracks in the system, such as the legal system or changing international norms, to challenge the dominance of the settling group and hence constantly destabilize the ethnocratic political order" (2003:24). In addition, of course, more obviously violent confrontations have taken place at the margins; Bedouin citizens have developed methods of resistance based largely on their physical refusal to leave the land they claim as their own. The state has employed a variety of violent tactics in response, leading to an ongoing confrontation in the Naqab.

Criminalization and Law Enforcement

As a result of judicial decisions on land title requirements, many of the Bedouin residents of the Naqab were mapped and categorized as trespassers invading state land and opposing development. Classified as citizens and yet conceived as administratively invisible or criminal, the Bedouins are trapped by a sophisticated regulatory architecture. Planning renders their residency illegal; judicial interpretation, procedural requirements, and active governmental counterclaims create insurmountable obstacles to land claims; and administrative bodies appear to offer suspicious compromises for what Bedouin citizens view as attempts by the state to dispossess them of their historical land. Since their claims are doomed to failure, their resistance to settlement and urbanization remains clear, and the land they view as theirs has been zoned otherwise, Bedouin residents of the unrecognized villages become potential criminals subject to law enforcement. They thus emerge only as "a trespasser, a lawbreaker or, at best, a creature taking its first steps toward socialization" (Shamir, 1996:237). These practices decontextualize the Bedouin condition by obscuring the state's role in constructing the situation, reconfiguring the Bedouins as criminals and as risks to the state rather than as communities engaged in a legal and political struggle with the state.

In January 2005, the Knesset took another step in criminalizing Bedouin presence on their ancestral land while simultaneously increasing the power of the ILA to enforce ownership rights over state and public land. An amendment to the 1981 Public Lands (Removal of Trespassers) Law added to the already wide range of authority delegated to the ILA with regard to Bedouin land and law enforcement in the Naqab. The ILA was granted the power to issue house demolition orders, spray crops with chemicals, uproot trees, and force evictions. Over the course of 2009, state authorities demolished 254 houses and destroyed crops on 45,000 dunams of land through plowing (Yagna, 2010).[62]

In conjunction, the law enforcement strategy and the counterclaim tactic utilized after 2003 strengthen the notion that the legal system is the "enemy" of the Naqab Bedouins, by making Bedouins visible only inasmuch as they are lawbreakers and not recognizing them as land-holders with legal rights. The law enforcement narrative includes assertions that "there is no feeling of law and order in the open lands of the Negev" (Havatzelet, 2006:6), that "a significant minority clearly feel they are not obliged to obey Israeli law" (Havatzelet, 2006:6), and that the Bedouin population takes advantage of lax enforcement to grab further land. As a result, the Bedouins are further encouraged to accept the administrative "solutions" fostered and monitored by the government.

Legal Claims and Resistance

Bedouin Arabs have historically both engaged with and resisted the Israeli state. In the most dramatic cases of resistance against the system, Bedouins—who have been deemed trespassers on the land they claim—have remained there despite both violent actions by the state against them and extraordinarily harsh living conditions.[63] Cooperation with the state has meant, for some families, relinquishing land claims in exchange for some compensation and assistance in moving to the Bedouin townships or simply to other land. These decisions can have additional consequences, including internal Bedouin disputes over claimed land (for example, if the government allocates to Bedouin families land that other Bedouins claim as their own).

Other modes of resistance that involve some engagement with the state include fighting for the recognition of unrecognized villages— a tactic that has resulted in limited recognition, but which has had other consequences (including the possibility that the state will map the newly recognized village in a reduced area, leaving certain families outside the village borders). As described above, Bedouin groups have also attempted to resist discriminatory planning measures by petitioning the courts and offering revised plans. Finally, Bedouin Arabs have contested state action through legal claims including and beyond land claims. Court cases seeking to remedy the conditions of life in the Naqab and discrimination against the Bedouin Arabs have covered a wide range of issues, including the rights to land, housing, health, and education, among others. Of these, the most unlikely to result in Bedouin victory have been those seeking recognition of land rights and recognition of unrecognized villages. Cases on the provision of health, education, and social welfare facilities have consistently been more successful than those addressing planning and housing rights; these cases are necessitated by the initial planning processes, which exclude Bedouin citizens, thus constructing the illegality of Bedouin residence and consequently denying them state services. Critically, the authors know of no instance in which a Bedouin party was victorious in a court case examining land claims.

The relationship between the Bedouin Arabs and the Israeli court system has a long history. Bedouin cases began reaching the courts in increasing numbers after the end of the military regime in 1966, as a result of two factors: the establishment of state-planned Bedouin townships in the late 1960s, and the land title settlement process created for land in the Restricted Area, which led to a series of land claims filed in the early 1970s. Some cases on land issues were brought without legal representation, as in the landmark case of *Al-Hawashla*. The strategy could be attributed to a naive belief that Bedouin land rights could easily be argued before the court based on the long history of possession and the robust nature of the traditional land system; in fact, however, the cases were consistent failures from the viewpoint of Bedouin claimants. Cases brought during this period were based solely on property rights and employed narrow legal arguments, with no human rights or discrimination claims.

With the rapid development of civil society organizations in Israel in the early 1990s, cases on behalf of the Bedouin community dealing with planning and services began to reach the Supreme Court in high numbers, but they focused largely on provision of services.[64] Filed collectively, the cases began to strategically deploy a human rights discourse. In cases of housing rights and recognition, petitions were filed on behalf of entire villages or neighborhoods, and included alternative zoning plans demonstrating the viability of officially recognizing the villages involved.[65] While some cases were partially successful and eased the life of some of the Bedouin community, they were incapable of resolving the structural inequality faced by Bedouins in the Naqab. As one resident of an unrecognized village stated in an interview, "We play the legal game. We are not equal and we are not at the same level. I know I will lose the game but I am playing. We know the results from the start."[66]

The Administrative Option: The Goldberg Commission

Parallel to the use of land and planning laws to control, segregate, and ghettoize the Bedouin community, the state has—through successful cases at the Supreme Court that virtually eliminated the possibility of Bedouin victory—promoted the idea that Bedouin claims should be addressed through negotiated agreements or administratively determined formulas in special committees. Since the alternative appears to be complete dispossession, the committees begin to appear as plausible sites for viable claims. At this point, however, a further condition of constraint on Bedouin claims based on asymmetrical power relations becomes clear: these state-appointed committees are tasked with resolving claims that are seen as against the state's perceived self-interest (since the Bedouins are understood alternately as outsiders or criminals and as obstacles to the national preoccupation with territorial and demographic Judaization). Throughout the years, dozens of cabinet resolutions and committees have been established to handle different aspects of the Bedouin case. The 1975 Albeck Committee constituted one of the most significant of these executive bodies; the 2008 Goldberg Commission was another. The state has treated the Bedouin community as exceptional (a community apart) and thus has furthered the community's marginalization from both the dominant Jewish society and the rest of the Palestinian Arab community in Israel.

Established by a cabinet resolution in July 2007, the Goldberg Commission was tasked with making recommendations for resolving land and housing issues affecting the Bedouin community. Over the course of six months in 2008, the Commission held dozens of public hearings, gleaning testimony from 117 witnesses, including activists, academics, experts, civil society representatives (local and international), and governmental representatives. In addition, 130 written submissions were made (Amara, 2008:230).

The Commission bears particular attention for several reasons. First, it demonstrates the tension between hegemonic state control of land distribution and an increasingly impatient and deprived indigenous community. As the most recent of the various Israeli governmental committees, it reflects the government's current understanding of viable "solutions" and of the tools considered appropriate for achieving such ends. Similarly, it demonstrates the ongoing conditions and ideological concerns animating the issue. Second, it offers both a sense of relative progress in its recognition of historical injustice and a stark demonstration of institutional inertia in its refusal to recognize Bedouin land rights. Third, it reflects inevitable tensions between a settler state and its indigenous population, as well as the complexity of simultaneously addressing the interests of the state and the needs of the citizenry.

Establishment

An Israeli governmental resolution calling for the creation of a body within the Ministry of Construction and Housing that would be responsible for formulating a comprehensive response to the Bedouin case led to the establishment of the Goldberg Commission and to the creation of a Bedouin Authority (to replace the BAA) tasked with implementing the Commission's recommendations.[67] In December 2009, the Goldberg Commission submitted its final recommendations to the Ministry of Construction and Housing. Following adoption of the report, the government appointed a committee to formulate an "action plan," including technical and legal suggestions for the implementation of the Commission's recommendations.[68] In early 2011, a draft of the implementation committee's report was leaked to the Israeli press. Its main recommendations included organizing land claims and compensation through legislation rather than executive action or ILA Council resolutions; offering the possibility to choose between pursuing a court case rather than legislative settlement, the price of which would be the loss of any compensatory option if the court case failed; and a suggested timeline of five years for claimants to settle their land claims, after which the claimed land would be registered as state land.[69] It should be noted that the government imposed budgetary and territorial limitations on the implementation of the Commission's report. Made public on June 23, 2008, a memorandum submitted to the Goldberg Commission by the Prime Minister's Office (and made binding by the resolution establishing the Commission) limited land available for the resolution of claims to 100,000 dunams.[70]

Although in certain ways representing a move forward in the long struggle to arrive at a viable resolution to Bedouin existence in the Naqab, the Goldberg Commission also reiterated and reconstructed a familiar set of moves with regard to law, land, bureaucracy, and planning. The Commission's recommendations reflect some openness to Bedouin claims and—most centrally—offer the possibility of recognition for some unrecognized villages. However, following precedents set by the Albeck Committee, the counterclaim strategy and numerous other governmental attempts to consolidate, urbanize, and largely ignore the Naqab Bedouin Arabs (albeit spoken in the language of "resolution" or "development"), the Goldberg Commission once again confirmed the impossibility of Bedouin claimants achieving satisfaction or justice in the Israeli courts and recommended a specialized solution as the only viable option. As described below, this approach permits description of the Bedouins as obstacles to development; expression of governmental sympathy for their "historical attachment" (never legally validated) to the Naqab; confirmation of inevitable failure in court (due to inadequacies of the Bedouins themselves in terms of their documentation and registration of land); and, finally, a proposed solution that reaffirms the sympathetic reading of Bedouin existence as difficult without any inquiry into the discriminatory quality of the state's application and interpretation of law.

Recommendations

The Commission's report recommended that land claims be settled through an extrajudicial process by which land committees would address the claims, determining whether the claimant had possessed and cultivated the claimed land (Goldberg Commission, 2008a: para. 85). For proven land claims, the Commission proposed settlement terms combining monetary and territorial compensation, based on a scheme involving a set amount of money per dunam in different categories of claimed land, which would entitle the claimant to roughly

20% of his claim in alternative land and 30% of his original land claim in monetary compensation.[71] As for the recognition of unrecognized villages, the report recommended recognition of villages with a "critical mass of residents" that are able to maintain themselves as municipal units and do not contradict the District Master Zoning Plan. If a village does not fulfill the conditions (or for any other "reasonable reason"), it may be moved elsewhere, to an area to be designated by the government (although the village in question may suggest alternative areas within six months of the decision). For recognition and relocation purposes, the Commission recommended a special planning committee tasked exclusively with the question of Bedouin settlements (Goldberg Commission, 2008a: paras. 126–128). At the same time, the report recommended new proposals for law enforcement with regard to Bedouin structures built without official permits (paras. 109–110).

The Goldberg Commission did make statements unusually supportive of the Bedouin cause, and it did in principle accept the narrative of the indigenous population—inasmuch as it acknowledged Bedouins' historical displacement by the Israeli army in the 1950s and the restriction against their return to their land (para. 18). It also acknowledged the fact that they had had valid reasons for avoiding land registration under both Ottoman and British rule. In recommending extrajudicial settlement, the Commission explicitly recognized the biases of the existing laws and their implementation by the judiciary, pointing to the inability to resolve the conflict within the judicial system. However, the Commission pointed out the difficulty of achieving success in the Israeli courts not as a critique of the system but rather as a tool to encourage Bedouin claimants to accept the Commission's recommendations and utilize new land claims committees rather than the court system. Thus, administrative strategies once again were the logical outlet for an indigenous population excluded from, and oppressed by, the regular court system. The Commission's report highlights the contrasts between the "formal" and "informal" (or "modern" and "native") land systems existing in settler areas throughout the world that have led to a situation in which

> the "modern Western" legal system does not recognize the ways locals organize their spatial relations to land as giving rise to property rights. Typically, settler states regard these native lands as public land, which can be disposed of by governments without the natives' approval or even knowledge. As a result, many natives have become trespassers on their own land. (Kedar, 2001:927)

Because the Bedouins have lacked sufficient documentary proof of ownership and since the state has had valid reasons "based on legal claims of law and precedent" (Goldberg Commission, 2008a: para. 29) to refuse any recognition without documentary evidence, the Commission noted that another solution must be found. Thus, the report offers a vague principle of Bedouin "historical attachment to the land" (para. 77), but explicitly resists any recognition of a prior legal right to the land. It then makes the assumption that the Bedouins cannot succeed in their claims in Israeli courts due to the apparent lack of law on their side and suggests a specialized system as an answer to the conundrum. While the practical effect might conceivably be to offer a more pragmatic and just solution to the Bedouins than they have received in the past, a certain continuity of assumptions and beliefs with its predecessors underpins the report.

The turn to pragmatic administration may be traced not only to the Albeck Committee's previously cited invocations to act in "good will" and to go "beyond the letter of the law," but even to prior Supreme Court language. Even in the Court, a claim to some source other than law is suggested in certain instances. For example, in one case, Bedouin petitioners requested a regular supply of electricity for the family or village of a small child who needed refrigerated injections for her cancer treatment. The Court dismissed the petition, concluding that no legal obligation required the provision of electricity; however, the Court added that "this young girl is struggling for her life, and in these circumstances no one can stand aside, even if he has no legal requirement to act."[72] As a result, the Court suggested that it would be wise to provide such informal assistance in this specific situation without requiring the state to provide electricity to the family.[73] The sense that only an extrajudicial set of actions could address the problems of the Bedouins remains a constant, as does the tendency to isolate each case in order to avoid setting a precedent. The sense that separate or informal measures are needed due to a moral rather than legal requirement creates a sense of exceptional circumstances rather than structural problems. In recognition of the myriad legal barriers facing the Bedouins (e.g., the Absentee Property Law, lack of documentary evidence proving land ownership, and inability to receive building permits), the government seeks solutions "outside the regular framework," while simultaneously using the law to pressure the Bedouins to participate in such alternative measures.

The text of the Goldberg Report provides a series of implicit or explicit reasons for the need to resolve the situation of the Naqab Bedouins in a sustainable manner: (1) bolstering Bedouin "trust in the state"; (2) managing demographic concerns; and (3) promoting development in the Naqab (Goldberg Commission, 2008a: para. 48). With regard to the first, the Commission urged the state to resolve the Bedouin case in order to prevent "Palestinization and Islamization" (para. 48). As the report underlines, "The Bedouins' belief in the state has been seriously compromised, and it cannot be re-established until a solution is found for this problem" (para. 26). The second concern appears in the report's mention of the high birthrate of the Naqab

Bedouins and its citation of scholarship, indicating that increased education for women and their integration into the regular workforce will reduce birthrates "in a population in which the birth rate is too high" (paras. 24–25). With regard to development, the report cites the 2006 position paper of the Council for National Security, which stated that "ownership claims which have not been settled for tens of years impede the development of whole areas of the Negev" in addition to permitting "uncontrolled geographic expansion of the Bedouins in the Negev" (para. 48). The Commission's objectives thus include both ideological and material elements, calculated to maintain a particular relationship between the Bedouins and the State of Israel and to facilitate the planning, management, and development of the geographic territory on which the Bedouins reside or claim land.[74]

The report reveals the potential for increased willingness on the part of Israeli state bodies to cede some land to the Bedouin Arab claimants (albeit perhaps out of concerns regarding demography or "Palestinization"), as well as the concomitant refusal to fully recognize a history of discriminatory practices and dispossession (which might raise broader questions about the treatment of all Palestinian citizens of Israel since 1948). Rather than deploying the language of human or indigenous rights, the report largely remains within the accepted narratives of the ethnocratic state, offering some compromises but seemingly retaining for the state both the power of the law (since Bedouin claims admittedly cannot make headway in Israeli courts) and that of history (since "attachment" is recognized, but customary law and historical (dis)possession are not). The action-plan team (Prawer and later Prawer-Amidror) that was appointed by the government to follow up on the implementation of the Goldberg Report has retreated from these recommendations to resolve the Bedouin question (see introduction, this volume).

Conclusion

The situation of the Bedouin Arabs of the Naqab developed due to a complex combination of Zionist ideology, Ottoman and Mandate policies, the structure of relations between Jews and Arabs in pre-1948 Palestine and subsequently in Israel, state interest in territorial consolidation and control of population, and the specificity of Israeli development plans, which at times combine the language of modernization with the actions of "Judaization." The ethno-national land approach followed by the Israeli state divides the formalities of political citizenship (the right to vote in free and fair elections, among others) from the structural (in)equality of land allocation. As a result, the Bedouin Arab citizenry (like the larger Palestinian citizenry) is conceptualized and located outside the national collective. Although the results are manifold, one of the most concrete is the comparison between the population of Palestinian Arabs, which has grown sixfold since 1948, and their land ownership, which has been halved in the same time period (Adalah, 2003).

In the case of the Bedouin Arabs of the Naqab, three particular modes of Israeli state action—emanating from the legislature, judiciary, and executive—have contributed to their dispossession and isolation. First, legislation expropriated Palestinian land in the aftermath of the 1948 War, and policies displaced many Bedouin citizens and frequently separated them from their claimed land. Later legislation established planning regulations and land rules that created "unrecognized villages" invisible on any map and denied state services. Second, a series of judicial decisions reinterpreted Ottoman and British land laws in ways that expanded the definition of *mawat* land while limiting the procedural, substantive, and evidentiary capacity of Bedouin claimants to prove land ownership. Finally, the combination of restrictive legislation and inevitable loss in adjudication funneled the Bedouin population toward a system of committees in which Bedouin citizens are separated from the broader population in ways that may be beneficial in individual cases, but which have their own consequences, including failure to challenge the system as a whole, isolating Bedouin citizens from other Palestinian citizens of Israel, and reinforcing separation from the Jewish majority. Thus, a process that began with legislative expropriation continued through narrowed judicial interpretations and active governmental counterclaims, bolstered by a planning system that rendered Bedouin residence illegal, as well as by governmental administrative bodies that offer what Bedouin citizens regard as problematic compromises with a state that continually seeks to dispossess them of their historical land.

Although the system often appears as a monolithic structure designed to prevent the exercise of Bedouin rights and to reconstitute their communal world, livelihoods, and history in a different image, in fact it is partially constituted by the ongoing negotiations between the state and its indigenous citizens (which includes the Israeli self-perception as a liberal democracy and the refusal by Bedouin claimants to abandon their land or their claims). Since the choices made by individuals or groups within the various Bedouin communities have consequences for their subsequent options, the system is not completely determined, although its general political parameters appear clear.

Resistance and contestation remain options for a Bedouin population that has become both more empowered and increasingly subject to violent law enforcement measures by the government, including a decision to increase house demolitions by three times in 2010, as well as increasing the submission of land counterclaims by the government (Yagna, 2010). Despite a difficult situation of uncertainty, violence, and discrimination, certain successes have been won by the Bedouin Arabs of the Naqab. In particular, at least thirteen unrecognized villages have gained recognition, and legal advocacy has forced the state to provide further services in the villages. The continuing residence of many Bedouins on their ancestral lands has been correctly interpreted as resistance to the state, and, as a result, the state interest in concentrating the Naqab Bedouin population in state-planned townships has continued to be at least partially thwarted. As described above, however, even victories have consequences. Recognized villages may be limited unilaterally by the state; individuals who remain on land the government claims as its own may face violence; cooperation may result in the further erasure of a history of dispossession by a state that views the settlement of claims as the effective extinguishing of alternative historical narratives; and legal victories in certain areas may distract from the structural violence experienced by the Bedouin population as a whole.

In light of ongoing land claims and Bedouin alienation from the state, some have suggested that a historical justice lens—as has been employed in other indigenous situations—might provide a more equitable resolution to the ongoing difficulties of Bedouin existence in the Naqab. Considering the structure of the land system and the character of the ethnocratic state, however, full resolution of Bedouin claims is likely to remain elusive.

REFERENCES

Abu Hussein, H., and McKay, F. (2003). *Access Denied: Palestinian Land Rights in Israel*. London: Zed Books.

Abu-Ras, T. (2006). "Land disputes in Israel: The case of the Bedouin of the Naqab." *Adalah Newsletter* 24:1–9.

Abu-Saad, I. (2008). "Introduction: State rule and indigenous resistance among Al Naqab Bedouin Arabs." *HAGAR Studies in Culture, Polity and Identities* 8(2):3–24.

Adalah. (2003). "Land and housing rights: Palestinian citizens of Israel." UN CESCR Information Sheet No. 3 (May). http://www.adalah.org/eng/intladvocacy/CESCR-land.pdf (accessed September 22, 2011).

———. (2007). Adalah and Bimkom request recognition of Attir Um-Akhiran and the preparation of a zoning plan for it. Press release,

November. http://www.adalah.org/newsletter/heb/nov07/4.php (accessed September 22, 2011) (Hebrew).

Amara, A. (2008). "The Goldberg Committee: Legal and extra-legal means in solving the Naqab Bedouin case." *HAGAR Studies in Culture, Polity and Identities* 8(2):227–243.

Bedouin Authority. (2011). Proposed Outline for Solving the Bedouin Settlement in the Negev. Draft No. 12, for signature. January 24. On file with authors.

Ben-David, J. (1996). *A Feud in the Negev: Bedouins, Jews, and the Land Dispute*. Ra'anana, Israel: Center for Studying the Arab Society in Israel (Hebrew).

Bunton, M. (1999). "Inventing the status quo: Ottoman land-law during the Palestine Mandate, 1917–1936." *The International History Review* 21(1):28–56.

———. (2007). *Colonial Land Policies in Palestine, 1917–1936*. Oxford: Oxford University Press.

Chatty, D. (ed.). (2006). *Nomadic Societies in the Middle East and North Africa: Entering the 21st Century*. Leiden: Brill.

Doukhan, M. (ed.). (1933–1936). *Laws of Palestine 1918–1925*. Tel Aviv: Rotenberg (Hebrew).

Falah, G. (1989). "Israel state policy towards Bedouin sedentarization in the Negev." *Journal of Palestine Studies* 18(2):71–90.

Forman, G. (2000). "The transformation of eastern `Emeq Yizre'el/ Marj Ibn `Amer and `Emeq Beit Shean/Ghor Beisan: Changes in population, settlement and land tenure due to the 1948 Palestine War and the establishment of the State of Israel." Master's thesis, University of Haifa. On file with authors.

Forman, G., and Kedar, A. (2004). "From Arab land to 'Israel lands': The legal dispossession of the Palestinians displaced by Israel in the wake of 1948." *Environment and Planning, D: Society and Space* 22:809–930.

Goldberg Commission. (2008a). Final report of the Commission to propose a policy for arranging Bedouin settlement in the Negev. December 11. http://www.moch.gov.il/ spokesman/pages/doverlistitem.aspx?listid=5b390c93-15b2-4841-87e3-abf31c1af63d&webid=fe384cf7-21cd-49eb-8bbb-71ed64f47de0&itemid=42 (accessed September 22, 2011) (Hebrew).

———. (2008b). Minutes of the Goldberg Commission. May 20. On file with authors (Hebrew).

Government of Palestine. (n.d.). *A Survey of Palestine, Prepared in December 1945 and January 1946 for the Information of the Anglo-Amer-*

ican Committee of Inquiry. Jerusalem: Government of Palestine. (Reprinted 1991, Washington, DC: Institute of Palestine Studies.)

Government of Palestine. (1937). "British response to the Jewish Agency regarding Bedouin land." Files of the British Government of Palestine, DCF/32-72.

Habitat International Coalition and Adalah. (2006). "Racism, racial discrimination, xenophobia and all forms of discrimination." Statement submitted to the UN Commission on Human Rights. http://www.adalah.org/eng/intl06/un-i6-jnf.pdf (accessed September 22, 2011).

Hamdan, H. (2005). "The policy of settlement and 'spatial Judaization' in the Naqab." *Adalah Newsletter* 11:1–7.

Havatezelet, Y. (2006). "Land disputes between the Negev Bedouin and Israel." *Israel Studies* 11(2):1–22.

Holzman-Gazit, Y. (2002). "Law as a status symbol: The Jewish National Fund Law of 1953 and the struggle of the fund to maintain its status after Israel's independence." *Tel Aviv University Law Review* 26:601–44 (Hebrew).

Horner, D. F. (1982). "Planning Bedouin settlements: The case of Tel Sheva." *Third World Planning Review* 4(2):159–176.

Human Rights Watch. (2008). *Off the Map: Land and Housing Rights Violations in Israel's Unrecognized Bedouin Villages*. New York: Human Rights Watch.

Israel Central Bureau of Statistics. (2010). "Statistical abstract of Israel." Table 2.8. http://www.cbs.gov.il/reader/shnaton/templ_shnaton.html?num_tab=st02_08&CYear=2010 (accessed September 22, 2011).

Israel Land Administration. (2007). "General information." http://www.mmi.gov.il/Envelope/indexeng.asp?page=/static/eng/f_general.html (last modified March 11).

———. (2009). "The Bedouin in the Negev." July 10. http://www.mmi.gov.il/static/HanhalaPirsumim/Beduin_information.pdf (accessed April 10, 2011).

———. (2011). "Reform in the Israel Land Administration." http://www.mmi.gov.il/static/Reforma.asp (last modified September 5) (Hebrew).

Kedar, A. (2001). "The legal transformation of ethnic geography: Israeli law and the Palestinian landholders 1948–1967." *Journal of International Law and Politics* 33:923–1000.

Kimmerling, B. (2001). *The Invention and Decline of Israeliness: State, Society and the Military*. Berkeley: University of California Press.

Marx, E. (2000). "Land and work: Negev Bedouin struggle with Israel bureaucracies." *Nomadic Peoples* 4(2):106–120.

Masalha, N. (2000). *Imperial Israel and the Palestinians: The Politics of Expansion*. London: Pluto.

McDonnell, Sir M. (ed.). (1934). *The Law Report of Palestine, 1920–1933*. Vol. 1. London: Crown Agents for the Colonies.

Meir, A. (1997). *As Nomadism Ends: The Israeli Bedouin of the Negev*. Boulder, CO: Westview Press.

Noach, H. (2009a). *The Bedouin-Arabs in the Negev-Naqab Desert: Response to the Report of the State of Israel on Implementing the Covenant on Civil and Political Rights*. Omer, Israel: Negev Coexistence Forum for Civil Equality.

———. (2009b). *The Existent and the Non-Existent Villages: The Unrecognized Bedouin Villages in the Negev*. Haifa: Pardes Press (Hebrew).

Porat, C. (2002). *The Negev: From a Desert to Cultivable Land, Negev Development and Settlement 1949–1956*. Beersheba: Ben-Gurion Heritage Institute, Ben-Gurion University of the Negev (Hebrew).

Prime Minister's Office. (2009). "Report on policy recommendation to solving the Bedouin Settlement in the Negev (Goldberg Commission)." January 18. http://www.pmo.gov.il/PMO/Archive/Decisions/2009/01/des4411.htm (accessed September 22, 2011) (Hebrew).

Shafir, G. (1989). *Land Labor and the Origins of the Israeli-Palestinian Conflict, 1882–1914*. Cambridge: Cambridge University Press.

Shamir, R. (1996). "Suspended in space: Bedouins under the law of Israel." *Law and Society Review* 30(2):231–257.

Shamir, R., and Ziv, N. (2001). "State-oriented and community-oriented lawyering for a cause: A tale of two strategies." In A. Sarat and S. Scheingold (eds.), *Cause Lawyering and the State in a Global Era* (pp. 286–304). New York: Oxford University Press.

Sharon, A. (2000). "Land as an economic tool for development infrastructure and significantly reducing social gaps." *Karkah* 50:10–21 (Hebrew).

Shlaim, A. (2009). *Israel and Palestine: Reappraisals, Revisions, Refutations*. London: Verso.

Swirski, S. (2007). *Current Plans for Developing the Negev: A Critical Perspective*. Tel Aviv: Adva Center.

———. (2008). "Transparent citizens: Israel government policy toward the Negev Bedouins." *HAGAR Studies in Culture, Polity and Identities* 8(2):25–45.

Swirski, S., and Hasson, Y. (2006). *Invisible Citizens: Israel Government Policy toward the Negev Bedouin*. Tel Aviv: Adva Center.

Weisman, J. (1970). "Land law, 1969: A critical analysis." *Israel Law Review* 5:379–456.

Yacobi, H. (2007). "The NGOization of space: Dilemmas of social change, planning policy and the Israeli public sphere." *Environment and Planning, D: Society and Space* 25:745–758.

Yagna, Y. (2010). "Demolition of unlawful buildings in the Bedouin community will be tripled in 2010." *Haaretz*, February 18. http://www.haaretz.co.il/hasite/spages/1150631.html (accessed September 22, 2011).

Yiftachel, O. (2003). "Bedouin-Arabs and the Israeli settler state: Land policies and indigenous resistance." In D. Champagne and I. Abu-Saad (eds.), *The Future of Indigenous Peoples: Strategies for Survival and Development* (pp. 21–47). Los Angeles: American Indian Studies Center, UCLA.

———. (2006). *Ethnocracy: Land and Identity Politics in Israel/Palestine.* Philadelphia: University of Pennsylvania Press.

NOTES

1. While many of the points in this chapter apply to the Bedouin Arab population of Israel as a whole, our arguments focus on the Bedouin Arabs of the Naqab. Thus, mention of "Bedouin Arabs" and "Bedouin citizens" should be understood as referring to the Bedouin population of the Naqab rather than the general Bedouin population in Israel.

2. Due to space constraints, this section offers only a brief introduction to the historical background pertinent to the Bedouin case. The history leading up to the specific events described here has been reported and analyzed in more literature than can be listed. For details on Israeli-Palestinian history with regard to the Bedouins, see Abu-Saad and Creamer (chapter 1, this volume). See also, more generally, Masalha (2000); Shlaim (2009).

3. A dunam is roughly equivalent to one-quarter of an acre.

4. Article 2 of the 1951 State Property Law stated that all property, movable and immovable, that belonged to the Palestine government during the Mandate became the property of the State of Israel as of May 15, 1948.

5. Land and other immovable property of the Palestinian Arab refugees of 1948 was transferred to the state, while an estimated 40%–60% of the land of those Palestinian Arabs who remained after 1948 and became Israeli citizens was expropriated.

6. Called the *siyag* in Hebrew (meaning "fence"), the Restricted Area was a roughly triangular region, located between the Israeli cities of Arad,

Dimona, and Beersheba, to which most of the remaining Bedouins were moved and confined after 1948. The area was under military rule until 1966. For more on the historical background of the Naqab Bedouins, on the unrecognized villages and townships, and on Bedouin resistance to Israeli policies, see Abu-Saad and Creamer (chapter 1, this volume).

7. JNF Memorandum of Association, art. 3(a).

8. The details of this purchase, including the price, are unknown (Holzman-Gazit, 2002; Yiftachel, 2006:139). According to Geremy Forman, one million dunams were later returned to the state when the JNF was unable to pay for their entire purchase. See Forman (2000:131).

9. As a result of legal challenges to the exclusionary practices of the ILA and the Jewish Agency, the system of discrimination is gaining a more sophisticated shape by employing selection committees to admit new residents to established settlements. See Supreme Court 6698/95, *Qaadan v. Israel Land Administration et al.*, 2000.

10. See Habitat International Coalition and Adalah (2006). See also the ILA official website, http://www.mmi.gov.il.

11. If implemented, a new Israeli land reform program could potentially have significant effects on the regime. Included in the reforms is a new requirement that the ILA Council include thirteen members, six of whom would be appointed by the JNF. For more, see Israel Land Administration (2011).

12. See Israel Land Administration (2007). The ILA operates under the authority of a governmental ministry, although different ministries have been responsible at different times. As of May 7, 2006, the ILA was under the Ministry of Construction and Housing; it was previously under the Ministry of Industry, Trade and Labor (Human Rights Watch, 2008: n. 56).

13. For a useful discussion, see Forman and Kedar (2004).

14. Forman and Kedar list the competing statistics:

> While estimates of Arab researchers and organizations have typically been between 5.7 million and 6.6 million dunams, former mandate and UNCCP [United Nations Conciliation Commission for Palestine] land official Sami Hadawi reached a figure of 19 million dunams by classifying "state" and "public" land within Arab village boundaries as refugee land. Israeli officials and researchers have consistently estimated between 4.2 million and 6.5 million dunams. (2004:812; citations omitted)

In addition, under the 1951 State Property Law, Israel nationalized all property, movable and immovable, that belonged to the British Mandate government, as well as all property with no owner, retroactively as of May 15, 1948 (Noach, 2009b:36).

15. The Development Authority was established under the 1950 Development Authority Law (Properties Transfer). It has also been responsible for providing housing to homeless Palestinians and transferring property to other public and national bodies, such as the JNF, municipalities, and governmental bodies.

16. Since the mid-1960s, the state has followed a policy of concentrating Bedouin citizens in urban areas, most of which have been constructed for that purpose. Seven Bedouin townships were established between the 1960s and the early 1990s.

17. The law included a compensation formula, but the amount of compensation offered for the expropriated land was far less than that given to Jewish settlers removed from the Sinai at the same time. The government of Israel designated NIS 245 million (at 2005 value) for the evacuated 7,000 Bedouins, while the cost of the evacuation of approximately 5,000 Jewish settlers from Sinai was NIS 3.4 billion (at 2004 value) for paid compensation and another NIS 2.1 billion for their resettlement in about nineteen agricultural localities. See Abu-Saad (2008); Shamir (1996). On the Peace Law, see Swirski and Hasson (2006:19–21).

18. Ordinance No. 9 of 1928, Government of Palestine, Compiled Laws, available at LLMC Digital Law Library, http://www.llmc-digital.org. The 1928 ordinance had set up the process for a nationwide cadastral survey and property rights registration in Palestine through an administrative and judicial process outlined in the ordinance.

19. Of the 3,220 claims, 2,478 are within the Restricted Area, where the number of claimants is 1,281. In addition, 389 of the claims (292 of them within the Restricted Area) involve more than one claimant (Ben-David, 1996:73, 75). Furthermore, 150,000–200,000 dunams of land were claimed in the Har Hanegev area outside the settlement area, mainly by the 'Azāzmah tribe; these lands, however, had been registered as state land since the 1950s. In addition, claimants also claimed about 500,000 dunams of grazing area, thus making the total claimed land about 1.5 million dunams.

20. On Ottoman land law and its adoption and revision by the British Mandate, see Bunton (1999).

21. The obligations of the land settlement officer under the ordinance were to be executed between several days and several months, depending on specific requirements, which might include declaring the land boundaries under settlement, preparing a list of claims and a list of rights, and publicizing such documents.

22. By suspending the land claims process, the government both avoided the potentially negative image of unilaterally seizing a massive amount of Bedouin land at one time and subsequently acted on the possibility that the Bedouins would be "motivated" by their loss in the 1984 *Al-Hawashla* case (see *infra* pp. 14–15) to accept a compromise based on compensation and new housing in the planned townships. The authors would like to thank Geremy Forman for suggesting this line of analysis.

23. Of the settled claims, approximately 150,000 dunams were settled through negotiation, while about 50,000 dunams were settled through court decisions (including judgments in absentia and claimants who preferred to reach a settlement out of court) (Goldberg Commission, 2008a).

24. See the testimony of Ilan Yishoron, Director General of the Bedouin Advancement Authority, in Goldberg Commission (2008b:123–126). According to Yahel Havatzelet (2006:13–14), former head of the Land Title Settlement Unit for the Southern District, the policy of counterclaims began in 2004; as of 2006, the state had won about forty cases covering 25,000 dunams of land, while a relatively small number of out-of-court agreements resulted in settlement of an additional 4,000 dunams.

25. See 1948 Law and Administration Ordinance, passed to maintain legal continuity after the establishment of the State of Israel. It provides that all existing laws would remain in force, subject to legal modifications resulting from either the state's establishment or subsequent legislation.

26. For example, the Ottoman authorities purchased the land on which the city of Beersheba was established from the Bedouin tribe of 'Az zmah in 1900. By 1948, the JNF and Jewish individuals had purchased about 60,000 dunams of Naqab land from Bedouin possessors (Porat, 2002:3)

27. See http://www.archive.org/stream/ottomanlandcode00turkuoft/ ottomanlandcode00turkuoft_djvu.txt for full text of the code.

28. Although both the Ottomans and the British attempted to institute land registration systems, neither the underlying principles nor the processes themselves were the same. Although the OLC categories remained relevant, the British system cannot be viewed simply as a continuation of the Ottoman one. Space constraints limit any further discussion with regard to the differences between the two. For further reading, see Bunton (2007:30–42).

29. Text available at the Yale Avalon Project website, http://avalon.law.yale. edu.

30. By April 30, 1947, the total area settled in Palestine, according to the records of the British Mandate Department of Land Registration, totaled 5,243,042 dunams, of which more than 5 million became the State of Israel (Government of Palestine, n.d.:241).

31. Text of the ordinance is available in Doukhan (1933–1936):304 (also available online at LLMC Digital Law Library, http://www.llmc-digital. org).

32. See Official Report, Colonial Office documents, 733/2, Government House, Jerusalem.

33. The authors would like to thank Oren Yiftachel for bringing this document to our attention.

34. If British land registration had been extended to the Naqab by the end of the Mandate, it is likely that the British would have registered at least two million dunams as belonging to the Bedouins: "Some 12,577 square kilometers lie in the deserts of Beersheba. It is possible that there may be private claims to over 2,000 square kilometers which are cultivated from time to time" (Government of Palestine, n.d.:257).

35. Civil Appeal 182/52, *Custodian of Absentee Property v. Zalman David*, 10(1).

36. Civil Appeal 518/61, *The State of Israel v. Tzalach Badaran*, P.D. 16(3) 1717 [1962].

37. Civil Appeal 323/54, *Ahmad Hamda v. Al Kuatli*, 10(2).
38. *The State of Israel v. Tzalach Badaran, supra* note 36.
39. Letter from the head of the ILA Ownership and Registration Department to Yosef Weitz, head of the ILA (May 29, 1964) (on file with the Israeli Central State Archive at 5733/C, 3520/11), quoted in Kedar (2001: n. 118).
40. The state was represented in this case by Pliya Albeck, from the Attorney General's Office, who drafted the Albeck Committee report for Mr. Binyamin Gur-Aryih, Advisor for Arab Issues within the Prime Minster's office (Ben-David, 1996:57).
41. Civil Appeal 218/74, *Salim Al-Hawashla v. The State of Israel*, P.D. 38(3) 141 [1984]. See also Swirski and Hasson (2006:10).
42. Kedar (2001) discusses several of these points (see especially pp. 953–964).
43. Article 2 of the 1928 Land Ordinance states that "'village' includes any village lands within or abutting on municipal area, a tribal area or any part thereof."
44. *Salim Al-Hawashla v. The State of Israel, supra* note 41.
45. Article 44(b) states that "The Court is not obliged to act in accordance with Ottoman Law provisions that prevent the Court from examining claims that are based on unregistered documents; neither is it obliged to act in accordance with the Ottoman Evidence Law" (authors' translation).
46. *Sanad* is a written document proving the sale and ownership over the land; *rahen* is the document proving the mortgage of the land. For more
46. on the use of land documents among Bedouins, see Kram (chapter 3, this volume).
47. The equity principle was incorporated into Israeli law through article 46 of the Palestine Order in Council: "[W]henever the solution to a question of law is not to be found in the local law, reference must be made to the rules of the common law and the principles of equity prevailing in England as a complementary source."
48. Supreme Court, *Haj Hassan Hammad v. Mgr. Barlassina*, October 15, 1936.
49. Civil Appeal (Tel Aviv) 1067/55, *Chamis Ibrahim Dabub Karkar v. Custodian of Absentee Property*, 1956 (11). See Kedar (2001:975).
50. Civil Appeal 274/62, *State of Israel v. Hussein Ali Suead*, 16(3) (cited in Kedar, 2001:968).
51. Although the Naqab Bedouin Arab citizens of Israel have a unique situation and history, they are also intimately connected to the history of the Bedouin Arabs throughout the region. In the interest of space, we cannot address these broader questions in this chapter. Others have addressed this history in a broader regional sense (see, e.g., Chatty, 2006; Meir, 1997).
52. No "hierarchy of suffering" among Palestinians in Israel is implied here; certainly, many Palestinian communities in Israel have experienced discrimination in land, planning, and housing (among other arenas). We merely seek to highlight the particularity of the Bedouin case. Neither

space nor relevance allow for a description of the nature of Palestinian citizens' existence in post-1948 Israel more generally. For details, see, e.g., Abu Hussein and McKay (2003); Kedar (2001:923).

53. In a frank statement on the unlikely possibility of Bedouin success in the Israeli legal system, the Commission concluded that "so far as the legal disagreement over land ownership is concerned, the Bedouins will also lose their case in the future" (Goldberg Commission, 2008a: para. 45).

54. Shamir (1996:237–238) clarifies that the legal conceptual scheme he suggests—that is, that the technologies of Israeli law constructed the Bedouins as a nomadic population with no real attachment to the land in opposition to the "social realm" of the broader Israeli (Jewish) community—did not itself *cause* state land seizures (which would likely have occurred regardless). Rather, the conceptualism both simplified land expropriation from the Bedouins, who unlike the broader Palestinian population were not read as "national enemies," and created a narrative that made the denial of Bedouin land rights part of the "message of progress and benevolence" that helped constitute Israeli identity.

55. See Yiftachel (2006), especially p. 142. There is a pending petition against this policy of selection committees. See Supreme Court 3552/08, *Kimpler et al. v. ILA et al.*, 2008. Petition and briefs available at http://www.acri.org.il/he/?p=1826.

56. Israeli Government Decision No. 2265, July 21, 2002 (Hamdan, 2005:2).

57. The plan was originally authored by an Israeli non-governmental organization, Daroma–Eidan Ha-Negev (Southward–The Negev Era).

58. See the ministry's official website, http://www.vpmo.gov.il.

59. One might note the irony in the use of "legal" to categorize the internationally illegal settlements in the Gaza Strip, contrasted with reference to the "illegal" housing of the Bedouins residing on their historical land.

60. On the eviction of the inhabitants of the unrecognized villages of Attir and Um-Alhiran in order to build two new Jewish settlements, see Adalah (2007).

61. Supreme Court 1991/00, *Abu Hamad et al. v. the National Planning Council et al.* The petition originated in an objection filed against the plan in 1994.

62. In April 2007, the Supreme Court outlawed the practice of crop spraying due to its damaging health and environmental impacts (Supreme Court 2887/04, *Abu Mdieghem et al. v. Israel Land Administration et al.*).

63. Although remaining on the land does constitute a resistance strategy in many cases, it is also a situation driven by necessity; in most cases, the Bedouin citizens have no alternative housing and would be effectively homeless if they abandoned their claimed land.

64. A more detailed description of service-related claims would require far greater space. For more information on the types of petitions filed in these cases, see, e.g., the petitions filed by the Association for Civil Rights in Israel (http://www.acri.org.il/eng) and by Adalah: The Legal Center

for Arab Minority Rights in Israel (http://www.old-adalah.org/eng/legaladvocacyoverview.php). Scholars have also noted the new trends (see, e.g., Yacobi, 2007:745).

65. *Abu Hamad et al. v. the National Planning Council et al., supra* note 61.
66. October 22, 2007. Names of individual and village have been kept confidential.
67. Israel Government Resolutions 631 (July 15, 2007), 1999 (July 15, 2007), and 2491 (October 28, 2007). The Commission consisted of eight members: a Supreme Court justice emeritus (chairperson), four public representatives appointed by ministers, and three governmental representatives.
68. Led by Ehud Prawer of the Prime Minister's Office and comprising eight individuals, the action and implementation team was appointed by the government on January 18, 2009, by Government Resolution 4411. The resolution emphasized that the Bedouin case is of national priority and stated that the outline set by the Goldberg Commission would serve to guide the action plan, whose task included addressing reservations outlined in the Goldberg Report by some of the Commission's members. See Prime Minister's Office (2009). Interview with Dudu Cohen, Israel, December 27, 2009. Cohen, who was previously the head of the Ministry of the Interior of the Southern District (Naqab) and a member of the Goldberg Commission, currently works in the planning department of the Abu Basma Regional Council.
69. The report made no suggestions with regard to current planning frameworks, despite the Goldberg Commission's recommendation that recognition be expanded. The draft also recommended further law enforcement measures (Bedouin Authority, 2011:3–9).
70. Of these 100,000 dunams, 25,000 dunams are required to be within the planning boundaries of existing Bedouin settlements and those currently planned. In his presentation to the Goldberg Commission, the director of the Bedouin Authority, part of the ILA, proposed a settlement scheme that totaled 100,250 dunams. See Goldberg Commission (2008b).
71. Those who prove their claims will receive an ownership portion of up to twenty dunams (Goldberg Commission, 2008a: para. 86). Claims greater than twenty dunams will be met as follows: 50% of every dunam above twenty will automatically go to the state (para. 102.) Of the remaining 50%, the claimant may receive up to 40% as land and the remainder (i.e., a portion greater than or equal to 60% of the 50%) in monetary compensation (para. 102). Only 8% of claims are for twenty or fewer dunams (para. 104). In certain cases (such as previous settlement agreements or land held by a third party), claimants will receive only monetary compensation (paras. 87, 90).
72. Supreme Court 8002/05, *El-Atrash v. The Minister of Health et al.*, para. 4, emphasis added. The case—and this specific language from the verdict—is quoted by the Goldberg Commission itself in its report (2008a: para. 65).

73. In fact, the Court took into account offers by several organizations to donate approximately NIS 20,000 to the family, supporting the idea that a private charitable donation was more appropriate than any Court-ordered provision by the state. As a result, the substandard conditions of Bedouin life are reconstructed as a regrettable fact rather than as a state responsibility.

74. The impulse to "solve" the Bedouin "problem" for reasons of state interest is not new (Shamir, 1996:250, with reference to the *Avitan* case). One of the more explicit versions may be found in Ariel Sharon's article of December 2000 (shortly before the beginning of his term as prime minister), in which he stated that

> In the Negev, we face a serious problem: About 900,000 dunams of government land are not in our hands but in the hands of the Bedouin population. . . . The Bedouin are grabbing new territory. They are gnawing away at the country's land reserves, and no one is doing anything significant about it. (Sharon, 2000, cited and translated in Abu-Ras, 2006:1)

Abstract

This chapter explores the legal history of land disputes between the State of Israel and the Bedouins in the Naqab (Negev). Israel does not recognize Bedouin land ownership rights and since 1948 has used a series of legal procedures to nationalize a large percentage of the land previously held by the Bedouins. The chapter examines Bedouin legal struggles for land ownership and explores the differences between the legal arguments of the state and those of the Bedouins. In doing so, it looks at Ottoman, British, and Israeli legislation and court rulings, as well as Bedouin legal mechanisms that determine ownership rights, including selling, leasing, and boundary marking.

The chapter offers new perspectives for understanding Bedouin struggles for land and the legal land disputes between Israel and the Bedouins by looking at the cultural, historical, and national aspects of these disputes. It challenges the traditional representation of Naqab Bedouins as "rootless nomads" with neither attachment to land nor ownership perception. It also challenges the lack of acknowledgment of Bedouin customary practices of land ownership within conventional legal and academic discourse. The chapter argues that the legal conflict over land reflects power imbalances between Israeli legal practices and Bedouin indigenous oral practices, and has been shaped by the national conflict between Israel as a Jewish state and the Bedouins as part of the Arab Palestinian minority in Israel. In this context, the chapter discusses the ways in which legal discourse (primarily through laws and court decisions) renders the national and historical aspects of the land dispute essentially invisible.

CHAPTER 3

The Naqab Bedouins:
Legal Struggles for Land Ownership Rights in Israel

Noa Kram

Introduction

The relations between Bedouins and the Israeli state, particularly concerning legal disputes over land ownership, can be analyzed within the context of state-indigenous relations.[1] The Bedouins are indigenous to the Naqab and have been living there for centuries; they were organized into nomadic and semi-nomadic tribes sustained by pasture, herds, and seasonal agriculture (Abu-Saad, 2008b; Marx, 1967).[2] As with other indigenous groups, land has played a central role in Bedouin history, livelihood, and culture, and is essential to both Bedouin identity and cultural viability (Abu-Saad, 2008b; Daes, 2001:8–9).

The conflict over land ownership is a core issue in relations between the Bedouins and the State of Israel. Israeli law does not recognize Bedouin claims for land ownership based on Bedouin customary law (Yiftachel and Kedar, 2000:73–74; Abu-Saad, 2008b). Since its establishment as a state, Israel has nationalized a large percentage of the land previously held by the Bedouins (Rozen-Zvi, 2004; Yiftachel, 2006).

This chapter is based on my current dissertation in Social and Cultural Anthropology at the California Institute of Integral Studies. I want to thank Professors Angana Chatterji and Ismael Abu-Saad for reading the dissertation proposal and for their comments and guidance. I also want to thank Professor Oren Yiftachel for discussing some parts of this chapter and providing editorial comments.

This chapter discusses the differences between the legal claims for land made by the Israeli state and those asserted by the Bedouins. It begins by describing Israeli courts' rejection of Bedouin claims for ownership. It also discusses the development of Bedouin customary law pertaining to land ownership since the nineteenth century, arguing that both the Ottoman and British rules recognized de facto and respected Bedouin land ownership based on Bedouin customary practices. Finally, the chapter provides a cultural, historical, and legal critique of Israeli state policies that reject Bedouin claims for land, and addresses the impact of the loss of land on the Bedouin community.

State and Bedouin Claims for Land
The Legal Claims of the Israeli State

The Israeli government claims that the majority of the land in the Naqab is state land and that the Bedouins do not have ownership rights but rather only partial holding rights (Swirski and Hasson, 2006:9–11). The state's legal claim is based on legislation, governmental decisions, and court rulings from the Ottoman, British, and Israeli governments. Ottoman and British laws regarding land rights in the Naqab remained in force under Israeli rule until they were replaced by the 1969 Land Law, which is still in effect today.

The 1858 Ottoman Land Code (OLC) classified land according to five categories. One of the categories was *mawat* ("dead" in Turkish), defined as uncultivated and uninhabited land located more than 1.5 miles from any town or village. *Mawat* land was classified as state property (Shamir, 1996; Forman and Kedar, 2004). The Ottoman law allowed the "revival" of *mawat* lands through cultivation: whoever transformed such territory into agricultural land could register it and subsequently gain ownership rights. The system thus encouraged land cultivation, in part as a means of increasing the Empire's tax income (Kedar, 2001; Rosen-Zvi, 2004:47; Yiftachel, 2003:31–32).

To consolidate land under governmental control, the British Mandate authorities replaced the Ottoman legislation on *mawat* land with the 1921 Mawat Land Ordinance (Kedar, 2001:923). The new law transformed the status of those who cultivated *mawat* lands from individuals entitled to ownership rights to potential trespassers. This was accomplished by declaring that a person who cultivates *mawat* land without administrative consent "shall obtain no right to a title-deed for such land, and, further, shall be liable to be persecuted for trespass" (Rosen-Zvi, 2004:47). The ordinance provided a narrow opportunity to register *mawat* land—within two months of the promulgation of the ordinance in February 1921—and stated that those who failed to register the land within this time would lose any ownership rights, since the land would be classified as state land (Rosen-Zvi, 2004:47).

The 1969 Israeli Land Law abolished the *mawat* category and determined that all such land would be registered as state property unless a formal legal title could be produced according to the Ottoman or British laws. The state argues that the last opportunity to register *mawat* land was under the British ordinance in 1921. Since most of the Bedouins did not register their land at that time, for a variety of reasons discussed below, the only option to prove ownership was to convince the Israeli judicial branches that the lands were not *mawat* land (Shamir, 1996:238–250; Falah, 1989:77; Yiftachel, 2003:31–32).[3]

The Legal Claims of the Bedouins

Since 1948, Bedouins have been filing land claims before Israeli courts in an attempt to register their land according to Israeli law. The courts have rejected Bedouin claims, stating that presence on the land does not itself suggest ownership rights. As of 2006, not a single court had awarded full ownership rights to Bedouins, effectively declaring the Naqab lands as *mawat* and therefore belonging to the state (Ben-David, 1996; Yiftachel, 2006:198). The Bedouin claimants have based their claims on historical rights according to Bedouin customary law, which have determined ownership based on long-term possession, inheritance, gift, or purchase. In most cases, the Bedouins claim that they have owned the land in question for generations, that they have cultivated the land continuously, and that the land therefore cannot be considered *mawat*. In some cases, they have based their claims on tax payment documents for land they held during the British and Ottoman eras. Additionally, Bedouins have argued that the fact that they sold land to Zionist organizations before 1948 proves their rights over the Naqab lands that they possessed and continue to possess (Ben-David, 1996, 2004:290; Arab Association for Human Rights, 2004).

Rejection of Bedouin Claims for Land in Israeli Courts

In *Al-Hawashla*,[4] a precedent-setting case regarding Bedouin land ownership, the Israeli Supreme Court rejected the appeal of ten Bedouins for recognition of their ownership over a number of plots and for permission to register the land in their name according to the 1969 Land Rights Settlement Ordinance [New Version]. The state claimed that the land should be classified as *mawat* land and, since the appellants did not have a legal title, that the land should be registered as state property according to the 1969 law. The appellants based their claim on rights that were passed down to them from previous generations and on their long-term possession and cultivation. They argued that the land was not neglected and should not be considered *mawat*.

The key question in the verdict was whether the land in question should be classified as *mawat* land. In order to classify it as *mawat*, the state had to prove that in 1858 the land was barren, was not possessed by anyone, and was more than 1.5 miles from the nearest town or village. The Bedouins argued that the land was cultivated, that a Bedouin village (Sir) did exist near the claimed land, and that in the middle of the nineteenth century their ancestors lived in Sir, which was located fewer than 1.5 miles from the plots. The Court rejected these claims. It stated that "in the said area there had been no village and no agriculture, and except for a visible Bedouin tent-encampment and wild vegetation the whole area was nothing but barren desert" (cited in Shamir, 1996:239). The Court declared the land as *mawat* and thus state land.

Representation of Bedouin History by the Courts

As this verdict shows, in defining legal land ownership rights, the Court relied on and constructed a particular historical representation of Bedouin society in the Naqab in the nineteenth century. Bedouins have been continually depicted by Israeli courts and the state in general as "rootless nomads" who "never resided permanently in any place whatsoever" (*Abu-Solb*), without attachment to land, without territorial perception of individual ownership, and without entitlement to land ownership.[5] The Naqab was described as "nothing but a barren desert" (*Al-Hawashla*).[6] This representation reproduces and constructs a specific historical narrative that legitimizes dispossession of Bedouin land (Shamir, 1996:236, 250–251; Abu-Ras, 2006:2).

In the last two decades, this representation has been challenged by some critical anthropological, historical, legal, and geographic scholarship (see S. Abu-Rabia, 2008; Abu-Saad, 2008a, 2008b; Kedar, 2004; Yiftachel, 2003, 2006; Meir, 1997, 2009; Rosen-Zvi, 2004; Shamir, 1996). These studies challenge the dominant state narrative and provide more complex historical accounts regarding the role of land within Bedouin society. In doing so, they emphasize "the strong sense of ownership and belonging" among the Naqab Bedouins (Shamir, 1996:236). These accounts demonstrate that from at least the second half of the nineteenth century, the Bedouins perceived themselves as landowners and had their own legal mechanisms to determine ownership rights, including selling, leasing, boundary marking, inheritance, and settling of land disputes. Furthermore, their ownership was recognized by factors external to Bedouin society—namely by Ottoman and British authorities, Arab peasants and merchants, and Jewish institutions (Shamir, 1996:235; Meir, 2009).

Development of Bedouin Customary Practices of Land Ownership

Bedouin Land Usage

The late Ottoman period (1858–1917)

Throughout the nineteenth century, the Bedouins were largely the only inhabitants of the Naqab. Ottoman rule did not interfere with Bedouin affairs, and Bedouins lived an "autonomous, if not independent, existence" (Bailey, 1980:80). In Bedouin areas, land was under tribal control and was used primarily for livestock, although there is evidence of agricultural activity as early as the late eighteenth century (Rosen-Zvi, 2004:83; Meir, 1997, 2006). Throughout the nineteenth and twentieth centuries, the extent of agricultural cultivation increased and intensified (Meir, 2006:53–64).

From the mid-nineteenth century, in the face of the threat posed to Ottoman sovereignty by European colonial powers, the Ottomans sought to stabilize the area and gain control over the Bedouin population (Rosen-Zvi, 2004:44).[7] As part of this policy, the Ottomans enacted the OLC, the first external law to interfere with Bedouin land affairs (Meir, 1997). By classifying uncultivated land as state property, the law encouraged transition to agriculture at the expense of pasturing. The integration of pasturing with agricultural use resulted in a more fixed and stable perception of territory by the Bedouins, and land became a base for agriculture and settlement (Rosen-Zvi, 2004:83; Meir, 1997:79; Ben-David, 1990:187–190).

The British Mandate (1917–1948)

The British Mandate government increased the process of land com-modification and sedentarization among the Bedouins. The Naqab region was affected by the European economy, and demand for agri-cultural products from the area radically increased the amount of agri-cultural activity undertaken by Bedouin communities (Meir, 1997:84–85).[8] The 1931 British census of Palestine pointed out that 89.3% of the Bedouins in the Naqab earned their livelihood through agricul-ture, while only 10.7% did so through livestock (Mills, 1931:334). During the British Mandate period, Bedouins cultivated about 600,000 dunams in drought years, and between 2 million and 3.5 million dunams in rainy years (Meir, 2006:62; Porat, 1996:12).[9] The shift toward agriculture attracted peasants who emigrated from Egypt looking for livelihood. In addition, around the turn of the century, Zionist organizations began to express interest in buying land from the Bedouins. The demand for land by Arab peasants and merchants and by Jewish organizations—a new phenomenon in the Naqab—also affected the market values of land. Leasing and selling land became increasingly common (Meir, 1997:83; Rosen-Zvi, 2004:83).

Parallel to the increase in land cultivation, a conception of private ownership (as opposed to collective tribal land) gradually emerged. Tribal land that had been collectively owned was divided into family and individual plots, and patterns of permanent agricultural settle-ment emerged. While grazing areas and water resources remained in communal possession, cultivated land was placed under family and individual ownership (Marx, 1967:82; Meir, 1997:86; Kressel, 2003:29). Alongside this shift to family and individual ownership of land, the acts of selling, leasing, and inheriting land became common, and customary practices of land ownership developed (Meir, 1997:80, 2006:64–66; H. Abu-Rabia, 2005; Shamir, 1996:235).[10] By 1948, the majority of the Naqab Bedouins were sedentarized, perceiving land as a base for settlement and agriculture. They cultivated most of the land in the Naqab that was suitable for agriculture. Some families moved seasonally with the herds to pastoral areas, while others remained in permanent places of residence (Marx, 1967; Rosen-Zvi, 2004:45, 82–85; Ben-David, 1990:190; Meir, 1997:79–81; Shamir, 1996:236).

This historical account challenges the representation of Bedouins as "rootless nomads" without a concept of individual land ownership, and shows that the Bedouins perceived themselves as landowners. In addition, such a contextualized account reveals the ways in which Naqab land was and is central to Bedouin history, culture, and livelihood. As Issachar Rosen-Zvi has argued:

> From this reconstructed historical narrative it is clear that the Zionist image of the Bedouin as nomads with no attachment to the land (or in its multicultural version— with a distinct conception of territory illegible to the Western mind), which justified practices of dispossession and segregation is not anchored in historical reality. (2004:85)

Bedouin Practices of Land Ownership

During the eighteenth and nineteenth centuries, several conflicts among different Bedouin tribes occurred over control of land and water resources. By 1890, the boundaries of land belonging to each tribe were delineated and known, and remained fixed until 1948. Ottoman authorities recognized the tribal territories and Bedouin possession of water resources and grazing areas (H. Abu-Rabia, 2005:24; Bailey, 1980:35–39; Porat, 1996:3). The boundaries between tribal and individual plots were marked by stones or difficult-to-move plants (Kressel, Ben-David, and Abu-Rabia, 1991:60–66). The Bedouins also had their own system of land registration. Plots were registered in a book kept by sheikhs (tribe chiefs), and registration included significant details regarding the land, its boundaries, and relevant transactions. This process gave land registration validity within Bedouin society (Porat, 1996:4; Kark, 2002:48). 'Ārif al-'Ārif, governor of the Beersheba district during the Mandate period, wrote about the land in the Beersheba area:

> Every inch of land is owned by someone and everyone knows his own land in spite of the absence of boundary fences. A strip of fallow or a strip of sown land carrying a crop different from the land on each side will serve as lines of demarcation. Clumps of Basul grown at certain points also serve to define ownership. There are fewer disputes over boundaries in Beersheba than in the towns and villages. (1944:180)

In the twentieth century, land transactions became common; Bedouins sold land among themselves, to Ottoman authorities, to Arab merchants, and to Zionist institutions (Porat, 1996:10, 15; Maddrell, 1990:5). The practice of writing a bill of sale was developed at the beginning of the twentieth century under the influence of merchants from Gaza and Hebron and of Zionist institutions. Those buyers were accustomed to receiving a document as part of any transaction, and they needed a document to register the land with the Ottoman, and subsequently the British, registry. Therefore, the practice of *sanad* ("bill of sale" in Arabic) became common. A written agreement between the sellers and buyers, the *sanad* included the names of the seller and the buyer; their addresses; the source of the rights over the land (inheritance or purchase); the location and boundaries of the land; neighboring territories, water sources, caves, gardens, or dams on the land; the date, price, and forms of payment; and the signatures of the buyers, sellers, witnesses, and the sheikh (Porat, 1996:10; H. Abu-Rabia, 2005:24; Kressel, Ben-David, and Abu-Rabia, 1991:51–54). As such, the *sanad* became a document with binding legal power. The British rule regarded it as sufficient documentation for land registration, and the Beersheba tribal court under the British Mandate used it to rule in land disputes (H. Abu-Rabia, 2005:25). In addition, in an arrangement called *rahen*, Bedouins leased or mortgaged their land, mostly in drought years when they needed money. The lease provided the right to cultivate the land, while the owners received one-third of the crops. Furthermore, a tribal court presided over land disputes. A steady increase in land transactions and disputes led to some judges specializing in such matters (H. Abu-Rabia, 2005:25; Bar-Zvi, 1991:146; Porat, 1996:12–13; Kressel, Ben-David, and Abu-Rabia, 1991:54–58).

To conclude, throughout the latter half of the nineteenth century and the beginning of the twentieth century, Bedouin society developed organized procedures for determining land ownership. Boundaries between different plots were known and respected, and an internal system regulated land ownership. This system included practices of inheritance, boundary marking, selling and leasing transactions, and procedures for a tribal court to address land disputes.

Recognition of Bedouin Land Ownership Prior to 1948

Ronen Shamir (1996) has argued that Israeli authorities' reliance on archaic Ottoman and British laws without regard for their historical and social context has constituted a means to appropriate Bedouin land in the Naqab. Neither Ottoman nor British governors interfered with Bedouin internal autonomy concerning land, and, in fact, neither regime substantively challenged Bedouin land possession. Only after 1948 were Ottoman and British laws used by the State of Israel as a means to confiscate land (Shamir, 1996:239–240).

In practice, both the Ottoman and British regimes—as well as the pre-state Zionist institutions—recognized Bedouin land ownership even after the 1858 and 1921 land ordinances came into effect (Abu Hussein and McKay, 2003:122; Shamir, 1996:239–240; Swirski and Hasson, 2006:10). Ottoman and British rulers collected taxes from Bedouin landowners, and British authorities received tax payment documentation as part of the land registration process. Both regimes recognized land-selling transactions and registered them in their respective land registries (Porat, 1996:5–11; Marx, 1982; Meir, 2006:44, 2009:826). For example, in 1900, Ottoman authorities purchased 2,000 dunams from the 'Azāzmah tribe to establish the city of Beersheba (Abu Hussein and McKay, 2003:112–113; Maddrell, 1990:5). In addition, in 1911, a Zionist organization purchased 6,000 dunams from the Bedouins in Jammama (Ruchama). The land had not been registered previously in the Ottoman registry; the Bedouins registered the land in their name to complete the transaction. Based on the transaction, the Ottoman registered the land in the name of the purchasers (Porat, 1996:17; Kark, 2002:44). Oren Yiftachel has argued that these purchases indicate that the Ottomans recognized Bedouin ownership and did not implement the 1858 Land Code in the Naqab area.[11] If the Ottoman governors had perceived the land as *mawat* (and thus belonging to the state), there would have been no reason either to register the land in the name of the Bedouins or to purchase the land from them.

Following Ottoman practice, the British Mandate government generally recognized de facto Bedouin ownership. According to Halil Abu-Rabia, when the Mandate took over the Naqab, the district governor met with Bedouin sheikhs to discuss their concerns. The sheikhs' main request was that their rights over land and water resources remain unaffected; Mandate authorities granted their request (H. Abu-Rabia, 2005:27).[12] Bedouins who wanted to register their land in the British land registry had the opportunity to do so during the 1930s and 1940s, although according to the 1921 British ordinance, the last opportunity to register *mawat* lands was in that year. British authorities also recognized Bedouin land sales and provided land titles to Arabs and Jews who bought land from the Bedouins (Porat, 1996:5, 9). By 1936, Jewish institutions had bought about 40,000 dunams; by 1947, the Jewish National Fund (JNF) alone had purchased about 65,000 dunams in the Naqab (Porat, 1996:15; Kark, 2002:102). When the Bedouins sold land to Jews, they first registered the land in their name in the British land registry. British officials recognized Bedouin ownership based on *sanad*, tax payments, neighbors' testimonies, and sheikhs' signatures (Porat, 1996:5, 11; H. Abu-Rabia, 2005); the Mandate government also issued certificates of registration for Jewish buyers of land. In these certificates, Bedouins are registered as the former owners of the land (Central Zionist Archives, 1938). Chiram Danin, who purchased land from the Bedouins for the Palestine Land Development Company during the 1930s, describes the purchase and registration process:

> This year, I purchased 400 dunams north of the military cemetery that were registered in the *tabu* [land registry office] in the name of the Palestine Land Development Company. . . . After the maps of Al-Sir land were prepared, the task of collecting signatures from the Bedouin owners and neighbors began. . . . When the maps and documents were signed by the owners . . . they were submitted to the *tabu* for registration. Afterward, an order from the government land division was given to register the land in the name of the Bedouin owners, and a special official arrived from Jerusalem to register the lands in English. (1990:172–173; author's translation)

In addition to registering the land for the purpose of property sales, Arab landowners in the Naqab registered 64,000 dunams in their names in the land registry (Fischbach, 2003:273). It is likely that the majority of the land was not registered within the two months in 1921 dictated by British law but rather registered gradually throughout the three decades of British rule. Documents from the Israeli military rule in the Naqab (1948–1966) also suggest that the British Mandate recognized Bedouin ownership of the lands in question. In 1966, Israeli military governor Sasson Bar-Zvi wrote that although the Naqab land had not been registered by the British authorities, Bedouin possession would remain intact, since the British authorities recognized their land rights. This recognition finds expression in the registration of Bedouin land in tax payment books and in British authorities' recognition of land transactions among the Bedouins and between Bedouins and other purchasers. In this way, the JNF purchased thousands of dunams and registered them in its name (Bar-Zvi, 1966).

These practices indicate that both pre-state Zionist organizations and the British Mandate recognized the authority and validity of traditional Bedouin ownership, as well as Bedouins' power to sell land. They also demonstrate that British authorities never fully implemented the 1921 Mawat Land Ordinance, allowed Bedouins to register land in their name even after the two-month period stipulated in the ordinance, and did not treat the land in question as *mawat*. As Ismael Abu-Saad writes in an article entitled "How Can We Be Called Intruders If We and Our Ancestors Have Been Living in the Naqab for Thousands of Years?":

> The government authorities claim the Bedouins do not own the land. But what can you do when, historically, the Bedouins never registered their land with the government land administration? Can this deny them ownership? The whole question of ownership of land is seen by the Bedouins as a kind of paradox. "How is it possible," ask the Bedouin, "that in the 1920s and 1930s, the Jewish National Fund and the Jewish Agency purchased land in the Naqab from its Bedouin owners, and today they're suddenly not the owners? What has changed?" (cited in Abu-Ras, 2006:2)

"What Has Changed?": Critiquing the Legal Claims of the State

The Invisibility of Customary Law

In defining land rights in the Naqab, Israeli law disregards Bedouin practices of land ownership and land use. Israel's official legal discussion is limited to the interpretation of Ottoman, British, and Israeli laws. Neither the issue of the applicability of Ottoman and British legislation to Bedouin culture nor the question of whether Bedouin society had its own valid legal system to determine ownership is discussed. As a result, current legal processes exclude Bedouin law, rendering it invisible and irrelevant to determining land rights. In other words, the Israeli legal system positions Bedouin law outside of what constitutes "law." This position was explicitly stated by the head of the Israeli Land Title Settlement Unit, who asserted that "the Bedouin ownership claims are not based on *legal grounds* but rather on *their own tradition* and the period of time they occupied the land, with limited documentation" (Yahel, 2006:11; emphasis added). Similarly, Hebrew University Professor Ruth Kark, in an expert opinion submitted on behalf of the state in 2010 as part of a land ownership trial, has claimed that "the Bedouins did not have an organized land system that could determine ownership" (author's translation).[13] Ignoring Bedouin law regarding land rights has meant, in practice, non-recognition of Bedouin culture and delegitimization of Bedouin claims for land. In a report to the United Nations (UN) Committee on the Elimination of Racial Discrimination, the Negev Coexistence Forum for Civil Equality argues, "By ignoring their traditional land ownership mechanisms, the Israeli judicial system effectively delegitimized and abolished any real chance for members of this group to win legal procedures regarding land issues in Israeli courts" (2006:12).

Several international norms emphasize governments' obligation to recognize indigenous peoples' right to land that they have traditionally occupied (Kedar, 2004; Daes, 2001). For example, article 26 of the UN Declaration on the Rights of Indigenous Peoples establishes the right of indigenous peoples to "own, use, develop and control" the "lands, territories and resources" they possess based on traditional ownership. The Declaration also calls on states to grant "legal recognition and protection" to these territories in conjunction with the "customs, traditions, and land tenure systems" of the relevant indigenous peoples.[14]

By contrast, the Israeli state uses the lack of Bedouin land registration during the Ottoman and British periods as a means to deny Bedouin ownership and as proof that the Bedouins did not perceive themselves as landowners. Reliance on the absence of such formal registration to delegitimize Bedouin claims for land ignores the historical and cultural context of the law and of Bedouin society. Israeli law, based on colonial legislation, legitimizes land titles as a means to constitute land ownership; Bedouin culture, however, as an oral culture, did not historically attach the same value to British and Ottoman land titles.

For a variety of reasons, Bedouins avoided registering their land under either the Ottoman or British systems. First and foremost, Bedouin communities did not adopt the Western system of land registration but rather continued to use their traditional mechanisms, including their own documentation, to determine land ownership (Negev Coexistence Forum for Civil Equality, 2006). They recognized each other's land ownership, and under British and Ottoman rule the absence of formal documentation did not threaten or undermine their control over land. Possession of lands without title was the norm prior to the title registration process initiated by the British. By the end of the Ottoman period, only 5% of the land in Palestine had been registered (Kedar, 2001:933; Maddrell, 1990:5). The Bedouins were suspicious of forced attempts to register their land, seeing these efforts as a means to turn them into taxpaying subjects of an external authority; in addition, such formal registration would expose them to the military draft. In addition, the British process of land registration did not reach the Naqab before the end of the Mandate. As a result, Bedouins did not have the opportunity to register their land as part of this organized procedure (Falah, 1989; Shamir, 1996:235, 241; Abu Hussein and McKay, 2003:113,121; Yiftachel, 2003:32).

(Re)Interpreting the 1858 Ottoman Land Law

Israeli authorities' reliance on the 1858 OLC as the basis for determining Bedouin land ownership is troubling for two reasons. First, the original code largely disregarded Bedouin cultural realities by enforcing the sensibility of the Ottoman Empire on the indigenous inhabitants. Second, the Israeli Supreme Court's interpretation of the code has reduced any potential flexibility of Ottoman practice to a narrow set of options for determining Bedouin land rights. With regard to the first issue, Avinoam Meir has argued that the OLC was forced on the Bedouins "through brutal disregarding of the cultural existence of the local indigenous population" (Meir, 2006:71). The law's definitions were not applicable to Bedouin society because they assumed a cultural context of permanent villages in which agriculture is the main form of livelihood. Within Bedouin society, land cultivation required neither permanent presence on the land nor continuous cultivation, and cultivation was carried out in patches according to weather and land conditions (Meir, 2006:49–55).

Beyond the problematic nature of the Ottoman code, however, the Israeli Supreme Court's interpretation of the *mawat* law has expanded the meaning of *mawat* beyond what was customary under the Ottoman and British rules, thus limiting the ability of Arab land claimants to gain ownership rights over land they had possessed (Kedar, 2001:953–954). As Alexandre (Sandy) Kedar argues, in the 1962 *Badaran* case, the Court determined that claimants who had not registered their land according to the 1921 ordinance could not revive the right to gain ownership, regardless of how long they had possessed and cultivated the land.[15] The ruling thus restricted claimants' possibilities for gaining ownership rights by relying on an interpretation of the British law that disregarded the actual practice of the British regime, which in fact allowed land registration after 1921 and never implemented the ordinance in a rigid fashion (Kedar, 2001:957–958). The *Badaran* decision essentially determined that "all unregistered land outside the confines of the mile and a half radius [created by the Ottoman Code] belonged to the State" (Kedar, 2001:969).[16]

In addition, the Supreme Court chose to interpret the Ottoman law requiring the existence of a permanent town or village prior to 1858 as *the only legitimate form of settlement* from which to measure the distance for the purpose of determining if the land is *mawat*. This interpretation ignores Ottoman provisions referring to an "inhabited place" as a form of settlement and was reached without any reliance on other legislation or precedents (Kedar, 2001:960–961). In other words, the Court interpreted the concept of "settlement" in a way that excluded many Bedouin forms of settlement (for example, the use of tents) from the definition of "village." This interpretation rendered pastoral economy and dwelling in tents as cultural practices that are not entitled for recognition (Shamir, 1996:239; Meir, 2006:68–70).[17] The Court's restrictive and exclusionary interpretation of the British and Ottoman *mawat* laws thus prevented the majority of land claimants from gaining ownership of the land—and stands in sharp contrast to the Ottoman and British authorities' de facto recognition of Bedouin land ownership.

Finally, the Israeli legal system declared the promulgation of the 1858 OLC as the decisive moment for determining Bedouin entitlement to land. By interpreting the law based on conditions prevailing in 1858 (when the law was passed) rather than on the situation in 1948 (when the law was adopted by the State of Israel), ninety years of Bedouin presence, culture, and land possession were brutally and strategically ignored (Meir, 2006:5)

Using "Traveler Literature" to Construct Naqab Land as *Mawat*

In *Al-Hawashla*, the Supreme Court based its findings primarily on Western travelers' literature, research, and maps from the nineteenth century. For example, the Court stated:

> The condition of the Negev in 1870 was researched by the scholar Palmer, who traveled in that area and closely studied the Negev condition. He found wilderness, ancient

ruins and nomad Bedouins, who did not particularly cultivate the land, did not plough the land and did not engage
in agriculture at all.[18]

In two 2010 verdicts, the Beersheba District Court similarly relied on
such literature to determine that the claimed land "was desolate area
from ancient times" (*Al-Asibi*) and that it was *mawat* "since it is distant
from a place of settlement and located in a desolate area" (*Al-Machdi*).[19]
This reliance on "traveler literature" to describe Bedouin settlements
and cultivation and to determine the Bedouins' legal rights over land
is particularly problematic since it conflates contemporary literature
with scientific research.

As Yiftachel points out in an expert opinion, most of the travelers
at the time were Christians who arrived in Palestine to trace the stories
of the Bible.[20] Their reports, therefore, must be understood as part of
a specifically Christian perception of the land rather than an overall
examination of the area. Such travelers and scholars writing about Palestinian society frequently explained in their prefaces that their epis-
temological point of departure was the Bible (Rabinowitz, 1998:18).
The majority of the researchers/travelers were Europeans who omitted
the local point of view. Thus, according to Dan Rabinowitz:

> The ethnographic knowledge collected in European lan-
> guages did not really address the people. It preferred to
> look through them. Their transparency was a convenient
> and elegant prism to look through what was much more
> interesting to the Europeans—the Bible. (1998:35; author's
> translation)

Rabinowitz argues that the random character of such descriptions does
not allow one to establish anthropological knowledge based on these
reports, since the main subject of the reports is the route of their tour
(1998:21). Furthermore, since the travelers sought permanent villages
similar to those in Europe, it is possible that other forms of settlement

or agriculture were, from their perspective, abnormal and meaningless (Meir, 2007:32–33).

Bedouins as "Other" to the Israeli Nation

The land conflict between the Israeli state and the Bedouins reflects the clash and power imbalance between modern Israeli legal practices and indigenous oral practices. The land disputes also have cultural and political aspects, as the clash of interests between indigenous and colonizing groups provides context for the law (Tsosie, 2003:7; Moore, 2005). The law reflects various social values and "may function to maintain unequal distribution of power or material wealth, or it may be used to bring about a more nearly equitable distribution of resources" (Nader, 2002:27–28).

The land conflict is part of a larger national conflict between Israel as a Jewish state and the Bedouins as part of the Arab Palestinian minority in Israel, and it involves questions of Bedouin citizenship in Israel.[21] At no point since its establishment has Israel perceived the Bedouin population as an integral part of the nation. Israel was established as a state for the Jews, with the aspiration of providing a safe homeland for them. The Bedouins, as with the rest of the Palestinians, were perceived as "other" to the national "self"—a potential "internal enemy" and "security threat" (Kimmerling, 2004:376–377; Reiter, 1995:47). Their histories, culture, traditions, and aspirations were not considered part of what constituted the "Israeli nation" but rather perceived as both an obstacle and a threat to the process of nation building (Yiftachel, 2003:24, 2008). For example, under the 1953 Land Acquisition (Validation of Acts and Compensation) Law, the state confiscated lands for the "urgent needs" of Israel, such as settlements, military zones, and industrial projects. Bedouins' need for land was not perceived as the "needs" of the state; indeed, the state aspired to concentrate the Bedouins on as little land as possible. Bedouins' exclusion from the nation is exemplified in an article by Ariel Sharon, published in December 2000, a few months before assuming his post as prime minister:

> In the Negev, we face a serious problem: About 900,000 dunams of government land are not in our hands, but in the hands of the Bedouin population. . . . The Bedouins are grabbing new territory. They are gnawing away at the country land reserves, and no one is doing anything significant about it. (2000:14)

Although Israel nominally grants Bedouins citizenship, and thus citizens' rights as individuals, the state excludes Bedouins from collective rights in the public realm by refusing to recognize their rights to land, cultural autonomy, or self-governance (Champagne and Abu-Saad, 2003:250–251; Kimmerling and Migdal, 1999:146; see Abu-Saad and Creamer, chapter 1, this volume).

State Policies Regarding Bedouin Land Ownership
The Broader Palestinian Context

Since 1948, most of the land previously held by Bedouins has been nationalized through a series of legal procedures. The Naqab Bedouins, both refugees and Israeli citizens, have lost most of their ancestral land (Yiftachel, 2003:32). The goal of the state's policies in the Naqab was to gain control of as much land as possible.[22] Israeli leadership viewed the region as a reservoir of natural resources, a site for industrial and agricultural development, and a valuable area for settling Jewish immigrants and establishing military bases. Numerous cities, towns, agricultural villages, and military areas were established on lands claimed by Bedouins (Swirski and Hasson, 2006:11, 49; Kedar, 2001:943; Porat, 2002:2–4).[23]

The Naqab land policy can be viewed as part of a broader policy toward land formerly possessed by pre-state Palestinians. As Kedar and Yiftachel have shown, the state's policies since 1948 have restructured territory and transferred land from Palestinians to Jewish individuals or state institutions. Most of the land currently held by the state was expropriated from Palestinian refugees. Before 1948, only about 7%–8% of the country's land was under Jewish ownership, with about 10% vested by the British regime. By 2000, the Israeli state held 93% of the land. After gaining control over the land, state authorities favored the Jewish population over the Arabs through state land allocations aimed at expanding existing Jewish settlements and building new ones, while at the same time excluding Arab settlements from the use of major portions of state land (Yiftachel, 2000; Kedar, 2001:923).

Non-Recognition of Bedouin Land Rights

In 1969, the state established a legal procedure for regulating claims for land in the Naqab. As part of this process, the Bedouins submitted ownership claims to the land settlement officer in the Ministry of Justice (Swirski and Hasson, 2006:15). The examination of these claims stopped in the mid-1970s, when the state accepted the recommendation of a governmental committee (the Albeck Committee) to halt the legal procedures and to try to reach a compromise with the Bedouins. The Albeck Committee did not recognize Bedouin ownership rights. Rather, it offered them, as a gesture of goodwill, compensation for the land they claimed, based on their willingness to give up their land claims and resettle in government-established towns. In some cases, the state agreed to grant them ownership of 20% of their claimed land and compensate them for the remaining 80%. Most Bedouins rejected this offer (Swirski and Hasson, 2006:16–18).

At present, a majority of the legal claims are still pending. The Bedouins have submitted approximately 3,200 claims related to about 991,000 dunams, of which the state has already registered 200,000 dunams in its name. The state has reached a settlement with the Bedouins for about 140,000 dunams; claims for about 650,000 dunams remain under dispute. In the last twenty years, and after the Israeli courts rejected Bedouins' legal claims for ownership, most Bedouins stopped trying to register their land in court. Instead, as a means to maintain their claims, they cultivated and built on the disputed land (Swirski and Hasson, 2006:16; Yiftachel, 2006:199). Bedouins constitute approximately 25% of the Naqab population; their land claims constitute about 5.4% of the Naqab area (Abu-Ras, 2006:6). Since 2003, the state has filed counterclaims to the ownership claims that the Bedouins submitted in the 1970s. By May 2008, about 450 counterclaims had been filed relating to about 180,000 dunams (see Amara and Miller, chapter 2, this volume).

One consequence of the land disputes has been the non-recognition of existing Bedouin villages. The villages sit on land that is either registered in the name of the state or under legal dispute, thus constituting forbidden zones for construction. The villages have not appeared on official maps and have not enjoyed access to basic infrastructure and services. Most of the villages have lacked connection to the power grid, proper sewage systems, paved roads, telephone lines, adequate health and educational facilities, and, in some cases, running water. The Bedouins have had the lowest socio-economic status among Israeli citizens, and about 50% of the population lives below the poverty line (Abu-Saad, 2008b; Almi, 2003; Swirski and Hasson, 2006:60–62; *Statistical Yearbook of the Negev Bedouin*, 2004).[24]

Conclusion: Historical Recognition and Cultural Survival

The history of the land dispute between Israel and the Naqab Bedouins marks the limitations of the Israeli legal system to engage with a culturally different legal system and to be inclusive of Bedouin history and culture. It also marks the potent refusal of Jewish nationalism to consider Bedouins as equal citizens and participants in the nation. As Thabet Abu-Ras argues:

> As long as the discourse of Israeli citizenship runs parallel to the boundaries of Jewish nationalism—and not to the country's geo-political boundaries—we will continue to speak about state land as the land of the Jewish people and perpetuate the existing image of the country's Arab citizens as land grabbers, in particular with regard to the Bedouin inhabitants of the Naqab. (2006:6)

Israeli law plays a central role in transferring land from Bedouin to state control and in legitimizing and normalizing the non-recognition of Bedouin land ownership. The legal discourse shifts the land disputes from a historical national conflict to a legal conflict between Bedouins as individuals and the state. As Forman and Kedar argue, by using legal arguments and jargon, laws and court decisions have "invisibalized" the political and historical context of the dispute (Kedar, 2001:928–929; Forman and Kedar, 2004).

The land on which the Bedouins have historically dwelled, literally and figuratively, is the ground from which they derive their unique identity. Disregarding Bedouin ownership of land and customary practices of land ownership entails delegitimizing Bedouin culture and history. Since land plays a critical role in Bedouin culture, the process of land dispossession has disrupted Bedouins' ability to maintain and develop their culture and society. In this context, the Bedouins' legal struggle for recognition of their land rights is part of a struggle for both historical recognition and cultural survival.

REFERENCES

Abu Hussein, H., and McKay, F. (2003). *Access Denied: Palestinian Land Rights in Israel.* London: Zed Books.

Abu-Rabia, H. (2005). "Empire follows Empire: Lands, culture and identity among the Negev Bedouin." *Mitan* 9:24–27 (Hebrew).

Abu-Rabia, S. (2008). "Between memory and resistance, and identity shaped by space: The case of the Arab Bedouins." *HAGAR Studies in Culture, Polity and Identities* 8(2):93–120.

Abu-Rabia-Queder, S. (2004). "Women, education, and control." *Adalah's Newsletter* 8:1–6.

———. (2005). "Struggle from marginality: Three generations of Bedouin women in the Negev." In H. Dahan-Kalev, N. Yanay, and N. Berkowitch (eds.), *Women of the South: Space, Periphery, Gender* (pp. 85–109). Beersheba: The Ben Gurion Research Institute, Ben-Gurion University of the Negev, and Xargol Publishers (Hebrew).

Abu-Ras, T. (2006). "Land disputes in Israel: The case of the Bedouin of the Naqab." *Adalah's Newsletter* 24:1–9.

Abu-Saad, I. (2008a). "Introduction: State rule and indigenous resistance among Al Naqab Bedouin Arabs." *HAGAR Studies in Culture, Polity and Identities* 8(2):3–24.

———. (2008b). "Spatial transformation and indigenous resistance: The urbanization of the Palestinian Bedouin in southern Israel." *American Behavioral Scientist* 51:1713–1754.

al-'Ārif, 'Ā. (1944). *Bedouin Love, Law and Legend.* Jerusalem: Cosmos Publishing Company.

Almi, O. (2003). *No Man's Land: Health in the Unrecognized Villages in the Negev.* Shaul Vardi, trans. Tel-Aviv: Physicians For Human Rights.

Amara, A. (2008). "The Goldberg Committee: Legal and extra-legal means to solving the Naqab Bedouin case." *HAGAR Studies in Culture, Polity and Identities* 8(2):227–245.

Anaya, S. J. (2000). *Indigenous Peoples in International Law*. New York: Oxford University Press.

Arab Association for Human Rights. (2004). "By all means possible: Destruction of the state of crops of Bedouin citizens in the Naqab (Negev) by aerial spraying with chemicals." July 26. http://www.arabhra.org/hra/SecondaryArticles/SecondaryArticlePage.aspx?SecondaryArticle=1457 (accessed June 28, 2011).

Bailey, C. (1980). "The Negev in the nineteenth century: Reconstructing history from Bedouin oral traditions." *Asian and African Studies* 14(1):35–80.

Bar-Zvi, S. (1966). Internal Military Correspondence, Beersheba District. Israeli Defense Forces Archive, 187-72/1970. Tel-Hashomer.

———. (1991). *The Jurisdiction among the Negev Bedouin*. Ma'abarot: Ministry of Defense Press (Hebrew).

Ben-David, J. (1990). "The Negev Bedouin: From nomadism to agriculture." In R. Kark (ed.), *The Land That Became Israel: Studies in Historical Geography* (pp. 181–195). New Haven, CT: Yale University Press.

———. (1996). *A Feud in the Negev: Bedouins, Jews, and the Land Dispute*. Ra'anana, Israel: Center for Studying the Arab Society in Israel (Hebrew).

———. (2004). *The Bedouin in Israel: Land Conflicts and Social Issues*. Jerusalem: Jerusalem Institute for Israel Research (Hebrew).

Central Zionist Archives. (1938). Certificates of Registration, Files L18/593 and L18/584. Jerusalem.

Champagne, D., and Abu-Saad, I. (eds.). (2003). "Concluding remarks and conference declaration." In D. Champagne and I. Abu-Saad (eds.), *The Future of Indigenous Peoples: Strategies for Survival and Development* (pp. 249–257). Los Angeles: American Indian Studies Center, UCLA.

Chatterji, A. P. (2009). *Violent Gods: Hindu Nationalism in India's Present; Narratives from Orissa*. Gurgaon: Three Essays Collective.

Daes, E-I. A. (2001). "Prevention of discrimination and protection of indigenous peoples and minorities: Indigenous peoples and their relationship to land." Final working paper prepared for the United Nations Commission on Human Rights. http://www.unhchr.ch/Huridocda/Huridoca.nsf/e06a5300f90fa0238025668700518ca4/78d418c307faa00bc1256a9900496f2b/$FILE/G0114179.pdf (accessed June 30, 2011).

Danin, C. (1990). "Memories from early days in Beersheba." Beersheba and Its Sites. *Ariel* 79–80:170–178 (Hebrew).

Dean, B., and Levi, J. M. (eds.). (2006). *At the Risk of Being Heard: Identity, Indigenous Rights, and Postcolonial States*. Ann Arbor: University of Michigan Press.

Falah, G. (1989). "Israel state policy towards Bedouin sedentarization in the Negev." *Journal of Palestine Studies* 18(2):71–90.

Fischbach, M. R. (2003). *Records of Dispossession: Palestinian Refugee Property and the Arab-Israeli Conflict*. New York: Columbia University Press.

Forman, G., and Kedar, A. (2004). "From Arab land to 'Israel lands': The legal dispossession of the Palestinians displaced by Israel in the wake of 1948." *Environment and Planning, D: Society and Space* 22:809–930.

Israel Central Bureau of Statistics. (2009). *Israel Statistical Abstract 60*. Jerusalem: Central Bureau of Statistics. http://www.cbs.gov.il/reader/shnaton/templ_shnaton.html?num_tab=st02_10x&CYear=2009.

Kark, R. (2002). [1974]. *Pioneering Jewish Settlement in the Negev 1880–1948*. Jerusalem: Ariel Press (Hebrew).

Kedar, A. (2001). "The legal transformation of ethnic geography: Israeli law and the Palestinian landholders 1948–1967." *Journal of International Law and Politics* 33(4): 923–1000.

———. (2004). "Land settlement in the Negev in international law perspective." *Adalah's Newsletter* 8:1–7.

Kimmerling, B. (2004). *Immigrants, Settlers and Natives: The Israeli State and Society Between Cultural Pluralism and Cultural Wars*. Tel-Aviv: Am Oved Press (Hebrew).

Kimmerling, B., and Migdal, J. S. (1999). *The Palestinian People*. Jerusalem: Keter Press (Hebrew).

Kressel, G. M. (2003). *Let Shepherding Endure: Applied Anthropology and the Preservation of a Cultural Tradition in Israel and the Middle East*. New York: State University of New York Press.

Kressel, G. M., Ben-David, J., and Abu-Rabia, K. (1991). "Changes in land usage by the Negev Bedouin since the mid-nineteenth century: The intra-tribal perspective." *Hamizrach Hahadash* 33:39–69 (Hebrew).

Maddrell, P. (1990). *The Bedouin of the Negev*. Report No. 81. London: Minority Rights Group.

Marx, E. (1967). *Bedouin of the Negev*. Manchester: Manchester University Press.

———. (1982). "'Is the Negev the Bedouin homeland?' Conversation with Professor Emanuel Marx." *Svivot Journal* 6. Sde Boker Institute. http://www.snunit.k12.il/beduin/arti/6.html (Hebrew).

Meir, A. (1997). *As Nomadism Ends: The Israeli Bedouin of the Negev.* Boulder, CO: Westview Press.

———. (2006). *Economy and Land among the Negev Bedouin: New Processes, New Insights.* Beersheba: The Negev Center for Regional Development, Ben-Gurion University of the Negev (Hebrew).

———. (2007). "Alternative examination of the roots of the land conflict in the Negev between the government and the Bedouin: Geo-legal aspects." *Karkah* 63:14–51 (Hebrew).

———. (2009). "Contemporary state discourse and historical pastoral spatiality: Contradictions in the land conflict between the Israeli Bedouin and the state." *Ethnic and Racial Studies* 32(5):823–843.

Mills, E. (1931). *Census of Palestine.* Vol. 1. Alexandria: Whitehead Morris Limited.

Moore, S. F. (2005). "Certainties undone: Fifty turbulent years of legal anthropology, 1949–1999." In S. F. Moore (ed.), *Law and Anthropology: A Reader* (pp. 346–367). Malden: Blackwell Publishing.

Nader, L. (2002). *The Life of the Law: Anthropological Project.* Berkeley: University of California Press.

Negev Coexistence Forum for Civil Equality. (2006). *The Arab-Bedouins of the Naqab-Negev Desert in Israel: Shadow Report Submitted to the UN Committee on the Elimination of Racial Discrimination.* Omer, Israel: Negev Coexistence Forum for Civil Equality.

Niezen, R. (2003). *The Origins of Indigenism.* Berkeley: University of California Press.

Noach, H. (2009). *The Existent and the Non-Existent Villages: The Unrecognized Bedouin Villages in the Negev.* Haifa: Pardes Press (Hebrew).

Porat, C. (1996). *From Wasteland to Inhabited Land: Land Purchase and Settlement in the Negev 1930–1947.* Jerusalem: Yad Izhak Ben-Zvi Press (Hebrew).

———. (2000). "The strategy of the Israeli government and the left parties' alternative plans towards solving the Bedouin issue in the Negev, 1953–1960." *Iyunim Bitekumat Israel* 10:420–476 (Hebrew).

———. (2002). *The Negev: From Wilderness to Green Fields; The Development and Settlement of the Negev 1949–1956.* Beersheba: The Ben-Gurion Research Center: Ben-Gurion University of the Negev (Hebrew).

Rabinowitz, D. (1998). *Anthropology and the Palestinians.* Ra'anana, Israel: The Institute for Israeli Arab Studies.

Reiter, I. (1995). "Between a 'Jewish state' and a 'state of its citizens': The Arabs in Israel in the era of peace." In J. Landau, A. Ghanem, and

A. Hareven (eds.), *The Arab Citizens of Israel Towards the Twenty-First Century* (pp. 45–60). Jerusalem: Magnes Press (Hebrew).

Rosen-Zvi, I. (2004). *Taking Space Seriously: Law, Space and Society in Contemporary Israel*. Burlington, VT: Ashgate Publishing Company.

Shamir, R. (1996). "Suspended in space: Bedouins under the law of Israel." *Law and Society Review* 30(2):231–257.

Sharon, A. (2000). "Land as an economic tool for developing infrastructure and significantly reducing social gaps." *Karkah* 50:10–21 (Hebrew).

Statistical Yearbook of the Negev Bedouin. (2004). Beersheba: The Center for Bedouin Studies and Development and the Negev Center for Regional Development, Ben-Gurion University of the Negev.

Swirski, S. (2008). "Transparent citizens: Israeli government policy toward the Negev Bedouins." *HAGAR Studies in Culture, Polity and Identities* 8(2):25–45.

Swirski, S., and Hasson, Y. (2006). *Invisible Citizens: Israel Government Policy toward the Negev Bedouin*. Tel-Aviv: Adva Center.

Tsosie, R. (2003). "Land, culture and community: Envisioning Native American sovereignty and national identity in the twenty-first century." In D. Champagne and I. Abu-Saad (eds.), *The Future of Indigenous Peoples: Strategies for Survival and Development* (pp. 2–20). Los Angeles: American Indian Studies Center, UCLA.

Working Group on the Status of Palestinian Women Citizens of Israel. (2005). "NGO alternative pre-sessional report on Israel's implementation of the United Nations Convention on the Elimination of all Forms of Discrimination against Women (CEDAW)." http://www.adalah.org/newsletter/eng/feb05/CEDAW.pdf (accessed June 30, 2011).

Yahel, H. (2006). "Land disputes between the Negev Bedouin and Israel." *Israel Studies* 11(2):1–22.

Yiftachel, O. (2000). "Lands, planning and inequality: The distribution of open space among Jews and Arabs in Israel." Position Paper, Adva Center: Information on Equality and Social Justice in Israel. http://www.adva.org/uploaded/karkaot%20tihnun%20&%20e-shivion.pdf (accessed September 4, 2011) (Hebrew).

———. (2003). "Bedouin-Arabs and the Israeli settler state: Land policies and indigenous resistance." In D. Champagne and I. Abu-Saad (eds.), *The Future of Indigenous Peoples: Strategies for Survival and Development* (pp. 21–47). Los Angeles: American Indian Studies Center, UCLA.

———. (2006). *Ethnocracy: Land and Identity Politics in Israel/Palestine*. Philadelphia: University of Pennsylvania Press.

Yiftachel, O., and Kedar, A. (2000). "Landed power: The making of the Israeli land regime." *Theory and Criticism: An Israeli Forum* 16:101–129 (Hebrew).

NOTES

1. For discussions of indigenous-state relations, see Dean and Levi (2006); Niezen (2003); Chatterji (2009).
2. According to the 2009 Israeli census, in 2008, about 168,000 Bedouins were living in the Naqab in seven state-established towns and forty-six villages (Israel Central Bureau of Statistics 2009).
3. This position was asserted by the governmental Albeck Committee, which addressed the question of Bedouin land rights in 1975. The position was adopted by the government in 1976, was endorsed by Supreme Court in 1984, and guided state authorities until the present (Swirski 2008:30–31; Shamir 1996:238–250). For further discussion of the legal claim of the state, see Yahel (2006).
4. Civil Appeal 218/74, *Salim Al-Hawashla v. The State of Israel,* P.D. 38 (3) 141 [1984].
5. Civil Appeal 518/86, *Abu-Solb v. Israel Land Authority*, P.D. 42 (4) 518 [1986].
6. *Salim Al-Hawashla v. The State of Israel*, *supra* note 4.
7. For further discussion of the Ottoman policies, see Rosen-Zvi (2004); Marx (1967); Meir (1997).
8. In 1903, Ottoman authorities established Beersheba as an administrative center and market town for surplus agricultural products. Traders from Gaza and Hebron moved to Beersheba and traded with the Bedouins. The economic profit gained from agricultural activities (for example, the demand for barley by the English beer industry) led some Bedouins to increase their agricultural activities (Rosen-Zvi 2004:84; Meir 1997:191).
9. One dunam equals a quarter acre.
10. Traditionally, while women did not inherit or own land, they did inherit livestock (al-'Ārif 1944:55–56). A gender analysis of land ownership is absent from existing literature regarding Bedouin society before 1948.
11. This argument was included as part of an expert opinion submitted to the Beersheba District Court in 2009 by Professor Yiftachel on behalf of the Al-Ukbi family in an ongoing land claim case. Civil Case 7161/06, *Al-Ukbi v. The State of Israel.* A copy of the expert opinion is on file with author.
12. For further discussion of the scope of recognition of Bedouin land owner-ship by the British Mandate, see Amara and Miller (chapter 2, this volume).
13. The opinion was submitted in the course of the *Al-Ukbi* case, *supra* note 11.

14. Declaration on the Rights of Indigenous Peoples, G.A. Res. 61/295, U.N. Doc. A/Res/61/295 (2007). For discussions of international norms pertaining indigenous land rights, their binding power, and the possible avenues for their implementation in the Israeli legal system, see Kedar (2004); Amara (2008:232–236); Noach (2009:22–26); Anaya (2000); Niezen (2003).

15. Civil Appeal 518/61, *The State of Israel v. Tzalach Badaran*, P.D. 16(3) 1717 [1962].

16. The Supreme Court also placed restrictions on gaining ownership rights over cultivated land within 1.5 miles from a village or town. For example, the Court required proof of actual cultivation of at least 50% of the parcel, markedly more stringent than the prior British requirement of proving only the agricultural *potential* of the land. See Kedar (2001:969–993).

17. In addition, the Court positioned the burden of proof that the claimed land is situated fewer than 1.5 miles from a town or village on the owners or possessors of the land (Kedar 2001:956).

18. *Salim Al-Hawashla v. The State of Israel*, *supra* note 4, p. 150; author's translation.

19. Civil Case 3316/04 *Al-Asibi v. The State of Israel* [2009]; Civil Case 4037/05 *Al-Machdi v. The State of Israel* [2009].

20. Yiftachel, expert opinion, *supra* note 11, para. 3(2).

21. In the literature, there are various theoretical approaches to conceptualizing the state's land policies toward the Bedouins. One approach conceptualizes the land dispute in a nationality framework, viewing the land policies within the broader context of state policies toward the Palestinians. Another approach emphasizes the particularity of the Bedouins as an indigenous semi-nomadic population. According to this approach, the Bedouins are not perceived as a "national threat," at least not to the extent of other Palestinians, and the land dispute is a conflict between a modern nation-state and its indigenous population. (Shamir, 1996; Kedar, 2001, 2004; Rosen-Zvi,2004).

22. Since the early days of the state, there was a resistance to the government's policy toward Bedouins in the Naqab. For further discussion, see Porat (2000).

23. For discussions of the main laws used to confiscate land in the Naqab, see Falah (1989:79); Shamir (1996:243); Ben-David (1996, 2004:287); Noach (2009).

24. Bedouin women are particularly affected by the loss of land. Traditionally, women played a central role in Bedouin livelihood and were responsible for herding, making carpets and tents, and harvesting crops. The loss of land has deprived them of their economic roles. According to traditional norms, women are not generally permitted to work outside the villages; thus, the majority of women are unemployed and economically dependent on men and state services (Working Group on the Status of Palestinian Women Citizens of Israel, 2005; Abu-Rabia-Queder 2004, 2005:89).

Abstract

This chapter analyzes the development of international human rights law regarding indigenous peoples and discusses the applicability of this legal regime to the situation of the Naqab (Negev) Bedouins. It begins by examining the legacy of colonialism in order to expose the historic roots of the marginalization and discrimination faced by contemporary indigenous groups, particularly with regard to pastoralists. The persistence of these injustices and the efforts of indigenous advocates have prompted the emergence of legal instruments that specifically address the rights of indigenous peoples. The chapter describes the legal advancements achieved by the International Labour Organization and the United Nations, as well as significant regional-level developments in Africa and the Americas. The chapter demonstrates that the history, culture, and lifestyle of Bedouin Arabs parallel those of other indigenous pastoral groups whose rights are protected by this legal framework. It argues that the Bedouins, as an indigenous people within the State of Israel, should enjoy the protections afforded by international human rights law. Statements by several United Nations human rights bodies criticizing the continued violation of Bedouins' rights reflect the fact that much remains to be done to transform these legal protections into a reality.

CHAPTER 4

International Law of Indigenous Peoples and the Naqab Bedouin Arabs

Rodolfo Stavenhagen and Ahmad Amara

Introduction

This chapter examines the international human rights framework insofar as it protects the rights of indigenous peoples. Some of the central questions in current debates revolve around determining which groups should be considered rights holders in this framework and specifying the scope and content of the contemplated rights. In many parts of the world, small societies of herders and pastoralists are characterized as indigenous peoples who subsist next to permanent agricultural settlements and are integrated, to various degrees, into existing nation-states. Many nomadic and semi-nomadic groups migrate seasonally over their traditional habitats, sometimes crossing international borders that represent recent legal and political realities but do not reflect their historical boundaries and land-use patterns. In

The authors would like to thank Daniel Saver for his invaluable assistance in writing this chapter, as well as Cosette Creamer and Zinaida Miller for reviewing an earlier draft of the chapter. Part of our research is based on the 2010 report *The Goldberg Opportunity: To Resolve the Question of the "Unrecognized" Villages in the Naqab/Negev, Israel*, which was prepared by an international fact-finding mission led by Habitat International Coalition and the Regional Council for the Unrecognized Villages. Professor Stavenhagen was a member of this mission. The report is available at http://www.hic-mena.org/documents/FFM%20report%20completex.pdf.

East Africa and the Middle East, numerous pastoralist groups struggle to maintain their cultural identities and customary economic activities, although the lifestyles of some of them have changed dramatically in recent years as a result of state policies. Such is the case of the Naqab Bedouins, whose traditional livelihoods and culture have been rapidly modified by state-driven processes of urbanization and industrialization. The international community, however, has recognized that such processes may violate the human rights of such groups.

The last quarter of the twentieth century witnessed significant developments aimed at protecting the human rights of indigenous peoples, including the promotion of indigenous forms of representation within national, regional, and international bodies. Indigenous groups and a number of international organizations have made this progress possible. Key among these achievements has been the adoption of the Declaration on the Rights of Indigenous Peoples, which was proclaimed by the United Nations (UN) General Assembly in September 2007 following more than twenty years of negotiation.[1] Earlier, in 1989, the International Labour Organization (ILO) adopted Convention 169 on Indigenous and Tribal Peoples.[2] Progress has also taken place at the regional level. The Inter-American Commission on Human Rights and the Inter-American Court of Human Rights have addressed cases involving indigenous rights, and as of 2011, the Organization of American States was debating a draft of the American Declaration on this topic.[3] Elsewhere, the African Commission on Human and Peoples' Rights has established a working group on indigenous peoples and has published several reports (see, e.g., African Commission on Human and Peoples' Rights, 2005). Another prominent body representing indigenous peoples has been the Saami Council, founded in 1956 in Europe. The Council has represented the Saami indigenous populations in Finland, Norway, Russia, and Sweden, and its representatives work closely with the governments of these countries (Korsmo, 1988:509–524).[4] Additionally, the Inuit Circumpolar Council was formed in 1977 by the Inuit People of Alaska, Canada, Chukotka (Russia), and Greenland to deal with their common problems.[5] Despite such developments, considerable violations of indigenous peoples' rights continue to occur, revealing that some of the protections enshrined in human rights instruments have existed merely on paper.

This chapter outlines the development of the international legal framework protecting the rights of indigenous peoples, making additional reference to relevant regional frameworks. Within these frameworks, we will discuss the situation of the Naqab Bedouin Arabs and their dispute over land rights with the State of Israel.

Colonization and State Building

The plight of indigenous peoples began attracting the world's attention in the nineteenth century, in the context of various colonial empires. Stories of the enslavement of native peoples in conquered lands, their arbitrary displacement and forced labor, their dispossession by European settlers, and their massacre became commonplace in numerous parts of the world. Sometimes colonial administrations established committees to investigate the more egregious incidents; in other instances, private missionary groups undertook humanitarian activities aimed at benefiting aboriginal communities. In the independent republics of Latin America, members of indigenous communities eventually received formal citizenship rights—though in practice, they remained victims of many kinds of discriminatory treatment. The U.S. and Canadian governments, for their part, negotiated numerous treaties with indigenous tribes even as these governments proceeded to appropriate indigenous lands and wealth, and violate those very treaties.[6] Similar processes of discrimination took place in other parts of the world. For example, in Australia and New Zealand, the Aboriginals and the Maori, respectively, were excluded from equal participation in the polity and civil society of the colonial settler communities, and only in recent years have their full rights been recognized (for more on Australia, see Sheehan, chapter 6, this volume; see also Ford, 2010).

Territorial expansion of nation-states often brought governments into conflict with tribal and indigenous peoples who remained outside of the dominant polity or were marginalized by the state administration. Such situations occurred in a number of Asian countries—for example, among the Ainu people in Japan, the tribal communities of the mountainous areas of northern Luzon in the Philippines, the hill tribes in a number of Southeast Asian states, and similar groups on the Indian subcontinent known collectively as Adivasis (see, e.g., Cornell, 1964; Prill-Brett, 1994; Clarke, 2001; Viswanath, 1997). Small semi-nomadic communities of hunter-gatherers in tropical forest areas and semi-arid grasslands were frequently treated in a similar manner by lowland agricultural dominant communities and centralized governmental administrations. Analogous conditions prevailed for centuries among the pastoralist herders of East Africa, the Arabian Peninsula, the desert lands of the Middle East, and the livestock grazing areas of Southwestern Asia. The territory and resources of these semi-nomadic groups provided their economic substance, pasture for their herds, and a place for regular migrating patterns depending on seasonal climate changes (see Chatty, 2006). Stable patterns of social reproduction emerged and prevailed among these societies for generations and were usually respected by rulers, colonial administrators, and governmental bureaucrats in faraway centers of power. These patterns continued undisturbed without drastic changes until modern times, when artificial state borders, drawn on military maps by the servants of imperial powers, divided and broke up traditional herding communities across the region. This new reality made it increasingly difficult for these indigenous groups to maintain their customary grazing and trading routes, as well as their alternate sites for seasonal agricultural subsistence activities (see, e.g., Mier and Tsoar, 1996:39–64; African Commission on Human and Peoples' Rights, 2005:12). The Naqab Bedouins are one such group (see Abu-Saad and Creamer, chapter 1, this volume).

In the modern political system dominated by nation-states, indigenous groups have often been among the most impoverished and politically marginalized groups, subject to adverse policies and practices. Common hardships faced by indigenous peoples have included the dispossession of land and natural resources, the logging of ancestral lands, forced urbanization, and the lack of cultural autonomy and recognition for many of their social and cultural practices and languages. In light of these hardships, there is a great need to draw on international legal protection for indigenous groups and to seek justice through mechanisms that promote cultural and economic autonomy, resource sharing, and land redistribution or compensation in an effort to correct historical injustices. The following sections will outline the different international and regional legal protections for indigenous peoples, with special emphasis on the Naqab Bedouin Arabs and the manner in which certain UN organs have treated their plight.

The Bedouin Arabs: Historical Background and Lifestyle

Traditionally, Bedouin Arabs have lived in small clusters on collectively held, semi-arid lands. The Bedouins are a predominantly desert-dwelling Arab people whose historic origins lie in the Arabian Peninsula and surrounding regions. Bedouin Arab tribes have lived in Palestine since at least the fifth century, though large-scale migration of Bedouin tribes into the rest of the Middle East and North Africa began during the centuries of Islamic expansion in the seventh century (Meir, 1997:74).

Bedouin tribes were generally mobile, often moving freely between Egypt, the Sinai, Palestine, and Saudi Arabia. During the Ottoman period (sixteenth to twentieth centuries), the Bedouin tribes of southern Palestine and the Sinai developed territorial regions within which they grazed their herds (Meir, 1997:75–76). During the second half of the nineteenth century, this system of land allocation evolved to include increased agricultural production and the privatization of tribal lands (Ben-David, 1990:188–194). Tribal territories were divided among subtribes led by individual sheikhs, and even further subdivided among specific communities and family units (Meir, 1997:75–78).

Ottoman efforts to exert control over the Naqab accelerated the processes of sedentarization and territoriality that the Bedouins had initiated independently earlier in the nineteenth century. Research suggests that pastoral nomads generally experience an ideological shift away from tribalism toward individualism during the sedentarization process. This shift manifests in a number of ways, one of which is increased territoriality, both for the tribe generally and for individual members (see Meir, 1997).

By the middle of the twentieth century, an estimated 95% of the Naqab Bedouins were settled agriculturalists, with only 5% exclusively dependent on a pastoral livelihood (Maddrell, 1990:4). Many of their settlements became villages well before the twentieth century. The British Mandate government issued an order in 1921 calling on Naqab inhabitants who cultivated, revitalized, and improved *mawat* ("dead") land to register their land. For a variety of reasons, the Bedouins largely chose not do so,[7] and their land remained unregistered in British records. The Supreme Court of Israel ruled sixty-three years later, in its *Al-Hawashla* decision, that Bedouins who had abstained from the 1921 land-registration opportunity and did not receive a certificate of ownership were no longer eligible to make claims to or register their land (for further discussion of how the Israeli legal system has dealt with Bedouin land claims, see Amara and Miller, chapter 2, this volume).[8]

The Bedouins, like many other indigenous groups, have undergone drastic changes in their lifestyles over a relatively short period of time. They have changed from nomadic or semi-nomadic herding to a more stable livelihood featuring increased agricultural production and urban employment. Only a few generations ago, Bedouin pastoralists were occupied mainly with the raising of livestock on uncultivated pasturelands, as distinguished from other forms of animal husbandry that rely primarily on the provision of cultivated fodder for livestock. In fact, the grazing needs of large herds—along with environmental factors, such as variation in rainfall and the presence of predatory animals—require a degree of mobility in all pastoral societies (Saltzman, 2004:1–6).

Despite governmental policies limiting the range and scope of pastoral practices available to them, Bedouin families today have adopted a variety of survival strategies that incorporate herding into an economically viable lifestyle (Ginguld, Perevolotsky, and Ungar, 1997:567–591). Yet such policies often force pastoral groups to adopt strategies that, while economically viable, may be ecologically detrimental (Meir and Tsoar, 1996:39–64).

The Bedouins of the Naqab have grown increasingly aware of their own "indigeneity," which has shifted perceptions of their land and territoriality. Recent forms of Bedouin opposition to governmental policies—including claims of legal title to traditional lands—have now been conceptualized as reflecting a process of indigenous resistance (see, e.g., Abu-Saad, 2005, 2008; Yiftachel, 2003). At the same time, negative governmental stereotypes of indigenous lifestyles have been used to thwart this resistance. For example, Western legal regimes like the one used in Israel tend to impose restrictive categories of time and space that give rise to a series of binary oppositions, favoring order/

agriculture over chaos/nomadism. Characterizations of the Bedouins as nomads have made Bedouin land claims based on indigenous rules of land ownership "invisible" to the Israeli legal system. Judicial decisions upholding these characterizations have justified the forced settlement of Bedouins in planned townships by reinforcing the imperative to settle and modernize Bedouins, who are perceived as chaotic and culturally backward (Shamir, 1996:231–258).

The rights of indigenous people, including their historical land rights, have been (and will be) a continuously evolving area of international law. Increasingly, legal challenges brought by indigenous groups in land disputes worldwide are affirming the tenure of lands used by peoples whose presence predates the state. This is also the case of the Bedouin community in Israel. The following section outlines the evolution of international and regional laws regarding indigenous peoples' rights.

International Legal Developments

The ILO and Indigenous Peoples

In its early years, the ILO concerned itself with the labor conditions of indigenous workers on colonial plantations and other enterprises. After the independence of numerous European colonies in the middle of the twentieth century, the ILO continued to monitor indigenous labor conditions in independent countries. In 1957, it adopted the Convention concerning the Protection and Integration of Indigenous and Other Tribal and Semi-Tribal Populations in Independent Countries.[9] Article 1 of the Convention adopts a broad definition of indigenous populations, noting that its provisions apply to

> (a) members of tribal or semi-tribal populations in independent countries whose social and economic conditions are at a less advanced stage than the stage reached by the other sections of the national community, and whose status is

> regulated wholly or partially by their own customs or tradi-
> tions or by special laws or regulations; [and]
> (b) members of tribal or semi-tribal populations in indepen-
> dent countries which are regarded as indigenous on account
> of their descent from the populations which inhabited the
> country . . . at the time of conquest or colonization.

Furthermore, the 1957 Convention instructs governments to assume responsibility "for developing coordinated and systematic action for the protection of the populations concerned and their progressive integration into the life of their respective countries."[10] Thirty-two years after the adoption of the Convention, the ILO concluded that the Convention's principal provisions were out of step with changing conditions of indigenous populations in many countries and that some of its articles were no longer applicable. After extensive consultations with governments, individual experts, and indigenous persons, in 1989 the General Conference of the ILO adopted Convention 169 on Indigenous and Tribal Peoples (ILO 169). ILO 169 increases protections for indigenous peoples and emphasizes states' obligations regarding their plans for and interaction with indigenous peoples. In terms of specifying the rights holders under the Convention, article 1(1) states that "[s]elf-identification as indigenous or tribal shall be regarded as a fundamental criterion for determining the groups to which the provisions of this Convention apply." Further, article 7 adds that "[t]he peoples concerned shall have the right to decide their own priorities for the process of development . . . and to exercise control, to the extent possible, over their own economic, social and cultural development." These two articles demonstrate the high level of importance that ILO 169 places on the principles of self-identification and decisional autonomy with regard to indigenous peoples.

While only twenty-two member states have ratified ILO 169 over the last twenty years, indigenous peoples worldwide consider the Convention to be one of the principal international legal instruments that can be invoked to protect their human rights.[11] Of particular importance is article 6 of the Convention, which seeks to avoid the paternalistic and domineering approaches often employed by governments toward indigenous peoples. Article 6 requires governments to develop mechanisms for ensuring consultation with and the participation of indigenous populations in all policy-making processes that affect them, instructing governments to, among other things, "consult the peoples concerned, through appropriate procedures and in particular through their representative institutions, whenever consideration is being given to legislative or administrative measures which may affect them directly."

The principles and rights set out in ILO 169 lend themselves well to the situation of pastoral peoples such as the Naqab Bedouins. Although Israel has not ratified ILO 169, core principles nevertheless should apply to indigenous peoples in any country. Regarding the right to consultation, for example, the Inter-American Court of Human Rights has stated that this applied to Suriname even though it has not ratified ILO 169.[12] Further, the continuing development of international law regarding the protection of indigenous peoples, and state practices in this respect,

> entails a sufficiently uniform and widespread acceptance of core principles to constitute a norm of customary international law. The relevant practice of states and international institutions establishes that, as a matter of customary international law, states must recognize and protect indigenous peoples' rights to land and natural resources in connection with traditional or ancestral use and occupancy patterns. (Anaya and Williams, 2001:55)

As norms of customary international law, then, ILO 169's principles could be invoked by the Naqab Bedouins to challenge Israel's indigenous policies.

For many indigenous peoples, no matter what their specific circumstances or livelihood, the right to be consulted about legislative or administrative measures that may affect them directly (or indirectly) is a main concern, particularly since this is the area in which their rights are most persistently violated. Since ILO 169 entered into force in 1999, the ILO's Committee of Experts has received an increasing number of complaints regarding states parties' non-compliance with this provision (see International Labour Organization, 2009:179–182).[13] Regardless of whether states have ratified ILO 169, numerous scholars and experts consider the Convention, as well as other non-binding international human rights instruments and standards, as being morally binding on all states (see, e.g., Anaya and Williams, 2001). This is also an interpretation increasingly adopted in specific cases by the human rights treaty bodies of the UN, and human rights commissions and tribunals elsewhere.[14]

The UN and the Rise of International Indigenous Activism

In 1982, the UN Economic and Social Council established the Working Group on Indigenous Populations within the structure of the UN Human Rights Commission. For two decades, this group studied the situation of indigenous populations around the world and began drafting a declaration on the rights of indigenous peoples, using the same general guidelines as many other UN declarations and conventions on human rights (see Engle, 2010:67–69). One of the highlights of the working group's activities was the presence of representatives of indigenous peoples from all over the world at its annual sessions in Geneva. Among the indigenous groups who gathered in Geneva at the UN sessions were not only subsistence farmers from intertropical regions, members of Indian reservations in North America, hunters and herders from the Extreme North, and hunter-gatherers from equatorial forests, but also semi-nomadic pastoralists and herders from the deserts and grasslands of North and Northeast Africa, as well as from Southwest Asian countries and the Middle East. They all participated as indigenous peoples, sharing common concerns and searching for solutions with the help of the international community of nations (see Charters and Stavenhagen, 2009). These indigenous representatives had the opportunity to explain their situation to UN diplomats and independent experts who gathered regularly at the working sessions of the Human Rights Commission.

Thus, indigenous peoples, including pastoralist communities, whose voices were previously unheard or who advocated for their rights in relative isolation were able to share their experiences with one another and collectively discuss their common problems. Soon they established an indigenous caucus that negotiated sensitive issues with governmental representatives and prepared position papers setting forth indigenous perspectives (see Muehlebach, 2001). The diplomats, in turn, became more aware of the general patterns of discrimination, marginalization, and social and cultural exclusion that so many indigenous groups were suffering.

Drafting a new human rights declaration for indigenous peoples was a long and painstaking process. Some state representatives argued that existing universal individual rights—a central concern of the UN since its founding—were sufficiently expansive in and of themselves, and to the extent that indigenous persons were covered and protected by these rights, there was no need for any other specific legal instrument (see Charters and Stavenhagen, 2009). Indigenous peoples argued that the universal and individualized rights of the human rights system often failed to sufficiently reflect their own particular identities, histories, and needs. Other specialists suggested that indigenous peoples' rights could well be protected by other UN instruments, such as the International Convention on the Elimination of all Forms of Racial Discrimination or the Declaration on the Rights of Persons

Belonging to National or Ethnic, Religious and Linguistic Minorities, which the UN General Assembly adopted in 1992 after many years of debate and negotiation.[15]

There was also the question of whether to include indigenous peoples under the protective layer of minority rights. On one side of the debate, states argued that rights pertained exclusively to individual members of minorities and not collectively to any particular group. In addition, they noted that most minority groups covered by the 1992 Declaration resided in more than one state (such as the case in post-socialist Eastern Europe) and that the UN could not in any way bring into question the territorial integrity and unity of its members (Daes, 2009:61–63). Thus, there was limited legal protection for members of minority groups from their respective governments with regard to ensuring the survival and use of their languages, the full exercise of their cultural freedoms, and the preservation of their religious beliefs and traditional ways of life.[16] On the other side of the debate, indigenous representatives and UN experts were adamant that the rights of indigenous peoples could not effectively be recognized, respected, and exercised if they were considered simply as individual members of just another ethnic or national minority. The indigenous argument derives less from a specific interpretation of universal individual rights and more from another source altogether: the rights of *peoples*.

With regard to the rights of peoples, common article 1(1) to the International Covenant on Civil and Political Rights (ICCPR) and the International Covenant on Economic, Social and Cultural Rights (ICESCR) states that "[a]ll peoples have the right of self-determination. By virtue of that right they freely determine their political status and freely pursue their economic, social and cultural development."[17]

In UN practice over the last sixty years, the right of all peoples to self-determination has related to the process of decolonization and the emergence of new independent states from the remains of former colonial empires. In its new version, the right of peoples to self-determination is anchored in the concept and language of human rights regarding these peoples' culture, traditions, and autonomy. As such, the right to self-determination is distinct from the rights of members of ethnic or other minorities, insofar as UN standards do not recognize minorities as distinct "peoples" within the meaning of the ICCPR or ICESCR (see Charters and Stavenhagen, 2009; Lâm, 2000).

In the years leading up to the adoption of the Declaration on the Rights of Indigenous Peoples, indigenous representatives at the Human Rights Commission insisted that their individual and collective rights belonged in the category of the rights of peoples because their identities, histories, and continuing relations with states put them in a situation quite similar, if not identical, to that of other formerly colonized and oppressed peoples. In support of this position, in 1996 the Working Group on Indigenous Populations developed four principles to take into account when defining indigenous peoples:

> (a) priority in time with respect to the occupation and use of a specific territory;
> (b) the voluntary perpetuation of cultural distinctiveness, which may include the aspects of language, social organization, religion and spiritual values, modes of production, laws and institutions;
> (c) self-identification as well as recognition by other groups or by state authorities as a distinct collectivity; and
> (d) an experience of subjugation, marginalization, dispossession, exclusion, or discrimination, whether or not these conditions persist. (Daes, 1996: para. 69)

The Human Rights Commission continued to elaborate on these principles for over a decade until 2006, when the newly structured Human Rights Council adopted a draft declaration on the rights of indigenous peoples. One year later, the draft was adopted as the Declaration on the Rights of Indigenous Peoples when the General Assembly adopted it easily with 143 member states voting in favor and only Australia, Canada, New Zealand, and the United States voting against it.[18]

The UN Declaration on the Rights of Indigenous Peoples

Like many other human rights declarations adopted by the UN, the Declaration on the Rights of Indigenous Peoples was the result of intense negotiations between member states. However, unlike other treaty negotiations, representatives of indigenous peoples were able to play an active role in the Declaration's production. Their lobbying efforts, public statements, persuasive skills, and stances on certain principles during the Declaration's incubation period of almost two decades allowed indigenous peoples to make valuable contributions to its drafting. The main concerns expressed by indigenous participants related to legal recognition of their specific identities; respect for their cultures and languages; the right to their lands, territories, and resources; and, particularly, the right to self-determination as peoples. This latter issue of the right to self-determination became a sticking point for a considerable period of time because numerous states refused to recognize the right to self-determination for indigenous peoples. The issue was finally resolved in article 4 of the Declaration, which states that "[i]ndigenous peoples, in exercising their right to self-determination, have the right to autonomy or self-government in matters relating to their internal and local affairs, as well as ways and means for financing their autonomous functions."[19] This article renders the right to self-determination a domestic rather than an international right—in other words, a right related to self-government and autonomy at the local level—and thus does not endanger state sovereignty (Engle, 2010:82–96).

The Declaration expands the protections that ILO 169 provides for indigenous peoples. It offers better protection regarding rights to territory, land, and resources. Article 26 of the Declaration emphasizes that "[i]ndigenous peoples have the right to the lands, territories and resources which they have traditionally owned, occupied or otherwise used or acquired" and the "right to own, use, develop and control the lands, territories and resources that they possess by reason of traditional ownership or other traditional occupation or use." More importantly, the Declaration places positive obligations on states to take preventive measures against assimilation (art. 8), discrimination, and displacement (art. 10) and to provide for redress, restitution, and fair compensation when redress is not possible, in cases of land confiscation and relocation or indigenous resources use (art. 28). The Declaration also requires not only of consultation, cooperation, and participation of indigenous peoples but also of their "free, prior and informed consent."[20] In the context of indigenous land claims, the right to free, prior, and informed consent refers to the idea that indigenous peoples have the right "to forbid, control or authorize activities that are on their lands and territories or that involve their resources" (Indian Law Resource Center, 2005:2). Furthermore, free, prior, and informed consent refers to the right of indigenous groups to make decisions about activities that, while taking place outside of their lands, may significantly affect their communities and human rights (Indian Law Resource Center, 2005:2).

In sum, the Declaration represents a substantive improvement on earlier international instruments and documents regarding the rights of indigenous peoples. Its interpretation and application has already begun in international jurisprudence and at the domestic level in some countries.[21] However, it is important to note that the Declaration asserts rights that indigenous peoples should have enjoyed a long time ago. In the words of one of the foremost experts on the international law regarding indigenous peoples, and current UN Special Rapporteur on the Rights of Indigenous Peoples:

It is precisely because the human rights of indigenous groups have been denied, with disregard for their character as peoples, that there is a need for the Declaration in the first place. In other words, the Declaration exists because indigenous peoples have been denied self-determination and related human rights. It does not create for them new substantive human rights that others do not enjoy. Rather, it recognizes for them rights that they should have enjoyed all along as part of the human family, contextualizes those rights in light of their particular characteristics and circumstances, and promotes measures to remedy the rights' historical and systematic violation. (Anaya, 2009:193)

Obviously, the true test of the Declaration's value will depend on its implementation by states.

Regional Legal Developments: Africa and the Americas

In addition to international norms, regional norms have also made strides in protecting the rights of indigenous peoples. Notably, regional instruments have formulated the rights of indigenous peoples in different ways due to the particularities of each region. These regional legal developments increase our understanding of the legal protections for indigenous peoples around the world.

The African Context

The concept of indigeneity in Africa differs from its conceptualization in Asia, the Pacific, and the Americas. In African countries, most indigenous peoples belong to a specific ethnic or tribal group, and all are indigenous to the African continent (Tomei, 2005:17). Until recently, the term "indigenous" was used generically by Africans in order to distinguish themselves from people of European descent linked to the former colonial administrations (African Commission on Human and Peoples' Rights, 2005:86–95). Thus, the peoples of the countries that achieved independence during the twentieth century were identified as indigenous to these countries. Yet, as the African Commission on Human and Peoples' Rights has pointed out, there are clear distinctions between majority and minority groups or between dominant and subordinate populations in many African states, and therefore the term "indigenous" can also be applied to some of the subaltern groups in those countries (African Commission on Human and Peoples' Rights, 2005:95–97). Groups such as hunter-gatherers and nomadic pastoralists are often subject to discriminatory policies due to their unique lifestyle and mode of subsistence. States traditionally considered the lands used by these groups as *terra nullius* (empty land or land belonging to no one), leading over the years to extensive land dispossession. Such policies seriously threatened the culture of these groups and endangered their livelihood systems, thus rendering them economically vulnerable (Tomei, 2005:17).[22] A joint study conducted by the ILO and the African Commission on Human and Peoples' Rights proposed the following characteristics for identifying indigenous groups in Africa:

- Indigenous peoples are socially, culturally and economically distinct.
- Their cultures and ways of life differ considerably from the dominant society and their cultures are often under threat, in some cases to the extent of extinction.
- They have a special attachment to their lands or territories. . . .
- They suffer discrimination as they are regarded as "less developed." . . .
- They often live in inaccessible regions, often geographically isolated [marginalized], both politically and socially.
- They are subject to domination and exploitation. . . .
- In addition . . . participants highlighted the primary importance of self-identification, whereby the people

themselves acknowledge their distinct cultural identity and way of life, seeking to perpetuate and retain their identity. (Thornberry and Viljoen, 2009:4–5)

Research indicates that African states demonstrate very little formal constitutional or legislative recognition of indigenous peoples. The terminology used in African legislation and policies to refer to those considered indigenous peoples under international law is inconsistent and even contradictory. However, a number of states have begun to recognize the specificities and particular needs of indigenous peoples and the need to develop laws, policies, and programs aimed at these groups (Thornberry and Viljoen, 2009:47–50). Without adequate state guarantees regarding their land, territories, and resources, indigenous communities have frequently become the victims of human rights abuses that in many cases have turned into violent conflict (see Stavenhagen, 2007: para. 52). For example, in East Africa the Maasai pastoralists of Kenya, Tanzania, and Uganda struggle to maintain rights over their traditional grazing areas, threatened by privatization, land-grabs by outsiders, and economic development activities that displace the Maasai from their subsistence habitat (African Commission on Human and Peoples' Rights, 2005:24–25).

The African Commission on Human and Peoples' Rights has stressed the importance of recognizing the overall subordination and dispossession of hunter-gatherers and pastoralists and the need to safeguard their fundamental collective human rights. The Commission has thus pointed out that in the African context, the term "indigenous" should be applied to these groups in light of their structurally subordinate position to other dominant groups and the state. Those who identify themselves as indigenous should be able to use this term to receive recognition not only as individuals but also as groups or peoples (African Commission on Human and Peoples' Rights, 2005:101–103). Of particular interest, because of its close cultural and ethnic relationship to pastoral herders in traditional Arab lands between the Mediterranean, the Red Sea, and the Arabian Gulf, is the Amazigh (or Berber) group, which

> constitutes the largest indigenous group on the continent. They are most populous in Morocco . . . and in Algeria. . . . In addition, the Amazigh are present in Tunisia, Libya and Egypt. The Tuareg, who live a more nomadic life-style associated with camels, are found in Niger, Mali, Burkina Faso, Algeria and Libya. Due to concerted campaigns of Arabisation and Islamisation in all North African States, the Amazigh identity is complex, and has become blurred and broadened. . . . A linguistically marked identity and an historical awareness ensure that their self-identification as "indigenous" is generally quite strong. (Thornberry and Viljoen, 2009:5)

The African Commission's position regarding indigenous rights was reflected in its 2010 ruling declaring that the Endorois peoples in Kenya could not be evicted from their traditional land. This case was groundbreaking, as it marked the first time that an international or regional tribunal found a violation of indigenous peoples' right to development and attempted to determine which peoples are indigenous in Africa, as well as the scope of their rights to land.[23] Additionally, some domestic courts have ruled against state policies evicting indigenous groups. In 2002, the High Court of Botswana ruled that the government could not evict a group of San Bushmen from their ancestral hunting grounds in the Central Kalahari Game Reserve;[24] and the South African Constitutional Court ruled in 2007 that the Nama people in Richtersveld had both communal land ownership and mineral rights over their traditionally used territory.[25]

The history and current condition of Bedouin Arabs share considerable similarities with other indigenous groups in Africa in terms of state policies, types of rights violations, and changing lifestyles as a result. Recognition of these similarities has triggered calls for a unified struggle to protect the rights of indigenous peoples everywhere. As summarized in a joint study by the International Work Group for Indigenous Affairs and the African Commission, the

> linking up to a global movement—by applying the term "indigenous peoples"—is a way for these groups to try to address their situation, analyse the specific forms of inequalities and repression they suffer from, and overcome the human rights violations by also invoking the protection of international law. (African Commission on Human and Peoples' Rights and International Work Group for Indigenous Affairs, 2006:11)

The Americas Context

Similar to Africa, the American region has witnessed significant developments regarding the protection of indigenous peoples' rights. Cases addressed by the Inter-American Commission on Human Rights and the Inter-American Court of Human Rights demonstrate the emergence of a new legal doctrine, one that is framed as the interpretation of the right to property as expressed in article 21 of the American Convention on Human Rights (Dannemaier, 2008). The Inter-American human rights bodies have argued that an indigenous community's ancestral land rights predate, and thus take precedence over, any modern state legislation concerning private land titles (Dannemaier, 2008). For example, in 2001 the Inter-American Court found in favor of the collective land rights of the indigenous Awas Tingni community against the state of Nicaragua.[26] This conception of ancestral land rights could be considered one manner of implementing the rights of indigenous peoples included in the UN Declaration on the Rights of Indigenous Peoples.

A number of domestic legal cases involving indigenous peoples have vindicated claims for recognition of collective land rights under a variety of circumstances. One well-known case concerns the Nisga'a of British Columbia, where the Canadian Supreme Court recognized indigenous land rights for the first time in 1973.[27] Another Canadian case in 1997 reasserted indigenous ancestral land rights,[28] similar to the Australian 1992 *Mabo* decision that recognized Aboriginal land titles, overthrowing the fiction of *terra nullius* adopted at the time of British colonization and used by the Australian government.[29] Similar cases have found in favor of indigenous communities in Belize, Malaysia, Paraguay, and Suriname.[30]

The development of legal protections for indigenous peoples at the international, regional, and local levels is a positive sign. Nevertheless, rights violations such as land dispossession, cultural assimilation, and forced urbanization have persisted with unfortunate regularity. It is apparent that the development of formal legal protections, while valuable, has severe limitations in practice due to insufficient implementation and application, and to stark imbalances in power relations between governments and indigenous communities. Overcoming this implementation gap requires increased political will on the part of governments. For example, the governments of Australia, Canada, New Zealand, and South Africa have recently undertaken efforts to address historical injustices against their indigenous peoples. Such attempts have taken a variety of forms, including special tribunals, legislation and constitutional protections, and the negotiation of special agreements with indigenous peoples. While these efforts are laudable, these states must continue to protect and promote the rights of their indigenous populations, and other states must follow suit.

The Indigenous Naqab Bedouin Arabs

The Declaration on the Rights of Indigenous Peoples does not define "indigenous," and in fact there is no one definition on which states and indigenous groups can agree. While this may seem problematic, the prevailing view in the international community is that no official definition is needed to ensure that the rights of indigenous groups are respected and protected. As a pragmatic matter, the four-factor definition set out by the UN Working Group on Indigenous Populations is widely accepted and followed internationally. As mentioned previously, this definition identifies the following four factors: priority in time; voluntary perpetuation of cultural distinctiveness; self-identification; and experience of subjugation, marginalization, dispossession, exclusion, or discrimination, whether or not these conditions persist (Daes, 1996).[31]

A recent ILO study describes the term "indigenous and tribal peoples" as

> a general denominator for distinct peoples who have been pursuing their own concept and way of human development in a given geographical, socio-economic, political and historical context. Throughout history, these peoples have struggled to maintain their group identity . . . and the control of their lands, territories and natural resources. (2007:3)

The ILO further points out that globalization has placed growing pressure on indigenous peoples' lands and resources (International Labour Organization, 2007:4).

The Naqab Bedouins self-identify as a population indigenous to the Naqab Desert since the fifth century, prior to the presence of Ottoman, British, and Israeli ruling authorities (Meir, 1997). The Bedouins' cultural distinctiveness from the Israeli Jewish majority and the ongoing marginalization and discrimination that the Bedouins suffer as a distinct collectivity are more than sufficient to grant them protection as an indigenous group under international law. Indeed, the Naqab

Bedouins share many common traits with indigenous peoples in other parts of the world, particularly with semi-pastoralists in other Arab-speaking countries in North Africa.

Following the expulsion and fleeing of the vast majority of Bedouins during the 1948 conflict, many of the remaining Bedouins were forcibly moved from their lands by Israeli army forces to the central part of the Naqab, in a demarcated area under military rule known as the *siyag* (enclosure), which comprises just 8% of the Naqab's geographical area (Shamir, 1996). Following the Bedouins' removal from their traditional habitats, Bedouin properties became vulnerable to seizure. After an eighteen-year phase of land confiscations and military rule, the government sought to make the appropriation of Bedouin lands permanent. For the Naqab, the policy prioritized

> the passage of a law for the settlement of the Bedouins and their transfer to permanent homes[,] . . . the speedy solution of the problem of compensation to be paid . . . for their land, which would aid in their early resettlement . . . [and] the encouragement by the state of Arab [Bedouin] migration to the cities of mixed population, to live there permanently with the help of the government. (Jiryis, 1976:12)

From the mid-1960s through the 1990s, the Israeli government planned and built seven townships to absorb the Bedouins into urban-style settlements (Tal a-Sabi', Rahat, Kseife, Ara'ra a-Naqab, Hura, Shqeb a-Salaam, and Laqiya). Settling in these townships required residents to disavow any claims to land taken by the state and to agree to terms excluding any freehold land tenure in the new towns. Despite their continued construction and expansion, these townships have lacked the basic services available to Jewish citizens in Jewish settlements (see Abu-Saad, 2005).

The recent Bedouin land claims concern only 778,856 dunams (194,741 acres)—a tiny percentage of the entire Naqab region (Ben-

David, 1996:73, 75).[32] In recent years, the Bedouins have possessed only 240,000 dunams (or 1.8% of the entire region), of which 180,000 dunams are the lands over which the Bedouin unrecognized villages sit (see Abu-Saad and Creamer, chapter 1, this volume). In other words, the residents of the unrecognized villages have resided on only 1.3% of the land in the Naqab, even though they have constituted 14.2% of the Naqab's citizens (Abu-Ras, 2006:6).

The situation of the Bedouin Arabs in the Naqab has been addressed on a number of occasions by UN human rights treaty bodies, which are charged with monitoring states' compliance with their treaty obligations. In their reports, these treaty bodies (also known as "committees") frequently include references to indigenous peoples, even though the committees tend to use local nomenclature to refer to such groups, rather than specifically defining them as "indigenous." For instance, the Human Rights Committee, which monitors member states' compliance with the ICCPR, has expressed its concern over

> the discrimination faced by Bedouins, many of whom have expressed a desire to continue to live in settlements in the Negev which are not recognized by the Israeli Government and which are not provided with basic infrastructure and essential services. The Committee recommends that members of Bedouin communities should be given equality of treatment with Jewish settlements.[33]

Furthermore, the Committee has noted that it "deplores the demolition of Arab homes," which it considers to conflict directly with several of Israel's obligations under the Covenant, including the right not to be subjected to arbitrary interference with one's home, freedom to choose one's residence, and equality before and equal protection of the law.[34]

With regard to the unrecognized villages, the Committee on Economic, Social and Cultural Rights, which monitors member states' compliance with the ICESCR, has expressed "deep concern" regarding the poor living conditions in these villages and their lack of recognition by the Israeli government.[35] The Committee has also expressed its "grave concern" over the practices of Israeli authorities against Bedouins in the unrecognized villages, who "are subjected on a regular basis to land confiscations, house demolitions, fines for building 'illegally,' destruction of agricultural fields and trees, and systematic harassment and persecution by the Green Patrol."[36] Furthermore, the Committee has taken note of discriminatory settlement policies of the Israeli state in other regions, remarking that "while Jewish settlements are constructed on a regular basis, no new Arab villages have been built in the Galilee."[37]

The Committee has expressed concern about ongoing land disputes in the Naqab and the government's proposed compensation scheme, noting that "the present compensation scheme for Bedouins who agree to resettle in 'townships' is inadequate."[38] The Committee's position, from an international human rights perspective, has been clear:

> The Committee further urges the State party to recognize all existing Bedouin villages, their property rights and their right to basic services, in particular water, and to desist from the destruction and damaging of agricultural crops and fields, including in unrecognized villages. The Committee further encourages the State party to adopt an adequate compensation scheme for Bedouins who have agreed to resettle in "townships."[39]

Current international human rights law and principles—including UN treaty bodies' interpretations of the content of human rights provisions, as explored above—is unequivocal. The Israeli government should recognize the historical land rights of the Bedouins. In extreme cases where it is impossible for Bedouin communities to return to their historical land, the state should provide just restitution and fair compensation. Bedouin Arabs should be free from discrimination and should enjoy their full rights as citizens; furthermore, the Israeli state should be responsive to the distinctive culture and lifestyle of Bedouins as an indigenous people. Any future state policies or decisions affecting Bedouin Arabs should be made through consultation, cooperation, and free and informed consent of the Bedouin community.

Conclusion

The development of international law throughout the twentieth and into the twenty-first century has clarified the scope of rights protected for indigenous peoples, including the rights to historical lands, to culture, and to natural resources. More importantly, it has better established indigenous peoples' right to take charge of their own destiny. Recognition of the self-identification of indigenous peoples is an important aspect of this, but perhaps more crucial is governments' obligation to ensure the consultation, participation, and free and informed consent of indigenous peoples regarding decisions and policies that affect their lives.

The adoption of the Declaration on the Rights of Indigenous Peoples marked an important milestone in global efforts to protect indigenous peoples' rights. Although the Declaration did not completely satisfy all indigenous groups' desire for a right to self-determination, it has empowered indigenous peoples in their struggles for justice. Recent developments at the regional level, in Africa and the Americas in particular, combined with domestic court cases supporting the rights of indigenous peoples, have contributed to the crystallization of international norms concerning indigenous peoples. The present international and regional legal framework aims both to preserve indigenous groups' lands, properties, and cultural heritage, and to address historical injustices committed against these groups following the establishment of the modern nation-state.

The Bedouins as an indigenous people are protected not only under universal human rights standards in general but also by particular international legal documents and principles concerning indigenous peoples. Israel should respect, protect, and fulfill the rights held by the Bedouin people, particularly the right to their traditional Naqab lands and the right to adequate housing in a manner that permits them to maintain their traditional way of life.

REFERENCES

Abu-Ras, T. (2006). "Land disputes in Israel: The case of the Bedouin of the Naqab." *Adalah's Newsletter* 24:1–9.

Abu-Saad, I. (2005). "Forced sedentarisation, land rights and indigenous resistance: The Palestinian Bedouin in the Negev." In N. Masalha (ed.), *Catastrophe Remembered: Palestine, Israel and the Internal Refugees* (pp. 113–142). London: Zed Books.

———. (2008). "Spatial transformation and indigenous resistance: The urbanization of the Palestinian Bedouin in southern Israel." *American Behavioral Scientist* 51:1713–1754.

African Commission on Human and Peoples' Rights. (2005). *Report of the African Commission's Working Group of Experts on Indigenous Populations/Communities.* Copenhagen: Eks/Skolens Trykkeri.

African Commission on Human and Peoples' Rights and International Work Group for Indigenous Affairs. (2006). *Indigenous Peoples in Africa: The Forgotten Peoples?* Copenhagen: Eks/Skolens Trykkeri.

Anaya, S. J. (2009). "The right of indigenous peoples to self-determination in the post-declaration era." In C. Charters and R. Stavenhagen (eds.), *Making the Declaration Work: The United Nations Declaration on the Rights of Indigenous Peoples* (pp. 184–198). Copenhagen: International Work Group for Indigenous Affairs.

Anaya, S. J., and Williams, R. A., Jr. (2001). "The protection of indigenous peoples' rights over lands and natural resources under the Inter-American human rights system." *Harvard Human Rights Journal* 14:33–86.

Ben-David, J. (1990). "The Negev Bedouin: From nomadism to agriculture." In R. Kark (ed.), *The Land That Became Israel* (pp. 188–194). New Haven, CT: Yale University Press.

———. (1996). *A Feud in the Negev: Bedouins, Jews, and the Land Dispute*. Ra'anana, Israel: Center for Studying the Arab Society in Israel (Hebrew).

———. (2004). *The Bedouins in Israel: Land Conflicts and Social Issues*. Jerusalem: Jerusalem Institute for Israel Studies (Hebrew).

Charters, C., and Stavenhagen, R. (eds.). (2009). *Making the Declaration Work: The United Nations Declaration on the Rights of Indigenous Peoples*. Copenhagen: International Work Group for Indigenous Affairs.

Chatty, D. (ed.). (2006). *Nomadic Societies in the Middle East and North Africa: Entering the 21st Century*. Leiden: Brill.

Clarke, G. (2001). "From ethnocide to ethnodevelopment? Ethnic minorities and indigenous peoples in Southeast Asia." *Third World Quarterly* 22(3):413–436.

Cornell, J. B. (1964). "Ainu assimilation and cultural extinction: Acculturation policy in Hokkaido." *Ethnology* 3(3):287–304.

Daes, E-I. A. (1996). "Standard-setting activities: Evolution of standards concerning the rights of indigenous people." Working paper. U.N. Doc E/CN.4/Sub.2/AC.4/1996/2.

———. (2009). "The contribution of the Working Group on Indigenous Populations to the genesis and evolution of the UN Declaration on the Rights of Indigenous Peoples." In C. Charters and R. Stavenhagen (eds.), *Making the Declaration Work: The United Nations Declaration on the Rights of Indigenous Peoples* (pp. 48–76). Copenhagen: International Work Group for Indigenous Affairs.

Dannemaier, E. (2008). "Beyond indigenous property rights: Exploring the emergence of a distinctive connection doctrine." *Washington University Law Review* 86:53–110.

Engle, K. (2010). *The Elusive Promise of Indigenous Development: Rights, Culture, Strategy*. Durham, NC: Duke University Press.

Ford, L. (2010). *Settler Sovereignty*. Cambridge, MA: Harvard University Press.

Ginguld, M., Perevolotsky, A., and Ungar, E. D. (1997). "Living on the margins: Livelihood strategies of Bedouin herd-owners in the northern Negev." *Human Ecology* 25(4):567–591.

Housing and Land Rights Network and Habitat International Coalition. (2010). *The Goldberg Opportunity: To Resolve the Question of the "Unrecognized" Villages in the Naqab/Negev, Israel*. Cairo: Housing and Land Rights Network. http://www.hic-mena.org/documents/ FFM%20report%20completex.pdf (accessed July 14, 2011).

Indian Law Resource Center. (2005). "Indigenous peoples' right of free prior informed consent with respect to indigenous lands, territories and resources." Workshop on Free, Prior and Informed Consent. U.N. Doc. PFII/2004/WS.2/6.

International Labour Organization. (2007). *Eliminating Discrimination against Indigenous and Tribal Peoples in Employment and Occupation: A Guide to ILO Convention No. 111*. Geneva: ILO. http://www.ilo.org/indigenous/Resources/Guidelinesandmanuals/lang--en/docName--WCMS_100510/index.htm (accessed July 14, 2011).

———. (2009). *Indigenous and Tribal Peoples' Rights in Practice: A Guide to ILO Convention No. 169*. Geneva: ILO. http://www.ilo.org/indigenous/Resources/Guidelinesandmanuals/lang--en/docName--WCMS_106474/index.htm (accessed July 14, 2011).

Jiryis, S. (1976). "The land question in Israel." *MERIP Reports* 47:5–20.

Korsmo, F. L. (1988). "Nordic security and the Saami minority: Territorial rights in northern Fennoscandia." *Human Rights Quarterly* 10(4):509–524.

Lâm, M. C. (2000). *At the Edge of the State: Indigenous Peoples and Self-Determination*. New York: Transnational Publishers.

Maddrell, P. (1990). *The Bedouin of the Negev*. Report No. 81. London: Minority Rights Group,.

Meir, A. (1997). *As Nomadism Ends: The Israeli Bedouin of the Negev*. Boulder, CO: Westview Press.

Meir, A., and Tsoar, H. (1996). "International borders and range ecology: The case of Bedouin transborder grazing." *Human Ecology* 24(1):39–64.

Muehlebach, A. (2001). "'Making place' at the United Nations: Indigenous cultural politics at the U.N. Working Group on Indigenous Populations." *Cultural Anthropology* 16(3):415–448.

Prill-Brett, J. (1994). "Indigenous land rights and legal pluralism among Philippine highlanders." *Law and Society Review* 28(3):687–698.

Saltzman, P. C. (2004). *Pastoralists: Equality, Hierarchy, and the State*. Boulder, CO: Westview Press.

Shamir, R. (1996). "Suspended in space: Bedouins under the law of Israel." *Law and Society Review* 30(2):231–257.

Stavenhagen, R. (2007). "Report of the Special Rapporteur on the situation of human rights and fundamental freedoms of indigenous people." U.N. Doc. A/62/286.

Thornberry, F., and Viljoen, F. (2009). *Overview Report of the Research Project by the International Labor Organization and the African Commission on Human and Peoples' Rights on the Constitutional and Legislative Protection of the Rights of Indigenous Peoples in 24 African Countries*. Geneva: ILO and African Commission on Human and Peoples' Rights.

Tomei, M. (2005). *Indigenous and Tribal Peoples: An Ethnic Audit of Selected Poverty Reduction Strategy Papers*. Geneva: ILO. http://www.ilo.org/indigenous/Resources/Publications/lang--en/docName--WCMS_100602/index.htm (accessed July 14, 2011).

United Nations. (2008). "United Nations Development Group guidelines on indigenous peoples' issues." February. http://www2.ohchr.org/english/issues/indigenous/docs/guidelines.pdf (accessed July 14, 2011).

United Nations General Assembly. (2007). General Assembly adopts Declaration on Rights of Indigenous Peoples. U.N. Press Release GA/10612, September 13.

United Nations High Commissioner for Human Rights. (n.d.). "The draft U.N. Declaration on the Rights of Indigenous Peoples." Leaflet No. 5. http://www2.ohchr.org/english/issues/indigenous/guide.htm (accessed July 14, 2011).

United Nations Permanent Forum on Indigenous Issues. (n.d.). "Advances in the recognition of indigenous rights since the adoption of the UN Declaration." Indigenous People Indigenous Voices fact sheet. http://www.un.org/esa/socdev/unpfii/documents/PFII8_FS1.pdf (accessed July 14, 2011).

Viswanath, C. K. (1997). "Adivasis: Protesting land alienation." *Economic and Political Weekly* 32(32):2016.

Yiftachel, O. (2003). "Bedouin-Arabs and the Israeli settler state: Land policies and indigenous resistance." In D. Champagne and I. Abu-Saad (eds.), *The Future of Indigenous Peoples: Strategies for Survival and Development* (pp. 21–47). Los Angeles: American Indian Studies Center, UCLA.

NOTES

1. Declaration on the Rights of Indigenous Peoples, G.A. Res. 61/295, U.N. Doc. A/Res/61/295 (2007). For a discussion of the negotiating process that resulted in the Declaration, see Charters and Stavenhagen (2009); Lâm (2000).

2. Convention concerning Indigenous and Tribal Peoples in Independent Countries, C169 I.L.O. (1989).

3. See, e.g., *Mayagna (Sumo) Awas Tingni Community v. Nicaragua*, Judgment, Inter-American Court of Human Rights (ser. C) No. 79 (August 31, 2001). For more information on the drafting process for the Inter-American Declaration, see the website of the Organization of American States Working Group to Prepare the Draft American Declaration on the Rights of Indigenous Peoples, http://www.oas.org/consejo/cajp/indigenous%20special%20session.asp.

4. See Saami Council website, http://www.saamicouncil.net.

5. See Inuit Circumpolar Council website, http://inuitcircumpolar.com.
6. For a discussion of the colonial encounter in Spanish and British America and the way in which the differences in these encounters shaped later indigenous advocacy, see Engle (2010).
7. For example, Bedouins might have elected to ignore the registration ordinance in order to avoid paying taxes, in order to avoid forced military service, or because there was no pressing need to register with the state, given the relative autonomy granted to Bedouin communities and the fact that they used their own traditional land ownership system. See Yiftachel (2003:32).
8. See Civil Appeal 218/74, *Salim Al-Hawashla v. The State of Israel*, P.D. 38(3) 141 [1984].
9. Convention concerning the Protection and Integration of Indigenous and Other Tribal and Semi-Tribal Peoples in Independent Countries, C107 I.L.O. (1957).
10. Ibid., art. 2.
11. For example, indigenous groups in Colombia and Chile have invoked ILO 169 in domestic courts to vindicate their right to consultation. See Corte Constitucional [Constitutional Court], October 15, 2009, Sentencia T-769/09, Expediente T-2315944 (Colombia); Corte de Apelaciones [Court of Appeals], Temuco, January 21, 2010, *Comunidad Palguín Bajo v. Comisión Regional de Medio Ambiente*, Rol de la causa: 1705-2009 (Chile).
12. *Saramaka People v. Suriname*, Preliminary Objections, Merits, Reparations, and Costs, Inter-American Court of Human Rights (ser. C) No. 172 (November 28, 2007).
13. For example, complaints were filed against Argentina, Bolivia, Brazil, Colombia, Denmark, Ecuador, Guatemala, Mexico, and Peru.
14. For example, the UN Office of the High Commissioner for Human Rights has stated that the Declaration carries "considerable moral force" even for states that do not ratify it (n.d.:1).
15. International Convention on the Elimination of All Forms of Racial Discrimination, G.A. Res. 2106 (XX), Annex, 20 U.N. GAOR Supp. (No. 14) at 47, U.N. Doc. A/6014 (1965); Declaration on the Rights of Persons Belonging to National or Ethnic, Religious and Linguistic Minorities, G.A. Res. 47/135, 40 U.N. GAOR Supp. (No. 49), U.N. Doc A/47/49 (1992).
16. This approach was also adopted by the Council of Europe in the 1995 Framework Convention for the Protection of National Minorities. Full text available at http://conventions.coe.int/Treaty/en/Treaties/html/157.htm.
17. International Covenant on Civil and Political Rights, G.A. Res. 2200A (XXI), 21 U.N. GAOR Supp. (No. 16) at 52, U.N. Doc. A/6316 (1966); International Covenant on Economic, Social and Cultural Rights, G.A. Res. 2200A (XXI), 21 U.N. GAOR Supp. (No. 16) at 49, U.N. Doc. A/6316 (1966).
18. Additionally, eleven countries abstained from the vote: Azerbaijan, Bangladesh, Bhutan, Burundi, Colombia, Georgia, Kenya, Nigeria, Russian Federation, Samoa and Ukraine. See United Nations General Assembly (2007).

19. Declaration on the Rights of Indigenous Peoples, *supra* note 1, art. 4.
20. One participating organization in the Permanent Forum on Indigenous Issues submitted the following understanding of free, prior, and informed consent:

    > For consent to be 'free,' it must be given without coercion, duress, fraud, bribery, or any threat or external manipulation. For consent to be 'prior,' it must be given before any significant planning . . . has been completed, and before each decision-making stage in the proposed activity's planning and implementation. . . . For consent to be 'informed,' it must be given only after the affected indigenous people is provided with all relevant information related to proposed activities in appropriate languages and formats, including information regarding indigenous rights under domestic and international law, the likely and possible consequences of the proposed activities, and alternatives to the proposed activities. (Indian Law Resource Center, 2005:2)

21. See, for example, a list of countries that made reference to the Decalaration in United Nations Permanent Forum on Indigenous Issues (n.d.).
22. Ethiopia's pastoralist population is estimated at 7–8 million; Kenya's approximately 6 million; and Tanzania's approximately 3.7 million.
23. *Centre for Minority Rights Development (Kenya) and Minority Rights Group International on behalf of Endorois Welfare Council v. Kenya*, 276/2003, African Commission on Human and Peoples' Rights (February 4, 2010).
24. *Sesana and Others v. Attorney-General* (2006) A.H.R.L.R. 183 (Botswana).
25. *Alexkor Ltd and Another v. Richtersveld Community and Others* 2003 (5) SA 460 (CC) (South Africa).
26. *Mayagna (Sumo) Awas Tingni Community v. Nicaragua, supra* note 3.
27. *Calder v. British Columbia*, [1973] S.C.R. 313 (Canada).
28. *Delgamuukw v. British Columbia*, [1997] 3 S.C.R. 1010 (Canada).
29. *Mabo v. Queensland* (No. 2) (1992) 175 CLR 1 (Australia).
30. *Maya Indigenous Community of the Toledo District v. Belize*, Case 12.053, Inter-American Commission on Human Rights, Report No. 40/04, OEA/Ser.L/V/11.122, doe. 5 rev. 2 (2004); *Sagong Bin Tasi v. The Selangor State Government*, (2002) 2 M.L.J. 591 (April 12, 2002) (Malaysia); *Saramaka People v. Suriname, supra* note 12; *Sawhoyamaxa Indigenous Community v. Paraguay*, Merits, Reparations and Costs, Inter-American Court of Human Rights (ser. C) No. 146 (March 29, 2006).
31. For a more extensive review of the various factors that have been considered in defining indigenous populations, see United Nations (2008).
32. Of the 3,220 land claims, 2,478 are within the *siyag*, where the number of claimants is 1,281. In addition, 389 claims (292 of which are within the *siyag*) involve more than one claimant. See Ben-David (1996:73, 75).
33. Human Rights Committee, Concluding Observations: Israel, U.N. Doc. A/53/40 (1998), para. 310.
34. Ibid., para. 320. Moreover, in 1999 the Committee on Economic, Social and Cultural Rights made similar comments on the situation of the Bed-

ouin in Israel. See Committee on Economic, Social and Cultural Rights, Concluding Observations: Israel, U.N. Doc. E/1999/22 (1999), para. 254.

35. Committee on Economic, Social and Cultural Rights, 1999 Concluding Observations, *supra* note 34, para. 252.
36. Ibid., para. 254.
37. Ibid.
38. Committee on Economic, Social and Cultural Rights, Concluding Observations: Israel, U.N. Doc. E/C.12/1/Add.90 (2003), para. 27.
39. Ibid., para. 43.

Abstract

The current global context includes increasing levels of violence against women; the growing feminization of poverty; the existence of entrenched systems of gender-based discrimination and prejudice; the use of cultural and religious defenses to violate women's rights, particularly their social and economic rights; and widespread impunity for violations of rights. With an eye toward this context, this chapter addresses the systemic and structural factors affecting women's right of access to adequate housing, focusing in particular on the impact of gender-based discrimination and violence against Naqab Bedouin Arab women. International human rights principles and standards reflect the recognition of the nexus between violence against women and various human rights, including women's equal ownership of, access to, and control over land; the (equal) rights to own property; and the right of access to adequate housing. Several United Nations human rights bodies have acknowledged that the lack of adequate housing is both a cause and a consequence of violence against women. Various reports confirm that forced relocation, forced eviction, lack of legal security of tenure, lack of effective remedies, and states' failure to address systemic inequalities have disproportionately affected women and their right to adequate housing. This chapter examines the international legal framework regarding women's right to adequate housing and shows how the Israeli government has fallen short of fulfilling its obligations in this respect.

CHAPTER 5

Continuum of Injustice:
Women, Violence, and Housing Rights

Rashida Manjoo

Introduction

The human right to adequate housing is the right of every woman, man, youth and child—to gain and sustain a secure home and community in which to live in peace and dignity.

(Miloon Kothari, United Nations Special Rapporteur
on Adequate Housing, 2001)

To live a life free from all forms of violence, oppression, discrimination, and insecurity is a right to which all persons are entitled by virtue of being human. Such an existence must be underpinned by societal norms and values of dignity, equality, non-discrimination, peace, and security, among others. The achievement of substantive civil, political, economic, social, and cultural rights is often dependent on the realization of the right to adequate housing. Furthermore, consideration of gender-based aspects of the right to housing and its indivisibility with other rights is crucial to maintaining a focus on relevant structural barriers.

This chapter addresses the systemic and structural factors affecting women's right of access to adequate housing, with a particular focus on the impact of gender-based discrimination and violence against women. International human rights principles and standards reflect the recognition of the nexus between violence against women and women's right to own, access, and control land, property, and adequate housing. Resolutions of the United Nations (UN) Commission on Human Rights and the UN Human Rights Council,[1] as well as reports of the UN Special Rapporteur on Violence against Women and the UN Special Rapporteur on Adequate Housing, acknowledge that the lack of adequate housing is both a cause and a consequence of violence against women, since the lack of adequate housing renders women more vulnerable to various forms of violence and limits women's options in their decisions to leave violent situations. Various reports confirm that forced relocation, forced eviction, lack of legal security of tenure, lack of effective legal remedies, and a failure by states to address systemic inequalities have disproportionately affected women and their right to adequate housing (see Kothari, 2001, 2003, 2004a, 2004b, 2005, 2006a, 2006b, 2008; Centre on Housing Rights and Evictions, 2000, 2002).

The Relationship between the Right to Adequate Housing and Other Human Rights

Through the adoption of an "indivisibility of rights" approach in international law, adequate housing has been defined as consisting of sixteen factors: legal security of tenure; availability of services, materials, facilities, and infrastructure; affordability; habitability; accessibility; location; cultural adequacy; access to land, water, and other natural resources; freedom from dispossession, damage, and destruction; access to information; participation; resettlement, restitution, compensation, non-refoulement, and return; privacy and security; access to remedies; education and empowerment; and freedom from violence against women.[2] The right to adequate housing applies to women as well as to men, and to individuals as well as to families— and the enjoyment of this right may not be subject to any form of discrimination.[3]

However, despite the universal nature of the right to adequate housing, multiple systemic and structural barriers obstruct women's enjoyment of it. These barriers are informed by historical, social, economic, and political contexts operating at the family, community, and state levels. Addressing women's access to adequate housing requires a gendered assessment of these contexts and the inherited legacy of such structural barriers.

South Africa offers an especially instructive example. Historically, both the colonial and apartheid governments restricted black urbanization in general and women's mobility in particular through the use of discriminatory labor and permit laws and policies. Such laws and policies made women's access to urban areas dependent on their relationships to men, as women were required to obtain permission from their husbands, partners, or fathers in order to visit or work in urban areas. Restrictions on mobility resulted in the denial of economic opportunities for women, since the industrial and mining sectors targeted the labor of African men and the influx control laws[4] reinforced this discrimination. A wide variety of factors, including high unemployment rates, limited employment in the mainly low-paid domestic sector, and women's unpaid care work due to the responsibility imposed on them through societal perceptions of gender roles, have had significant implications for women's economic realities and their right of access to adequate housing. The lack of health and educational services has also affected women's economic access and mobility, which in turn has led to the denial of housing rights due to the lack of access to credit and the inability to afford housing (see Walker, 1990, 1991; Albertyn, 1994; Bazilli, 1991; Liebenberg, 1995). In addition, South Africa's historical norm was to allocate state housing to families via the male household head. This discrimination against single-female-headed households resulted in large numbers of women living in informal settlements, with few or no services and no security of tenure.

South Africa's post-1994 environment is vastly different. It includes the adoption of a gender-sensitive constitution; a recognition that systemic and structural factors would continue to negatively affect women, and thus that affirmative action was necessary for the promotion and protection of women's rights; and the development of a focused land-reform program that includes land redistribution, restitution, and tenure reform. The government has passed numerous laws providing land for the landless, restoring land to people dispossessed of their land due to racially discriminatory laws and practices, extending security of tenure, and providing legal guarantees against forced evictions.[5]

Globally, a number of factors within the social context impede women's access to housing, including patriarchy, customary and religious laws and practices, and violence against women. These factors affect women's security of tenure by "preventing women from owning, inheriting, leasing, renting or remaining in housing or on land, placing women in a threatening situation involving the possible loss of their abode" (Centre on Housing Rights and Evictions, 2000:9). Worldwide, patriarchal norms and values dictate gender roles and relations, albeit in differing degrees in different contexts. Discrimination, disadvantage, and inequality underpin the functioning of patriarchy, and they negatively affect women's access to adequate housing.

The use of law—whether state, customary, or religious—to impede access to housing or deny security of tenure is another global reality. Often, despite antidiscrimination provisions in laws, family and community practices nonetheless lead to women being denied access and security of tenure. Violence against women, by both state and non-state actors, is also a barrier to achieving the right to adequate housing and security of tenure. There is a "reciprocal relationship between violence against women and women's adequate housing" in which "the lack of adequate housing can make women more vulnerable to various forms of violence and, conversely, violence against women can lead to the violation of women's rights to adequate housing" (Kothari, 2006b: para. 32). It has also been argued that violence protection and prevention measures are effective only when other economic and social rights, including the right to "adequate housing, food, water, education, and health," are also addressed (Erturk, 2009: para. 72).

Forced eviction disproportionately affects women due to the particular association of women with the home and housing in many cultures (Erturk, 2009: para. 8). Women are frequently responsible for their families' economic, physical, and psychological well-being, thus making forced eviction "a form of gendered violence" (Erturk, 2009: para. 76) and protection from forced evictions a key element of the right to housing (Kothari, 2005: para. 50). Furthermore, governments often fail to incorporate a gender perspective when assessing the needs and adequacy of housing, thereby further deepening the structural barriers that women face. As one human rights organization has stated:

> Women's housing rights are not peripheral issues—they are central to improving the lives of women and girls throughout the world. Housing rights violations are not gender neutral and they impact women in gender specific ways. Beyond basic shelter, for many women housing is a place of employment and social interaction, and a place to care for children. For women in particular, housing rights are intimately connected to their security, health, and wellbeing. (Centre on Housing Rights and Evictions, 2009)

In the context of Naqab Bedouin Arab communities, the issue of state-sponsored forced evictions presents an added challenge due to the ongoing vulnerability of Israel's Bedouin community. Individuals most at risk of such evictions are those with little political or economic power and who commonly suffer rights violations, such as indigenous groups, ethnic and racial minorities, and women (Centre on Housing Rights and Evictions, 2002:7–8). Thus, Bedouin women find themselves in a doubly vulnerable position.

Despite a strong international legal framework on housing rights, the norms and standards of equality and non-discrimination in the housing sphere remain a myth rather than a reality for many women around the globe. The following section addresses the international norms and standards applicable to housing rights. This is followed by an exploration of the economic, social, and cultural contexts and realities of Bedouin women in Israel. The chapter concludes with an analysis of the adverse consequences of inequality, discrimination, forced evictions, and violence.

The International Legal Framework

The protection, promotion, and fulfillment of civil, political, economic, social, and cultural rights require a holistic and intersectional approach. This section explores the international legal standards relating to women's rights, with a particular focus on their right to adequate housing and their right to be free from all forms of violence, both public and private. The Convention on the Elimination of All Forms of Discrimination against Women (CEDAW), which Israel ratified in 1991, lays out comprehensive legal standards.[6] These standards have been interpreted and monitored by the CEDAW Committee in its general recommendations and its concluding observations on states parties' reports. Further legal standards have also been set out in the Universal Declaration of Human Rights and the International Covenant on Economic, Social and Cultural Rights.[7]

Equality and Non-Discrimination

A number of international legal instruments include provisions on equality and non-discrimination on the basis of sex. Of these, CEDAW is the most prominent; however, the actual application of CEDAW's provisions remains a challenge. CEDAW is based on the principles of non-discrimination and of de jure and de facto equality.

Article 1 of CEDAW forbids both direct and indirect discrimination, which has the effect of "impairing or nullifying the recognition, enjoyment, or exercise . . . on a basis of equality of men and women . . . [of] human rights and fundamental freedoms." Provisions on direct discrimination include both intent to carry out and the result of differential or subordinate treatment for women,[8] whereas indirect discrimination requires only a discriminatory result, which has a disproportionate effect on women.[9]

Article 2 of CEDAW requires states to ensure de jure equality in national laws, in the behavior of public institutions, and in the behavior of individuals. Article 3 stipulates the de facto equality requirement. Under the same article, women are entitled to fundamental freedoms and equality in all fields, including civil, political, economic, social, and cultural. States must ensure and protect these rights (art. 3) and take "all necessary measures at the national level aimed at achieving the full realization of the rights" (art. 24). In particular, CEDAW broadly requires states to condemn discrimination against women (art. 2(f)); to take measures to eliminate it in all areas, including in economic and social life (art. 13) and in marriage and family relations (art. 16); to ensure the full development and advancement of women (art. 3); to take measures to eliminate bias and practices based on women's inferiority (art. 5); to accord women equality before the law, including equal rights to conclude contracts and administer property (art. 15); and to ensure that rural women participate in and benefit from rural development on an equal basis with men and enjoy their right to enjoy adequate living conditions, particularly with regard to housing and related services (art. 14(2)).

Adequate Standard of Living

The Universal Declaration of Human Rights holds that "everyone has the right to a standard of living adequate" for health and well-being, including "food, clothing, housing, medical care and necessary social services" (art. 25(1)). Articles 3 and 11 of the International Covenant on Economic, Social and Cultural Rights "recognize the [equal] right of everyone to an adequate standard of living," including "adequate food, clothing and housing" and "the continuous improvement of living conditions." States parties have an obligation to take appropriate steps to ensure the realization of this right. In its general comments, the Committee on Economic, Social and Cultural Rights has elaborated on the meaning of this provision, noting that the right to housing "should be seen as the right to live somewhere in security, peace and dignity" and is "integrally linked to other human rights."[10] The Committee has also recognized the "particular vulnerability" of women "to acts of violence and sexual abuse when they are rendered homeless" by forced evictions.[11]

The UN Human Rights Council has affirmed that adequate housing is a component of the right to an adequate standard of living, stating that adequate housing "is a key element for fostering family integration, contributing to social equity and strengthening the feeling of belonging, security and human solidarity."[12] The Council has further noted that states must "enable all persons to obtain shelter and access to affordable housing and access to land, *inter alia*, by taking appropriate measures . . . with special emphasis on meeting the needs of women."[13] On the relationship between the right to adequate housing and violence against women, the UN Commission on Human Rights has stated that it is "*convinced* that the lack of adequate housing can make women more vulnerable to various forms of violence, including domestic violence, and in particular that the lack of housing alternatives may limit many women's ability to leave violent situations."[14] The Commission has held that forced evictions violate the right to adequate housing and constitute "a gross violation of human rights."[15] The Commission has also urged states to "eliminate [the] disproportionate impact" of forced evictions on women.[16]

Health and Education Rights

The CEDAW Committee's General Recommendation 24 encourages governments to recognize the connection between women's health, education, and standard of living.[17] As defined in CEDAW, the right to health includes "access to adequate health care facilities" and access to "information, counseling and services in family planning" (art. 14(2)(b)). States are obliged to ensure that women receive "appropriate services" before, during, and after pregnancy (art. 12(2)). The CEDAW Committee has elaborated on these measures in its general recommendations and has linked violence against women to the right to health. Violence against women endangers women's health, and article 12 of the Convention requires states to "take measures to ensure equal access to health care" for women who have experienced violence.[18] States must pay special attention to women from "vulnerable and disadvantaged" groups, including women who are migrants, refugees, internally displaced, or indigenous.[19] The socio-economic status of women who are exposed to different forms of violence may also negatively affect their access to health care.[20] Furthermore, women are more susceptible to mental health problems if they are victims of "gender discrimination, violence, poverty, armed conflict, [or] dislocation."[21] States must report on their attempts to eliminate barriers to women's access to health-care services, such as the "distance from health facilities and the absence of convenient and affordable public transport."[22] Article 14 mandates that states provide rural women with adequate health-care facilities and "take all appropriate measures to ensure adequate living conditions, particularly housing, sanitation, electricity and water supply, transport and communications."[23] Adequate living conditions are necessary to ensure "the prevention of disease and the promotion of good health care" for women.[24] States should implement a "comprehensive national strategy" that promotes women's health, responds to violence against women, and ensures "universal access for all women to a full range of high-quality and affordable health care."[25]

The CEDAW Committee's General Recommendation 24 also recognizes that access to health care reduces female students' dropout rates and that education raises women's awareness of health issues.[26] CEDAW requires states to eliminate discrimination against women and to ensure equal rights for women in education (art. 10). Education includes "pre-school, general, technical, professional and higher technical education" and vocational training (art. 10(a)). Women's access to education and overall quality of education (defined in terms of curricula, examinations, and books) should also be the same as men's (art. 10(a)). Women should have equal opportunities for winning scholarships and other grants (art. 10(d)), for obtaining higher and continuing adult education (art. 10(e)), and for accessing sports and physical education (art. 10(f)). All facets of the right to education should be available for women in both urban and rural areas (art. 10(a)).

Indigenous Women's Rights

The UN Declaration on the Rights of Indigenous Peoples,[27] adopted in 2007, further strengthens the protection of indigenous peoples' right to "the lands, territories and resources which they have traditionally owned, occupied, or otherwise used or acquired" and declares that "[s]tates shall give legal recognition and protection to these lands, territories and resources" (art. 26(1)). The Declaration recognizes that the freedoms and rights contained therein are equally guaranteed to indigenous women (art. 43) and that particular attention should be paid to the rights and special needs of indigenous women—as well as to those of elders, youth, children, and disabled persons—in undertaking "special measures for the immediate, effective and continuing improvement of their economic and social conditions, including in the [area of] housing" (art. 22). With regard to forced evictions, article 10 provides that "[i]ndigenous people shall not be forcibly removed from their lands or territories" and that "[n]o relocation shall take place without the free, prior and informed consent of the indigenous peoples concerned and after agreement on just and fair compensation." The Declaration also protects the cultural rights of indigenous groups by clarifying that both individuals and groups have the "right not to be subjected to forced assimilation or destruction of their culture" (art. 8).

Other relevant applicable treaties include the International Covenant on Civil and Political Rights, which prohibits governments from arbitrarily and unlawfully interfering in a woman's privacy, family, and home;[28] the International Convention on the Elimination of All Forms of Racial Discrimination, which requires states to prevent racial segregation and to guarantee to all women—without distinction as to race, color, or national or ethnic origin—the equal enjoyment of the right to housing;[29] and the Convention against Torture, which obliges states to prevent actions that amount to cruel, inhuman, or degrading treatment.[30]

Violence against Women

Significant progress has been achieved in recent years in the international legal response to violence against women, resulting in the explicit recognition of violence against women as a human rights concern. Although CEDAW does not address violence against women specifically, except in relation to trafficking and prostitution (art. 6), many of its antidiscrimination clauses protect women from violence. In its General Recommendation 19, the CEDAW Committee further interprets article 1 of the Convention, stating that discrimination against women includes gender based-violence, meaning "violence that is directed against a woman because she is a woman or that affects women disproportionately."[31] Violence includes coercion, acts, or threats to inflict physical, mental, or sexual harm or suffering, and other "deprivations of liberty."[32] Violence denies a woman her fundamental freedoms and human rights, including the right to be free from torture and cruel, inhuman or degrading treatment or punishment, the right to liberty and security of person, the right to equality in the family, and the right to the highest standard attainable of physical and mental health.[33]

States must prevent public actors from perpetrating violence and must "act with due diligence" to prevent violence and punish perpetrators of violence.[34] The CEDAW Committee's General Recommendation 12 notes that governments are required to protect women "against violence of any kind occurring within the family, at the work place or in any other area of social life."[35] The 1993 Declaration on the Elimination of Violence against Women[36] and the 1994 UN Commission on Human Rights resolution to appoint a Special Rapporteur on Violence against Women[37] represent a political consensus at the UN level to address the challenges of promoting and protecting women's human rights generally, with a particular focus on addressing the pervasive problem of violence against women. States have a responsibility to eliminate violence against women through various measures, including legal and policy frameworks, responsive criminal justice systems, the provision of social services, and the creation of economic empowerment policies. The due diligence standard requires states to promote the right to be free from all forms of violence, both private and public, and to develop and implement prevention, protection, punishment, and compensation laws, policies, and programs.[38]

The country reports of the Special Rapporteur on Adequate Housing have recognized the "interlinkages between violence against women and women's right to adequate housing" (Kothari, 2008: para. 99), noting that these linkages "are unambiguous, given that the right to adequate housing also implies having access to a safe and secure house" (Kothari, 2006a: para. 100). The Rapporteur has further stated:

> Violence against women and housing violations are inextricably linked as causes and consequences of each other. Just as inadequate housing in the slums leads to risk of violence, a situation of domestic violence can lead to a woman being deprived of housing. (Kothari, 2004a: para. 45)

The Rapporteur has noted that "domestic violence [is] likely to increase in situations of stress," particularly in "cramped housing and living conditions," and that governments should address these conditions (Kothari et al., 2006: para. 104(f)).

Violations of Naqab Bedouin Arab Women's Human Rights[39]

This section briefly identifies the violations of Bedouin women's rights that occur at the hands of both state and non-state actors. An intersectional approach to identifying human rights violations is essential, as rights are interconnected, interdependent, and indivisible. This section examines several categories of rights violations: legal; economic, social, and cultural; violence against women; health; and education.

Legal

With regard to the Bedouin community, the Israeli state, through its acts and omissions, has created or failed to remedy intolerable living conditions created by policies of forced eviction, home demolitions, and forced urbanization. The government has also failed to provide essential services and infrastructure and has failed to recognize or protect existing land and housing rights. This is particularly true for Bedouin women, whose lives—for economic, social, cultural, and political reasons—are intimately bound to their homes and lands. As Nadera Shalhoub-Kevorkian aptly argues:

> The home is where women most acutely invest their time, build their safety nets . . . and carry on with their life responsibilities. Once the home is destroyed, women are left with the metaphoric and symbolic burdens [besides the material loss] of not having a sense of safety and place of belonging. . . . The destruction of the home changes women's previous gender roles sharply and requires them to face new challenges. (2006)

As indigenous women from an ethno-religious minority group and a culture that itself is built around patriarchal principles, Bedouin women of the Naqab have been particularly vulnerable to discrimination and other rights violations by both state and non-state actors. That vulnerability has been compounded for women who are survivors of forced evictions and domestic violence; widowed, divorced, separated, elderly, single, or young; disabled; or heads of households (see Kothari, 2006b: para. 30).

The housing available to Bedouin women in unrecognized villages and permanent townships has arguably failed to satisfy most of the sixteen adequacy criteria specified under internationally accepted norms and standards. Forced evictions and home demolitions have deprived women of legal security of tenure, subjected them to violence by state actors, and resulted in the destruction, damage, and loss of possessions. In both rural and urban areas, the state has failed to provide adequate infrastructure, services, information, remedies, education, and empowerment opportunities for Bedouin women.

Economic, Social, and Cultural

Bedouin women have been adversely affected by Israel's policies of forced resettlement, urbanization, and house demolitions. In some cases, Bedouin socio-cultural norms have exacerbated the problem. It is clear that the government has neglected to consider such norms when formulating its resettlement policies applicable to the Bedouin community. Despite some commonalities, women in the townships have faced different challenges from women in the unrecognized villages, thus requiring separate attention.

Israel's forced urbanization policy and its resettlement of Bedouin communities (see Abu-Saad and Creamer, chapter 1, this volume) has resulted in the loss of the traditional and productive role in agriculture and herding that Bedouin women previously filled, thus rendering them "merely" caretakers of the household (Gottlieb, 2008:53). Bedouin townships lack proper infrastructure and public services, such as sewage systems, adequate health and educational services, public transportation, and designated industrial zones. The townships have not provided sufficient employment opportunities for Bedouins, particularly women. According to Suleiman Abu-Bader and Daniel Gottlieb, 32% of Bedouins in southern Israel participate in the labor force—but when looking at women specifically, this number drops to 10% for those living in townships and less than 7% for those from unrecognized villages (Abu-Bader and Gottlieb, 2008:130).

Furthermore, since housing plots in the towns have been smaller and closer together than those in traditional Bedouin villages, different families have been forced to live in greater proximity to one another (Fenster, 1999:236). Traditional settlements consist of the home and the surrounding area, usually inhabited by extended family members (Fenster, 1999:229; Zaher, 2006:2; Working Group on the Status of Palestinian Women in Israel, 2006:75). This disruption of the familiar spatial design of villages through forced relocation has led to new challenges for Bedouin women. The reality of more densely populated residential areas of the towns has also increased the likelihood of new and unfamiliar public encounters and forbidden interactions between women and men of different family and tribal groups. Thus, in the towns, women have lived in culturally inadequate housing that they had no part in designing and that offers insufficient privacy and security. Tovi Fenster argues that women are thus more likely to be driven out of the one space over which they once wielded the most power and influence: the home and its surroundings (1999).

In the case of house demolitions and forced evictions, homeless families often have had to move in with extended family in the unrecognized villages or in the Bedouin towns, resulting in a significant expansion of women's caretaking responsibilities. In such cases, resources are spread more thinly and men's intrusion into women's private sphere becomes more frequent. Such factors can amplify frustrations and tensions and lead to acts of violence against women within the home (Zaher, 2006:6). As was shown in the context of the Occupied Palestinian Territories, an environment of uncertainty and stress before and after the forced eviction of Palestinian families led to an increase in domestic violence (see Amnesty International, 2004: pt. III). This seems to also be true in the context of the unrecognized villages, adding to the violence already conducted against Bedouin women by Israeli police forces during the evictions themselves (Gottlieb, 2008).

Violence against Women

As observed by the Special Rapporteur on Adequate Housing, the lack of adequate housing, as well as other obstacles to resettlement, creates tension within the family, which "often manifests itself as domestic violence" (Kothari, 2005: para. 67). The living conditions that are the result of inadequate housing can be conducive to violence (Coomaraswamy, 2000: para. 69). Overcrowded, unsanitary housing conditions combined with poverty and unemployment cause elevated stress levels, decreased tolerance, and a resulting higher risk of domestic violence (Coomaraswamy, 2000: para. 59). The Rapporteur has argued that when women suffering from persistent poverty "are forced to live in inadequate and insecure housing and living conditions," such conditions are themselves a form of violence (Kothari, 2006b: para. 32). Forced evictions can exacerbate gender disparities in society and in the family, and women can find themselves in a more perilous position due to an increased risk of gender-based violence (Kothari, 2004b: para. 44).

The impact of state-sponsored violence during and after house demolitions manifests in numerous ways. In addition to physical violence, evictions and demolitions inflict acute psychological violence on Bedouin women, the effects of which are unmistakable. Governmental bulldozers demolish more than concrete, metal, or cloth structures—they demolish women's sphere of power and their social networks. A woman's sense of personhood can be damaged, as evidenced by the recurring theme of humiliation in the testimonies of women affected by demolitions.[40] State violence also exposes women to unwanted male interactions that, in violating Bedouin cultural norms, aggravate the shame that women experience.

Bedouin women have also reported experiencing increased levels of domestic violence after eviction, which may be the result of additional stress within the family (Physicians for Human Rights Israel, 2008). Destabilization of family life occurs after forced relocation and creates an environment conducive to domestic, physical, sexual, or psychological violence (Coomaraswamy, 2000: para. 53; Kothari, 2004b: para. 56). Incidents of domestic violence occur more frequently after forced relocation, when women suffer the most (Coomaraswamy, 2000: paras. 53, 55). Women are generally responsible for acquiring "food, fuel, and fodder" for their families and will thus have an increased workload as a result of the scarcity of these items after forced relocation (Kothari, 2004b: para. 52). Violence continues after resettlement due to "loss of self-esteem among men" resulting from "loss of land and livelihood," which then "manifests itself in violence against the women in [a man's] home" (Kothari, 2004b: para. 57). When the land assigned for resettlement makes it difficult for communities to continue their traditional way of life, women are prevented from exercising their usual responsibilities, leading to a devaluation of their roles and increased violence against them (Coomaraswamy, 2000: para. 55). Women's opportunities for new employment are limited due to "their lower level of skills, education, exposure, and mobility" (Kothari, 2004b: para. 51). In addition, women may have more difficulty adjusting to relocation because of their "restricted mobility and lack of access to the public domain" (Kothari, 2004b: para. 54). They also tend to rely more heavily on social networks than men. Therefore, when these networks are destroyed after forced relocation, women may suffer trauma as a result of loss of the security and emotional and childrearing support that these networks provide (Kothari, 2004b: para. 55).

According to Physicians for Human Rights–Israel (2008), one out of two Bedouin women experiences assault at some point in her life; in the unrecognized villages, two out of three women experience assault. One in four Bedouin women is exposed to violence at least once a year (Physicians for Human Rights–Israel, 2008). Of those who experience violence, 62% seek help, but only 8% seek it from an official agency (Physicians for Human Rights–Israel, 2008).[41] As a result of the assault, abuse, and deprivation of personal resources, Bedouin women "display high levels of psychological distress which may manifest as low self-esteem, depression, somatization, anxiety and emotional disorders" (Physicians for Human Rights–Israel, 2008). Formidable cultural barriers affect women in both rural and urban communities. As members of the Palestinian minority, Bedouin women mistrust the Israeli police force, which has a history of treating Palestinians as a security threat, and often with violence. They also face the severe social stigma that comes with reporting domestic and sexual violence: within Bedouin communities, such acts are seen as private matters and, in the case of sexual violence, damaging to a woman's "honor." Reporting violence without adequate assurance of anonymity and protection can thus prove extremely dangerous for them (see Working Group on the Status of Palestinian Women in Israel, 2006:29–32).

According to Shalhoub-Kevorkian, who works extensively with Palestinian women facing the threat of house demolitions in the Palestinian Occupied Territories, women live with constant tension, a situation that carries a host of problematic consequences. For example, women do not sleep in pajamas because they are afraid of transfer, evictions, and demolitions. Women live in constant uncertainty about whether they will have a house to come home to, so they are afraid to go out. Furthermore, in the name of protection, men restrict them further. The home becomes a site of resistance against Israeli policies of house demolition, as well as an additional place to box women both into the domestic realm and into greater oppression.[42]

Health

Women's right to health is significantly affected by forced evictions, poverty, decreased access to water, and limited health services. Violence begins before the eviction process in the form of psychological stress (Coomaraswamy, 2000: para. 57). This stress is a result of living in constant fear of eviction and "reach[es] such extreme levels that . . . [it] is comparable to forms of cruel and inhuman degrading treatment" (Kothari, 2005: para. 50). Such psychological stress increases during eviction—when women are often targeted—and demolition of houses (Coomaraswamy, 2000: para. 57). After an eviction, women also take on the burdens of caretaking in the case of injury, and they suffer increased poverty, loss of adequate housing, and lack of community support (Coomaraswamy, 2000: para. 57). They also suffer from loss of "livelihoods, relationships, support systems[,] . . . breakdown of kinship ties, physical and psychological trauma and . . . increased morbidity and mortality" (Coomaraswamy, 2000: para. 43).

A 2003 study found that of 202 Bedouin women (from both state-planned and unrecognized settlements), 47% were anemic, 53% suffered from urinary tract infections, and 31% suffered from depression (Gottlieb, 2005). Infant mortality rates in the unrecognized villages are "three times the local average and about twice the average for the Israeli Arab population" (Gottlieb, 2005). Until 1994, Israel provided no health services to people living in the unrecognized villages (Gottlieb, 2005:16). Only after years of litigation before the Supreme Court did state authorities recognize unrecognized villages' need for health services, and the government subsequently provided partial health services. Barriers to obtaining substantive health-care services continue to include long travel distances; lack of public transportation; social and cultural norms that sometimes prevent women from traveling long distances without male company; inadequacy of services provided; the high cost of services; and language and other gendered barriers that affect women's ability to obtain health services (Physicians for Human Rights–Israel, 2009; Al-Krenawi, 2004:46–47). There is evidence that 62% of Bedouin women are illiterate in Hebrew, 59% lack oral communication skills in Hebrew, and 50% of physicians and administrative assistants working with Bedouins do not speak Arabic (Physicians for Human Rights–Israel, 2009:22). Signs providing information about clinic hours and materials providing health information are available primarily in Hebrew (Physicians for Human Rights–Israel, 2009:22).

Inadequate housing and insecure tenure frequently lead to overcrowded, unsanitary housing conditions. An important aspect of "living conditions" is that of the right to water, which, according to the

Special Rapporteur on Adequate Housing, is "indispensable for a dignified human life and for realizing other human rights, in particular the rights to food, health and housing" (Kothari, 2003: para. 43). The absence of running water in the unrecognized villages and the lack of garbage collection services exacerbate the health hazards for residents of the villages generally, and women in particular, putting residents "at risk of dehydration, infectious intestinal diseases, skin diseases and eye infections. Water of poor quality can cause parasitemia and dysentery, typhoid fever, cholera and hepatitis" (Physicians for Human Rights–Israel, 2008:47).

Women and female children often spend a significant amount of time obtaining water when it is not easily accessible (Physicians for Human Rights–Israel, 2008:47). As the Special Rapporteur on Violence against Women has noted, access to clean water can "address some of the root causes of poverty and gender inequality that fuel violence against women" (Erturk, 2009: para. 98). Access to water has been linked to "improved school attendance for girls, as they become free to go to school rather than being obliged to fetch water for their families" (Erturk, 2009: para. 98). It also "improves income-generating opportunities and access to economic resources that are known to lessen women's vulnerability to violence" (Erturk, 2009: para. 98).

Education

The Israeli government permits Jewish schools to be divided into secular and religious schools, where the latter includes a sex-segregated system; however, the government does not allow the Arab school system to segregate girls and boys (Abu-Rabia-Queder, 2006). In a study comparing Bedouin girls who remained in school with those who have dropped out, Sarab Abu-Rabia-Queder concluded that Israel's policy of imposing mixed-gender schools that fail to account for cultural restrictions discriminates against Bedouin girls by effectively depriving them of their right to education (2006:14). Further, since there have been no high schools in the unrecognized villages, students must walk and commute long distances to attend school. Many parents have refused to allow girls to travel these distances alone, and they frequently have prohibited their daughters from attending high schools outside the villages. This has largely been due to the fear that interaction with boys, or community perceptions of such interactions, will destroy girls' "honor" (Abu-Rabia-Queder, 2006:9–12). Abu-Rabia-Queder's study suggests that many of the parents of the girls who drop out of school, as well as the girls themselves, do not oppose education per se and see all-girls' schools as a viable solution (2006:13–14). This is apparent in the findings of a 2009 survey, which showed that while the school enrollment rates of girls from the unrecognized villages reached 85.8% in elementary school, it dropped to 38.7% in high school.[43]

Although the percentage of school enrollment and higher education attainment among Bedouin women has improved in recent years, the results are still alarming, particularly with regard to the disparity in enrollments between Bedouin towns and the unrecognized villages. According to a 2004 survey, 67% of Bedouin women surveyed had obtained some form of education (Al-Krenawi, 2004:28). In unrecognized villages, only 41% of women surveyed had obtained some form of education (Al-Krenawi, 2004:28). Furthermore, only 6% of women surveyed in the unrecognized villages had obtained higher education, compared to 17% of women surveyed in the recognized villages (Al-Krenawi, 2004:28).

The unrecognized Bedouin villages have lacked educational facilities and infrastructure, constituting a major limiting factor for the education of Bedouin girls (and boys) living in those villages (*Statistical Yearbook of the Negev Bedouin*, 2004). The schools in unrecognized villages have been "makeshift" and respond to "immediate, temporary needs for temporary education" (Abu-Rabia-Queder, 2008:384). These schools have had no electricity, water, or equipment (such as libraries, laboratories, or learning aids), and there have been no paved roads to school, which, together with the weather, has proven a serious hindrance to regular school attendance (Abu-Rabia-Queder, 2008:384). In some cases, high schools for Bedouins have been as far as twelve kilometers from the children's homes.[44] Many girls have had to walk or travel in mixed-sex buses, leading parents to determine that it is too dangerous to permit their daughters to attend school (Abu-Rabia-Queder, 2006:5). As Abu-Rabia-Queder suggests, in addition to the lack of infrastructure, the lack of segregated schools has been largely responsible for the high dropout rate among girls, and Israel's coeducation policy "essentially discriminates against Bedouin women, creating obstacles to their education while Bedouin men have undeterred access to schooling" (2006:14).

In summary, Israel's forced urbanization and forced eviction policies have negatively affected the Bedouin community, particularly Bedouin women, at many levels, including in the areas of education, health, violence, and culture. In the case of forced evictions, women have not been able to afford to build appropriate living quarters due to the high costs of demolition and the inadequate and insufficient employment opportunities available to them.[45] In the unrecognized villages in the Naqab, gender roles have forced women to shoulder the responsibility of "rebuild[ing] the household 'out of the rubble,'" physically and financially, after a demolition (Physicians for Human Rights–Israel, 2008:68). Food safety has also been a challenge for women because demolitions leave them "without options for proper storage, refrigeration, and preparation" of food (Physicians for Human Rights–Israel, 2008:71). Women in the Naqab have reported "los[ing] their economic independence" and becoming "more reliant on the men in their community" after forced evictions and demolitions, as well as experiencing a general loss of self-esteem and sense of security (Centre on Housing Rights and Evictions, 2002:16). Also, many Bedouin women living in towns have been unable to find work because no employment initiatives were established in these towns (Fenster, 1999:242). This has led to a loss of status for Bedouin women, who in the village played a vital role in supporting their families by milking goats, preparing food, weaving tent material, and helping with agricultural work—tasks that have been rendered either unnecessary or impossible in light of Israel's land confiscation and forced urbanization.

Additionally, the lack of infrastructure has influenced women's accessibility to health services and education. As Abu-Bader and Gottlieb assert, "[a]dequate infrastructure is crucial to the development of the economy and of the [Bedouin] population's living standard" (2009:29). Recent improvements in education have been due to an increase in the number of schools in the unrecognized villages and of new high schools in the newly recognized villages;[46] however, this has been far from sufficient, and the Israeli government must undertake greater efforts in order to meet the country's national educational achievement standards.

Conclusion

The five core human rights treaties mentioned above, which Israel has ratified, provide ample legal protection of indigenous women's rights to adequate housing and to be free of all forms of violence. However, Israel's treatment of indigenous women in the Naqab has been in clear violation of these legal standards. Through its laws and policies of discrimination, non-recognition, dispossession, eviction, and demolition, Israel has jeopardized Bedouin women's rights to adequate housing, to education, to health, and to be free from violence, among others. In addition, the government's policy of forcibly urbanizing Bedouin women rather than allowing them a choice between traditional settlements and relocation to towns or cities has directly contravened its obligations to ensure its inhabitants freedom to choose their residence. The resulting living spaces have paid no respect to women's social, cultural, economic, and spatial needs, creating for many a more restricted—and, in some cases, more violent—life.

Israel submitted its most recent report to the CEDAW Committee in 2005. In its concluding observations, the Committee discussed the rights of Israeli Arab women generally and Bedouin women in particular with regard to education, health, and housing. It notes that Israeli Arab women have been in "a vulnerable and marginalized situation, especially in regard to education and health,"[47] and urges the Israeli government to take "urgent measures" to address this problem.[48] The Committee recommended that Israel "allocate adequate resources" to improve Arab women's health and suggested that it pay special attention to the problem of infant mortality.[49] Furthermore, the Committee advised Israel to "take effective measures to eliminate discrimination against Bedouin women" and "enhance respect for their human rights through effective and proactive measures" in the areas of education and health.[50] In other, earlier concluding observations, the Committee also noted the alarming school dropout rates of Bedouin girls and recommended that Israel allocate "adequate resources . . . for school facilities" and for scholarship programs.[51]

The various forms of dispossession, dehumanization, and oppression experienced by indigenous peoples generally and Bedouin women in particular can be summed up by a young Bedouin woman's words of determination:

> We will stand for what is ours. I will stay here even between rocks. . . . We will stay here even if they [try to] throw us into the Dead Sea. . . . Even if they demolish, you build again and thus continue your life.[52]

This woman's statement exposes the alienation that Bedouin Arabs experience in Israel despite their formal status as Israeli citizens. In addition, it reflects domestic injustice, Bedouin invisibility, and lack of political will both in Israel and in the international community to improve Bedouins' reality. Despite extensive international laws and standards, there has been a lack of substantive protection for Bedouin women. There is a question that must be raised: Is justice both blind and deaf when it comes to addressing the violations of Bedouin women's human rights?

REFERENCES

Abu-Bader, S., and Gottlieb, D. (2008). "Education, employment and poverty among Bedouin Arabs in southern Israel." *HAGAR Studies in Culture, Polity and Identities* 8(2):121–136.
———. (2009). "Poverty, education and employment in the Arab-Bedouin Society: A comparative view." Society for the Study of Economic Inequality, Working Paper Series. http://www.geog.bgu.ac.il/fastSite/coursesFiles/bedouins/bader-article.pdf (accessed September 27, 2011).
Abu-Rabia-Queder, S. (2006). "Between tradition and modernization: Understanding the problem of female Bedouin dropouts." *British Journal of Sociology of Education* 27(1):3–17.
———. (2008). "Does education necessarily mean enlightenment? The case of Palestinian Bedouin women in Israel." *Anthropology and Education Quarterly* 39:381–400.
Albertyn, C. (1994). "Women and the transition to democracy in South Africa." In C. Murray (ed.), *Gender and the New South African Legal Order* (pp. 39–63). Cape Town: Juta Legal and Academic Publishers.
Al-Krenawi, A. (2004). *Awareness and Utilization of Social, Health/Mental Health Services Among Bedouin-Arab Women, Differentiated by Type of Residence and Type of Marriage.* Beersheba: The Center for Bedouin Studies and Development, Ben-Gurion University of the Negev.
Almi, O. (2003). "No man's land: Health in the unrecognized villages in the Negev." Physicians for Human Rights–Israel. http://www.phr.org.il (accessed May 30, 2010).

Amnesty International. (2004). "Israel and the Occupied Territories: Under the rubble; House demolition and destruction of land and property." http://www.amnesty.org/en/library/info/MDE15/033/2004 (accessed July 22, 2011).

Bazilli, S. (ed.). (1991). *Putting Women on the Agenda*. Johannesburg: Ravan Press.

Centre on Housing Rights and Evictions. (2000). *Sources 5: Women and Housing Rights*. Geneva: COHRE.

———. (2002). *Violence: The Impact of Forced Eviction on Women in Palestine, India and Nigeria*. Geneva: COHRE.

———. (2009). COHRE statement on International Women's Day: Women around the world bear the brunt of the global economic and housing crisis. Geneva, March 8.

Classens, A., and Cousins, B. (eds.). (2008). *Land, Power and Custom: Controversies Generated by South Africa's Communal Land Rights Act*. Cape Town: UCT Press.

Coomaraswamy, R. (2000). "Report of the Special Rapporteur on violence against women, its causes and consequences." U.N. Doc. E/CN.4/2000/68/Add.5.

Cwikel, J., Lev-Wiesel, R., and Al-Krenawi, A. (2003). "The Physical and Psychosocial Health of Bedouin Arab Women of the Negev Area of Israel: The Impact of High Fertility and Pervasive Domestic Violence." *Violence Against Women* 9(2):240–257.

Erturk, Y. (2009). "Report of the Special Rapporteur on violence against women, its causes and consequences, Addendum: Political economy and violence against women." U.N. Doc. A/HRC/11/6/Add.6.

Fenster, T. (1999). "Space for gender: Cultural roles of the forbidden and permitted." *Environment and Planning, D: Society and Space* 17:227–246.

Gottlieb, N. (2005). "Accessibility and utilization of antenatal care among the Arab Bedouin of the unrecognized villages of the Negev Desert/Israel." www.phr.org.il/uploaded/article-file_1157442731903.doc (accessed July 28, 2011).

———. (2008). "Reconstruction: The voices of Bedouin-Arab women on the demolition of their homes in the unrecognized villages of the Negev." *HAGAR Studies in Culture, Polity and Identities* 8(2):47–64.

Kothari, M. (2001). "Report of the Special Rapporteur on adequate housing as a component of the right to an adequate standard of living, submitted pursuant to Commission resolution 2000/9." U.N. Doc. E/CN.4/2001/51.

———. (2003). "Annual Report of the Special Rapporteur on adequate housing as a component of the right to an adequate standard of living, and on the right to non-discrimination, submitted in accordance with Commission resolution 2002/21." U.N. Doc. E/CN.4/2003/5.

———. (2004a). "Adequate housing as a component of the right to an adequate standard of living, Addendum, Mission to Kenya." U.N. Doc. E/CN.4/2005/48/Add.2.

———. (2004b). "Annual Report of the special Rapporteur on adequate housing as a component of the right to an adequate standard of living." U.N. Doc. E/CN.4/2004/48.

———. (2005). "Women and adequate housing: Study by the Special Rapporteur on adequate housing as a component of the right to an adequate standard of living." U.N. Doc. E/CN.4/2005/43.

———. (2006a). "Report of the Special Rapporteur on adequate housing as a component of the right to an adequate standard of living, Addendum, Mission to the Islamic Republic of Iran." U.N. Doc. E/CN.4/2006/41/Add.2.

———. (2006b). "Women and adequate housing; Report by the Special Rapporteur on adequate housing as a component of the right to an adequate standard of living, and on the right to non-discrimination." U.N. Doc. E/CN.4/2006/118.

———. (2008). "Report of the Special Rapporteur on adequate housing as a component of the right to an adequate standard of living, Addendum, Mission to Spain." U.N. Doc. A/HRC/7/16/Add.2.

Kothari, M., et al. (2006). "Report of the Special Rapporteur on extrajudicial, summary or arbitrary executions, Philip Alston; the Special Rapporteur on the right of everyone to the enjoyment of the highest attainable standard of physical and mental health, Paul Hunt; the Representative of the Secretary-General on human rights of internally displaced persons, Walter Kälin; and the Special Rapporteur on adequate housing as a component of the right to an adequate standard of living, Miloon Kothari: Mission to Lebanon and Israel." U.N. Doc. A/HRC/2/7.

Liebenberg, S. (ed.). (1995). *The Constitution of South Africa from a Gender Perspective*. Cape Town: Community Law Centre.

Ntsebeza, L., and Hall, R. (eds.). (2007). *The Land Question in South Africa: The Challenges of Transformation and Redistribution*. Cape Town: HSRC Press.

Physicians for Human Rights–Israel. (2008). "I am here: Gender and the right to health in the unrecognized villages in the Negev."

http://www.phr.org.il/default.asp?PageID=133&ItemID=157 (accessed July 23, 2011).

———. (2009). "The bare minimum: Health services in the unrecognized villages in the Negev." http://www.phr.org.il/default.asp?PageID=157&ItemID=340 (accessed July 23, 2011).

Shalhoub-Kevorkian, N. (2006). "House demolitions: A Palestinian feminist perspective." Jerusalem Center for Women. http://www.topicsandroses.com/spip.php?article272 (accessed July 23, 2011).

Statistical Yearbook of the Negev Bedouin. (2004). Beersheba: The Center for Bedouin Studies and Development and the Negev Center for Regional Development, Ben-Gurion University of the Negev.

UNIFEM. (n.d.). *CEDAW Briefing Kit.* Bangkok: UNIFEM CEDAW Southeast Asia Programme. http://cedaw-seasia.org/resource_documents.html#briefingkit (accessed July 23, 2011).

Walker, C. (1990). "Women and gender in Southern Africa to 1945: An overview." In C. Walker (ed.), *Women and Gender in Southern Africa to 1945* (pp. 1–22). Cape Town: David Philip; London: James Currey; Bloomington: Indiana University Press.

———. (1991). *Women and Resistance in South Africa.* 2nd ed. Cape Town: David Philip; New York: Monthly Review Press.

Working Group on the Status of Palestinian Women in Israel. (2006). "The status of Palestinian women in Israel: The alternative NGO report to the UN Committee on the Elimination of Discrimination against Women."

Zaher, S. (2006). "The Right of Arab Bedouin Women to Adequate Housing and Accommodation." *Adalah's Newsletter* 23:1–6.

NOTES

1. The UN Commission on Human Rights, established in 1946, was replaced by the Human Rights Council in 2006.

2. Committee on Economic, Social and Cultural Rights, General Comment 4, U.N. Doc. E/1992/23, annex III at 114 (1991), reprinted in *Compilation of General Comments and General Recommendations Adopted by Human Rights Treaty Bodies*, U.N. Doc. HRI/GEN/1/Rev.6 at 18 (2003), secs. 6 and 8; International Covenant on Economic, Social and Cultural Rights (ICESCR), G.A. Res. 2200A (XXI), 21 U.N. GAOR Supp. (No. 16) at 49, U.N. Doc. A/6316 (1966), art. 2(2); Kothari (2006b: sec. 11).

3. Committee on Economic, Social and Cultural Rights, General Comment 4, *supra* note 2, sec. 6; ICESCR, *supra* note 2, art. 2(2).
4. The term "influx control" refers to legal measures that the government used from 1923 to 1986 to regulate the inflow of black African people into urban areas, allowing black people access to towns only for the purpose of serving white labor needs.
5. See generally Constitution of the Republic of South Africa, 1996; Extension of Security Tenure Act 62 of 1997; Prevention of Illegal Eviction from and Unlawful Occupation of Land Act 19 of 1998; Interim Protection of Informal Land Rights Act 31 of 1996. See also Ntsebeza and Hall (2007); Classens and Cousins (2008).
6. Convention on the Elimination of All Forms of Discrimination against Women (CEDAW), G.A. Res. 34/180, 34 U.N. GAOR Supp. (No. 46) at 193, U.N. Doc. A/34/46 (1979).
7. Universal Declaration of Human Rights, G.A. Res. 217A (III), U.N. Doc A/810 at 71 (1948); ICESCR, *supra* note 2.
8. CEDAW, *supra* note 6.
9. Ibid.
10. Committee on Economic, Social and Cultural Rights, General Comment 4, *supra* note 2, para. 7.
11. Committee on Economic, Social and Cultural Rights, General Comment 7, U.N. Doc. E/C.12/1997/4 (1997), para. 11. In paragraph 3, the Committee defines "forced eviction" as the involuntary removal of a person from her home or lands, without the provision of or access to legal and other forms of protection.
12. Human Rights Council, Adequate housing as a component of the right to an adequate standard of living, Resolution 6/27 (December 14, 2007), preamble.
13. Ibid., para. 4(h).
14. Commission on Human Rights, Women's equal ownership, access to and control over land and the equal rights to own property and to adequate housing, Resolution 2005/25 (April 15, 2005), preamble.
15. Commission on Human Rights, Forced evictions, Resolution 1993/77 (March 10, 1993).
16. Commission on Human Rights, Women's equal ownership of, access to and control over land and the equal rights to own property and to adequate housing, Resolution 2003/22 (April 22, 2003), para. 7.
17. CEDAW Committee, General Recommendation 24 (20th session, 1999), para. 28.
18. CEDAW Committee, General Recommendation 19 (11th session, 1992), para. 19.
19. Ibid., para. 6.
20. Ibid., para. 12(b).
21. Ibid., para. 25.
22. Ibid., para. 21.
23. Ibid.
24. Ibid.

25. CEDAW Committee, General Recommendation 24, *supra* note 17, para. 29.
26. Ibid., para. 28.
27. Declaration on the Rights of Indigenous Peoples, G.A. Res. 61/295, U.N. Doc. A/Res/61/295 (2007).
28. International Covenant on Civil and Political Rights, G.A. Res. 2200A (XXI), 21 U.N. GAOR Supp. (No. 16) at 52, U.N. Doc. A/6316 (1966), arts. 17, 26.
29. International Convention on the Elimination of All Forms of Racial Discrimination, G.A. Res. 2106 (XX), Annex, 20 U.N. GAOR Supp. (No. 14) at 47, U.N. Doc. A/6014 (1965), arts. 3, 5(d)(iii).
30. Convention against Torture and Other Cruel, Inhuman or Degrading Treatment or Punishment, G.A. Res. 39/46, Annex, 39 U.N. GAOR Supp. (No. 51) at 197, U.N. Doc. A/39/51 (1984), art. 16. See also Committee against Torture, Conclusions and Recommendations: Israel, U.N. Doc. CAT/C/XXVII/Concl.5 (2001), para. 6(j) ("The Committee expresses concern about . . . Israeli policies on house demolitions which may, in certain instances, amount to cruel, inhuman or degrading treatment or punishment.").
31. CEDAW Committee, General Recommendation 19, *supra* note 18, para. 6.
32. Ibid.
33. Ibid., paras. 7(b), (d), (f), (g).
34. Ibid., paras. 8, 9.
35. CEDAW Committee, General Recommendation 12 (8th session, 1989).
36. Declaration on the Elimination of Violence against Women, G.A. Res. 48/104, 48 U.N. GAOR Supp. (No. 49) at 217, U.N. Doc. A/48/49 (1993).
37. Commission on Human Rights, Question of integrating the rights of women into the human rights mechanisms of the United Nations and the elimination of violence against women, Resolution 1994/45 (March 4, 1994).
38. Commission on Human Rights, Elimination of violence against women, Resolution 2000/45 (April 20, 2000).
39. This section is based in part on research conducted by Harvard Law School students between 2007 and 2009 under the supervision of Ahmad Amara.
40. Interview with Nadera Shalhoub-Kevorkian, Jerusalem, October 25, 2007. See also Gottlieb (2008).
41. In addition, a 2003 study found that 48.3% of Bedouin women were exposed to physical violence by persons known to them. While over 60% of those women sought some help, only 8% sought assistance from formal medical, legal, or law enforcement agencies (Cwikel, Lev-Wiesel, and Al-Krenawi, 2003:249; see also Working Group on the Status of Palestinian Women in Israel, 2006:30).
42. Interview with Nadera Shalhoub-Kevorkian, Jerusalem, October 25, 2007.
43. These findings are among girls aged 20 and younger. See Abu-Bader and Gottlieb (2009: table 3).
44. Adalah: The Legal Center for Arab Minority Rights in Israel, Petition to the High Court of Justice, H.C. 2848/05 (2005). http://www.adalah.org/eng/legaladvocacycultural.php#2848.

45. When demolishing homes, Israeli state authorities charge the homeowners for demolition-related expenses, such as the cost of using the bulldozers.
46. About ten villages are in the process of being recognized by the state, and more infrastructure is currently being developed in these villages. See Abu-Saad and Creamer (chapter 1, this volume).
47. CEDAW Committee, Concluding Observations: Israel, U.N. Doc. A/60/38, Part II (2005), para. 255.
48. Ibid., para. 256.
49. Ibid.
50. Ibid., para. 260.
51. CEDAW Committee, Concluding Observations: Israel, U.N. Doc. A/52/38/ Rev.1, Part II (1997), para. 176.
52. Dunya E. N., from Bir Almshash Village, interviewee, cited in Gottlieb (2008:59).

Abstract

This chapter explores the case for recognizing the property rights of the Bedouins, as indigenous peoples of the Naqab (Negev). Israel is a common-law country resulting from the British Mandate and is a member of the group of multicultural states, such as former British colonies Australia and Canada, that have indigenous peoples residing within their national boundaries. The developing native title jurisprudence in settler states, particularly Australia, provides a comparative legal framework for Israeli courts, which, thus far, have been unwilling to recognize Bedouin claims to property.

The chapter argues that the State of Israel commits an arguably fundamental jurisprudential error when it attempts to look back beyond the country's common-law heritage to earlier Ottoman laws. The law immediately preceding Israel's creation—and not a raft of multifarious laws and legal regimes reaching much further back—is recognized by international law as comprising the body of law of the newly established state. The chapter subsequently demonstrates that significant advances in common-law native title jurisprudence, including the watershed 1992 *Mabo* decision and subsequent cases of the Australian High Court, represent a persuasive body of case law that should inform Israeli jurisprudence in the area of Bedouin property.

CHAPTER 6

Applying an Australian Native Title Framework to Bedouin Property

John Sheehan

Introduction

[A]lready in the nineteenth-century Bedouin were developing alternative sites for winter and summer abode within their territories, located relative to seasonal grazing needs into different environments around which grazing activities revolved. That is, these sites were recognized as permanent bases. They reflected orderly patterns of grazing migration and camping, with grazing zones and ranges. These were highly constrained by the boundaries of tribal territories or by inter-group treaties and agreements that began to shape up from the mid-nineteenth century.

(Meir, 2009:832)

The property rights of indigenous peoples—such as the Bedouins of the Naqab (Negev) Desert—have always been a conundrum for countries whose land law is rooted in British common law.[1] Israel is one such state, having been the subject of the British Mandate. Indeed, British common law arguably emerged in 1917 with the conquest of Ottoman Syria, which included lands that would become the Palestine Mandate. The Bedouins also survive in other parts of the former Mandate area, such as Syria (Leybourne, 1997) and Jordan (Madanat, 2010).

The Naqab Bedouins are indigenous, semi-nomadic desert peoples characterized since the nineteenth century as semi-sedentary, with activities of a mainly agricultural nature being carried out on their traditional lands. In recent years, about half of them live in villages considered "illegal," and have thus been deprived of several basic rights. They have an ancient form of tenure markedly similar to that of indigenous nomads throughout the world, such as the indigenous (also known as Aboriginal) peoples of Australia.

The territories within which Bedouins have exercised their rights are similar to those of other semi-nomadic and nomadic peoples, and unsurprisingly rely on natural boundaries for delineation and the exclusion of others. Within these territories exists a constellation of traditional rights and interests, some of which are analogous to common-law notions of property and some of which are *sui generis* (unique). Confounding this tenurial picture are rights that do not distinguish between the temporal and the spiritual—concepts unknown to modern European societies, which regard land merely as a tradable commodity.

Among indigenous communities, property is not necessarily individually owned; rather, it is often held communally. In fact, individual ownership, and even clan ownership, is frequently eschewed. However, empirical evidence suggests that contemporaneity of tenures is not unknown, with a mixture of communal, joint, and individual landholding modes within particular societies persisting in various parts of the indigenous world. The absence of a taxonomic homogeneous panarchy of indigenous tenures is not unexpected, with subsidiary individualization of tenure possibly an expression of pre-contact possessive individualism, particularly evident in Australian indigenes (discussed below).

Like other indigenous societies, the Naqab Bedouins have seen themselves as part of the land and do not envisage a comfortable separation between themselves and their land. Accordingly, the property rights of the Bedouins are ordinarily not alienable beyond the Bedouin community. This predicament lies at the heart of the conundrum for Anglo-Israeli common-law notions of property, which place a monetary value on all conceivable types of property rights, be they freehold, leasehold, licenses, easements, or *profits-à- prendre*. Nevertheless, sales of Bedouin lands to non-indigenes are not unknown, especially during the Ottoman and British Mandate periods, which demonstrate that significant parts of Bedouin society have been in transformation from semi-nomadic to complete sedentarization.

This conundrum of Anglo-Israeli common law, however, is no longer evident in other common-law countries, where the "alien" rights and interests of indigenous semi-nomadic and nomadic peoples have steadily gained recognition. The main thrusts behind such recognition can be found in two jurisprudential developments: firstly, through the International Court of Justice's (ICJ) 1975 decision demolishing the *terra nullius* notion and, secondly, through benchmark cases, particularly the Australian High Court's 1992 *Mabo* decision, according the land rights of indigenous peoples the respect deserved in domestic law.[2] Notwithstanding such jurisprudential developments in other common-law countries, the State of Israel has been unwilling to reach an accommodation similar to that demonstrated by other comparable jurisdictions, such as Australia.

The Israeli government's visceral unwillingness to undertake a similar approach is arguably a product of the ongoing Israeli-Palestinian conflict, the *leitmotif* (dominant theme) that has stigmatized traditional Bedouin land tenure in the eyes of the state (see Amara and Miller, chapter 2, this volume).

The following sections explore the prospect for recognizing Bedouin property rights, particularly in light of relevant international and comparative law.

Characteristics of Indigenous Property

When Augustus Caesar returned to Rome in 29 BC from Egypt, the restoration of the property rights of the Roman citizenry was crucial for the new but autocratic Augustan Empire because, "[t]o the Romans, security of tenure was a moral as much a social or economic good" (Holland, 2004:382).

Such action was necessary because much earlier, in 49 BC, Gaius Julius Caesar and his legionaries had crossed the Rubicon, the narrow stream marking the border between the Roman Province of Gaul and Italy. In crossing the Rubicon and illegally marching on Rome, Caesar had overturned such prized values as "private property" and "rights before the law," resulting in the eventual collapse of the Roman Republic (Holland, 2004:xxi).

Figurative re-crossings of the iconic Rubicon to establish yet again such values in modernity were attempted through the French and American revolutions (Holland, 2004:xxii); however, ancient concepts of property (especially those within the aegis of deep property,[3] such as indigenous property rights) still remain stubbornly elusive. Indeed, the characteristics of indigenous property are slowly being revealed as imbued with inherent complexity and pervasive cultural baggage. However, indigenous property is not incomprehensible; a unique world of property rights is emerging with a genius that is sometimes indefinable and yet often disconcertingly intelligible in its simplicity. Any attempt to uncover indigenous property rights through the lens of deep property necessitates a peeling of the layers comprising the elemental land property right, many of which remain inchoate.

Importantly, interrogation of these layers may need to occur repeatedly, using different lenses, if we are to understand the characteristics of indigenous property and the reasons for its complexity. Such inquiries may be placed on a seemingly vulnerable theoretical limb on the extremity of current thinking around property and what it means. Yet, in the process of doing so, recent property theory and formal property law are richly extended.

Any inquiry into institutional aspects of the nature and behavior of property rights reveals questionable assumptions derived from the parent discipline of economics. Greater exploration is needed into theoretical positions outside the mainstream paradigm in order to reveal some of the failures between theory and reality experienced in property. Such institutional aspects of property are key to understanding economic behavior and how it permits inquiry into the nature of property-related institutions.

However, the survival of ancient property-related institutions in settler societies such as Israel demonstrates the aforementioned failure between theory and reality experienced in property. Traditional semi-nomad order, albeit partially transformed, reveals the dyschronous property rights existing in Israel, especially where the Bedouins have adopted a pluralist lifestyle that accommodates both customary and market-based approaches.[4]

Indigenous property-related institutions in other common-law countries, such as Australia, can help shed light on the Bedouins' plight. Australia's indigenous institutions were described with great insight by Justice Richard Blackburn in his ruling in *Milirrpum v. Nabalco Pty Ltd*:

> The evidence shows a subtle and elaborate system highly adapted to the country in which the people led their lives, which provided a stable order of society and was remarkably free from the vagaries of personal whim or influence. If ever a system could be called "a government of laws, and not of men", it is that shown in the evidence before me.[5]

Hence, an institutional focus inexorably leads to the law and demonstrates the relevance of legal thought to the understanding of property, notably in the context of indigenous property rights.

Interrogating Indigenous Property Rights

Traditional legal research can be distinguished from the research approach used for property rights, which of necessity is at a jurisprudential level indistinguishable as a multidisciplinary part of broader social sciences, especially for indigenous property rights. Property rights in many post-colonial common-law countries evidence cultural blindness, with fundamental flaws in conceptions of property. To comprehend the complex matrix of property rights requires a multidisciplinary appreciation of colonial history, international law, and the pragmatic responses of post-colonial legal regimes.

Legal research traditionally focuses on the identification of either broad principles or specific *ratio decidendi* (reason for deciding) through statutes, common law, case law, legal commentary, and refereed articles in law journals, and unsurprisingly this positivist[6] research approach is used for the legal specificity of property.

However, property rights research differs markedly from traditional legal research, notably because positivism can provide only a partial understanding of property rights. Arguably, the often flawed nature of specific property rights can be more adequately canvassed through an interrogation of issues such as the source of property-related laws, their purpose, and their operation. Furthermore, the epistemology of the authority behind specific laws must be uncovered, particularly regarding the reasoning behind the choice of a particular approach over another. In modern nation-states, private property rights are ordinarily protected from arbitrary interference, in particular compulsory acquisition, except by statutory fiat coupled with compensation.

The interrogation of law in this manner invariably uncovers shortcomings and unforeseen consequences after the enactment of a particular law, sometimes many decades later. Nevertheless, examining whether the intent of a specific property-related law is just (or, alternatively, unjust and hence wrong) raises broader definitional issues, which, as stated earlier, can be indistinguishable from broad moral issues of the social sciences. Courts' increasing recognition of customary land tenures is one example of how common law, indigenous customary law, and statute law have coalesced outside of positivism, incorporating notions of kinship—ideas that are more familiar to anthropologists than to lawyers (Enright, 1991:4).

Increasingly, modern societies expect their law to recognize indigenous or customary title. In Australia, such recognition occurred more than two centuries after British colonization, with the High Court's decision in *Mabo & Ors v. The State of Queensland.*[7] Recognition of native title has also resulted in indigenous peoples in Australia affirming a connection with their "ancestral lands," seeking to return to those lands in order to pursue "a way of life that is informed by fundamentally different value systems" (Altman, 2009).

In addition, emerging property rights such as Australian native title are slowly transforming statutory law, and in turn being more clearly defined through partial codification. Such codification through statute as a method for resolving indigenous or customary issues has been demonstrated by Australian courts, which have stressed the primacy of legislation whereby the common law gains relevance to the extent that it informs legislation.[8]

With legislation as the starting point for the definition of emerging (but ancient) property rights, such as indigenous customary tenures, the scope of the rights and interests capable of being legally recognized is also established.[9] Ordinarily, property rights are the expression of a relationship between an individual or group and the land (or other natural resource) in terms of rights and interests. Unsurprisingly, codifying statute law often requires indigenous communities to express their relationship with the land in terms of such rights and interests, and it is this requirement that has presented significant difficulties for the judiciary in recognizing relationships where "the spiritual or religious is translated into the legal."[10]

There are certain aspects of indigenous cultural heritage that will not be recognized as customary land tenures, and it is important to note that intellectual indigenous property has been distinguished from land tenures by the Australian courts.[11] Clearly what is and what is not customary land tenure, and when it suffers impairment or even extinguishment, and what might or might not be compensable, are all issues being slowly resolved by the Australian courts. Arguably, the inexorable incorporation of customary land tenures into received and post-colonial property law is a process whereby the common law is encompassing indigenous custom and kinship.

Importantly, property rights in many common-law countries are the legacy of a historical colonial process creating flawed property rights. Research on how these legal property rights were formed in the colonial (settler) milieu reveals that these rights have been either reinforced or modified by subsequent post-colonial statutes and case law. Furthermore, property rights in some common-law countries can be culturally blind, often resulting in fundamentally flawed property relationships between the state and its citizens, such as Israel and the Naqab Bedouins.

As demonstrated above, an extraordinary depth of research is required to comprehend the complex matrix of property rights in many post-colonial common-law nations, including Israel. This approach necesitates a multidisciplinary appreciation of colonial history, international and comparative law, and the seemingly pragmatic response of post-colonial societies to specific property issues.

A Common-Law Framework for Indigenous Property Rights

At the outset, property rights appear to be a homogeneous legal notion in both the developed and developing world. However, this apparent homogeneity as a legacy of colonialism is grossly misleading, in much the same way as the world's current enchantment with the chimera of a homogeneous economic and legal framework for international business investment. Similarly, the conventional view of unlocking "dead capital" in the developing world, as proposed by Hernando de Soto, urges the creation of homogeneous "formal property" (de Soto, 2000:15, 231). However, this view has been criticized as too simplistic and grossly overestimating the cadastral and bureaucratic capacity of most developing countries (Molebatsi et al., 2004:151).

Property rights in the developing (and developed) world are "paperised" (Molebatsi, 2004:149) in ways that suggest a significant misunderstanding of the specific needs of states' indigenous peoples, highlighting deeply embedded flaws in notions of property rooted in colonial legacies. However, there was no misunderstanding by the colonizers that dispossession hinged on the use of law to create or negate property rights such that

> [o]ne relatively constant element of dispossession has been the use of law in effecting and/or normalizing the outcome. The central role of legislation in such situations derives from the fact that the provision, or, alternatively, the transformation or negation of property rights, is invariably institutionalized by some type of law. It is surprising, then, that the role of legislation in the dispossession of displaced ethnic and national groups has not received greater academic attention. (Forman and Kedar, 2004:810)

Not only does the negation of indigenous property rights and the transfer of control to colonizers confirm the imported property rights regime, but also

> [s]ettlers' law and courts attribute to the new land system an aura of necessity and naturalness that protects the new status quo and prevents future redistribution. Formalistic legal tools play a meaningful role in such legitimization. Courts apply "linguistic semantics, rhetorical strategies and other devises" to disenfranchise Indigenous peoples. (Kedar, 2003:415)

More so, the property of the conquered is often regarded as "public land" (Kedar, 2003:414), which can be utilized by the state without consulting the traditional owners. For example, during Israel's 2005 withdrawal from the occupied Gaza Strip, the government disregarded traditional Palestinian owners of the lands of the Jewish Israeli settlements.[12]

Using the Lens of International Law

The surviving traditional property rights of the Naqab Bedouins present a significant concern for the state because, as Israeli citizens, Bedouins can draw on applicable comparative law, such as Australian native title jurisprudence, in their claims for tenure recognition. Israel became a common-law country in 1917, when the British Army occupied Palestine after defeating the Turks. Israel thus shares the common law with Australia and other former British colonies and possessions.

This historical judicial connection also draws Anglo-Israeli law to "another formal and highly important source of law" (Tamir, 2006)—namely, judicial precedents from other common-law countries, such as Australia. In particular, crucial decisions such as *Mabo* (described above) in which the Australian High Court reexamined established notions of Anglo-Australian property rights. This reexamination was the culmination of a series of significant jurisprudential developments, particularly the aforementioned ICJ advisory opinion in the *Western Sahara* case on the concept of *terra nullius* under international law. In this opinion, the ICJ also commented on issues surrounding Western Sahara's self-determination during the decolonization process, specifically its legal ties with Morocco and Mauritania.

Broadly, international rules regarding territorial sovereignty are based on Roman law provisions governing ownership and possession, and the different methods of acquiring territory under international law are derived from Roman rules of property (Schoenborn, 1929:333). Roman law notions of property, however, are quite different from property concepts within the common law, a distinctive English legal system originating in the twelfth century that arose primarily from case law based on very old local customs. Arguably, the common law drew little influence from Roman law.

Nevertheless, the concept of territorial sovereignty finds its roots in the notion of title, or the factual and legal conditions under which territory is deemed to belong to one particular authority or another. In other words, it refers to the existence of those facts required under international law to entail the legal consequences of a change in the juridical status of a particular territory (Brownlie, 1990:123–124).

The ICJ has noted that the word "title" encompasses any evidence that may establish the existence of a right and the actual source of that right.[13] In this sense, title to territory under international law is a very fact-specific inquiry.

International law does recognize a category of territory—*terra nullius*—over which there is no sovereign. The expression *terra nullius*, like other concepts of territorial sovereignty under international law, derives from classical Roman law, under which the doctrine of *occupatio* (seizing) conferred ownership to the discoverer of an object that was *res nullius* (belonging to nobody). Such seizing must be performed by the state, must exercise effective control, and must be intended as a claim of sovereignty over the area (Shaw, 1997:333). In post-Renaissance Europe, this doctrine was conveniently applied to states' acquisition of territory. Territory that was *res nullius* could be lawfully acquired by a state through simple occupation, and uninhabited territory was always uncontroversially classified as *terra nullius*. Over time, the categories of territory that were considered *terra nullius* were expanded to include certain kinds of inhabited territory. Whether or not inhabited land was included within such expanded notions of *terra nullius* depended on the degree of political development and other characteristics of the inhabitants of the land in question.

For example, in 1885, states attending the Berlin Conference declared most of the African continent as *terra nullius*, on the basis that the continent's inhabitants were supposedly incapable of governing themselves. The ICJ, in a case concerning South Africa's sovereign right to control South West Africa (now Namibia), declared the characterization of African territory by the Berlin Conference participants as *terra nullius* a "blunder." The Court noted that as early as the sixteenth century, Vitoria had written that Europeans could not obtain sovereignty over the Indies by occupation because the Indies were not *terra nullius*. Similarly, the African peoples had "founded states and even empires of a high level of civilization," and thus much of the African continent could not be considered *terra nullius*.[14]

This issue of whether a particular territory had been *terra nullius* at the time of its colonization was raised in the ICJ's *Western Sahara* case. Spain's colonization of Western Sahara had begun in 1884, when Spain claimed a protectorate over Río de Oro, although Spain had established a presence in the territory during the fifteenth and sixteenth centuries. Western Sahara remained a Spanish colony—the Spanish Sahara—until 1976. In 1966, the United Nations (UN) General Assembly encouraged the territory's decolonization on the basis of the right to self-determination, and it invited Spain, in consultation with neighboring states Mauritania and Morocco, to "determine . . . the procedures for the holding of a referendum under UN auspices with a view to enabling the indigenous population of the territory to exercise freely its right to self-determination."[15] After some delay, Spain agreed to hold a referendum in the Spanish Sahara under UN supervision in 1975. Then King Hassan claimed the territory of Western Sahara for Morocco on the basis of "historic title" predating Spain's colonization of the territory. Mauritania made a similar and overlapping claim. In order to assist in the process of resolving these competing claims and proceed with decolonization, on December 13, 1974, the UN General Assembly requested that the ICJ provide an advisory opinion on the following questions:

- At the time of its colonization by Spain, was Western Sahara (Río de Oro and Sakiet al-Hamra) land belonging to no one (*terra nullius*)?
- If not, what legal ties existed between this territory and the Kingdom of Morocco and the Islamic Republic of Mauritania?

The ICJ clearly saw its role as establishing whether international law at the time of colonization would have considered Western Sahara *terra nullius*. There is an emphasis that *terra nullius* was a legal term used in connection with the mode of territorial acquisition known as "occupation," viewed legally as an initial peaceful acquisition of sovereignty over territory otherwise than by cession or succession. The Court noted that state practices during the period of colonization indicated that territories inhabited by tribes or peoples having a social or political organization were not regarded as *terra nullius*.[16] It should be noted, however, that the ICJ's interpretation of international law at the time of Spanish colonization ran counter to the beliefs of some writers during that period (see Lindley, 1926:11–20; Westlake, 1894:141–142). It should be further emphasized that the Court did not reject the legal concept of *terra nullius* in its entirety— rather, it simply determined that this concept was not applicable to the territory of Western Sahara at the time of its colonization, based on specific facts indicating a certain level of social or political organization by the indigenous inhabitants.

Of particular relevance to the Naqab Bedouins is the ICJ's view that Western Sahara was being utilized almost exclusively by nomads, pasturing their animals or growing crops where conditions were favorable, and that common rights of pasture were enjoyed by the occupants. However "some areas suitable for cultivation, on the other hand, were subject to a greater degree to separate rights" such as water holes, which were considered property of the tribe that "put them into commission," although they were open to all for use.[17] The Court found that "at the time of colonization Western Sahara was inhabited by peoples which, if nomadic, were socially and politically organized in tribes and under chiefs competent to represent them."[18] The Court also emphasized the actions and subjective beliefs of the colonial state. It found that Spain, in colonizing Western Sahara, was not attempting to establish its sovereignty over a *terra nullius* but rather "taking the Rio de Oro under his [Spain's] protection on the basis of agreements which had been entered into with the chiefs of the local tribes."[19] Thus, the Court stressed that Spain had recognized independent tribes of this territory and did not rely on any claim to the acquisition of sovereignty over a *terra nullius*.

For territories inhabited by tribes or peoples having a social or political organization, the acquisition of sovereignty was thus not generally considered as effected unilaterally through "occupation" of *terra nullius* by original title but rather through agreements concluded with local rulers. Although the word "occupation" was used by Spain, it was used in a non-technical and non-legal sense:

> [It] did not signify that the acquisition of sovereignty through such agreements with authorities of the country was regarded as an "occupation" of a *terra nullius* in the proper sense of these terms. On the contrary, such agreements with local rulers, whether or not considered as an actual "cession" of the territory, were regarded as derivative roots of title, and not original titles obtained by occupation of *terra nullius*.[20]

Therefore, in the eyes of the Court, European colonizers exploited the notion of *terra nullius* not only for questionable assertions of sovereignty but also as a legal device to ignore the pre-existing property rights of the indigenous people of Western Sahara, and indeed elsewhere throughout the world. *Terra nullius* created a category of title to property that wholly favored the settler society at the expense of indigenous inhabitants. As a result, the 1975 Advisory Opinion of the ICJ was approved in the 1992 *Mabo* decision providing crucial background for rejecting any notion that Australia was unoccupied at the time of British arrival.[21]

Early U.S. Jurisprudence

In addition to the 1975 Advisory Opinion of the ICJ, the High Court of Australia was influenced significantly by the much earlier decision of the U.S. Supreme Court in *Johnson v. M'Intosh*,[22] a case from 1823 in which the exclusive right of a discovering sovereign to extinguish Native Americans' interests in their land was recognized under common law by the Court. In *M'Intosh*, the Supreme Court explored the issue of conflicting rights of settlers and aboriginal peoples, and adopted a compromise now known as "native title" or "aboriginal title" under the common law. In this case, the Court upheld a grant by the United States over the claims of a private purchaser from the Native American tribes of the same lands, holding that "discovery gave title" to the discovering nation.[23] The Court recognized that these lands had been inhabited at the time of discovery, but rejected the use of legal doctrines of conquest, instead creating a "new and different rule."[24] The Court recognized Native Americans as "rightful occupants of the soil" but held that the state had an "absolute title . . . to extinguish that right" and might even "grant the soil, while yet in possession of the natives."[25] The Court did not suggest that this arrangement was "just" but rather noted that it was the only possible or pragmatic accommodation of the interests of both settlers and Native Americans.[26] Thus, the pragmatic compromise between settler and indigenous interests necessitated an inferior and subordinate status for native title and denied the indigenous inhabitants equality before the law (see Bartlett 1995:285).

M'Intosh established two levels of property rules governing rights in American lands: the discovery rule that regulated inter-European claims and the rules to regulate relations between discoverers and the natives. The discovery rule itself prevented Native Americans from selling to other colonizing states. Native Americans were not stripped of all property rights but retained what Chief Justice John Marshall labeled the "Indian title of occupancy," which could be extinguished only by purchase or conquest. The precise content of the Indian title of occupancy under *M'Intosh* is not entirely clear, however. Included in this title of occupancy was the power to sell to the discovering sovereign lands that a tribe had previously conveyed to someone else. But the most important question for the Native Americans, given that they could sell full title only to the U.S. government, was whether they could refuse to sell. The Court ultimately determined that the United States could divest the natives of title only via purchase or conquest. The word conquest was subsequently limited to "defensive wars" or those fought for some other "just cause."[27]

After India, the United States is arguably the second largest common-law country in the world; it was thus unsurprising that the Australian Court, in *Mabo*, recognized the importance of the 1823 *M'Intosh* decision. Both the 1975 ICJ opinion and the *M'Intosh* decision underpin *Mabo*, although the subsequent enactment of Australia's 1993 Native Title Act created "a pathway to recognition less difficult than" (French, 2008:3) expending a decade to obtain a common-law judgment, as was the case in *Mabo*. Thus, both case law and statute have contributed to the establishment of the conception of property, known as "native title," into the existing matrix of proprietary interests in land under Anglo-Australian law.

The Content of Native Title

The recognition of surviving native title in Australia created a need to also recognize the likely content of these indigenous rights and interests in Australia as a bundle of legal rights that may or may not be capable of separate existence,[28] especially when only partially commuted or impaired by the state. Under current native title jurisprudence, such indigenous rights can constitute contemporaneous communal, joint, and individual titles:

> The community, the largest possible native title owning entity, is in fact the society whose laws and customs are in question. The group is smaller, and will ordinarily have a fluctuating membership (so, of course, will the community). The individual is the smallest possible native title owning entity.[29]

There is currently only limited understanding of how indigenous rights and interests can be characterized within Anglo-Australian law, and hence made more readily approachable legally. Nevertheless, the suggested native title content of communal, joint, and individual titles[30] constitutes a familiar tenurial approach (Rigsby, 1998:35). However, if only for the narrow purposes of compensation, an urge exists to overcome any conceptual property strictures, a reality described by Justice Robert French as a need to "shake off the difficulties of . . . [native title] origins in a common law judgment" (French, 2008:4).

In order to assess the impact of violations of indigenous property rights, and in turn determine appropriate compensation for such violations, it is necessary to disaggregate these rights. To ascertain the content of a specific native title, disaggregation simply involves a studious examination of the various rights (communal, joint, or individual) in the bundle of indigenous property rights. Approaching the core of native title in this manner is also consistent with other collectively held property rights in Anglo-Australian property law. Arguably, indigenous rights arc analogous to the entitlement of an association to compensation for the use of its land by individual association members. In such cases, the association's rules would permit individual members to use the land for different purposes and with differing intensity, sometimes contemporaneously. Adopting a core native title allows compensation to be assessed at the subgroup or individual level—in other words, separately from compensation for the collective. To avoid difficulties with orthodoxy, it is necessary to note the *sui generis* nature of native title, which arguably permits disaggregation.

Assisting this disaggregation approach, case law throughout the common-law world over the past two centuries has addressed the multifaceted nature of compensation arising from compulsory state acquisition of non-indigenous property rights. Importantly, various Australian courts have awarded compensation for the loss of intangible rights and usufructs, evidencing an empathetic approach to entitlement and compensation. In *March v. City of Frankston*, for example, the Victorian Supreme Court held that additional compensation in the manner of *solatium*[31] was warranted as "some amount to cover inconvenience and in a proper case distress caused by compulsory taking."[32]

Subsequently, in *RK Morgan Holdings Pty Ltd v. Melbourne & Metropolitan Board of Works*, the Court stated that "a claim is made for solatium founded on intangible or non-pecuniary disadvantages."[33]

Arguably, an approach to assessing the worth of indigenous rights and interests could utilize analogies from non-indigenous property rights, such as *profits-à-prendre*. There would of course be a need to enhance such analogies to account for the spiritual and cultural dimensions embedded in indigenous rights, perhaps by way of additional compensation in the form of *solatium*. Eight years prior to the *Mabo* decision, the spirituality of indigenous property rights was addressed in *Hackshaw v. Shaw*,[34] which described this aspect of the indigenous world as "inherited spiritual custodianship" (Sir William Deane cited in Stephens, 2002:48). Subsequently, in *Gerhardy v. Brown*,[35] the Australian High Court advanced the following useful explanation of this spirituality:

> To the extent that one can generalise, their society was not institutionalised and drew no clear distinction between the spiritual and the temporal. The core of existence was the relationship with the responsibility for their homelands which were neither individual or clan "owned" in a European sense but which provided identity of both in a way which the European settlers did not trouble to comprehend and which the imposed law, based on an assertion of terra nullius, failed completely to acknowledge, let alone to protect . . . almost two centuries on. (Stephens, 2002)

However, caution must be exercised in constructing analogous compensation entitlement enhanced for spirituality and culture, as there is no agreement on the survival of "intense spirituality" (Duffy, 2005), which today can realistically be asserted only by a minority of indigenous Australians who still view their land with enchantment rather than as a commodity. Nevertheless, an analogical approach inexorably leads to the view that *solatium* may be the closest equivalent to spiritual value within Australian property compensation law. Current awards of compensation based on the notion of *solatium* are pitifully small,[36] and any proper analogy to spirituality would require *solatium* to be significantly increased. Such action would clearly be necessary in order for *solatium* to properly account for spiritual values.

The above Australian discourse, while preponderantly structuralist in form, seeks to avoid any attempt to rigidify indigenous rights and interests. Jurisprudential language is still ill-equipped to describe the multifarious and often exotic indigenous notions of culture and spirituality embedded in native title. The unanticipated but overdue recognition in *Mabo* of indigenous rights and interests has so outpaced property theory and practice that improvisation drawn from compensation analogies is almost obligatory when considering compensation for the violation of native title.

Such an analogical approach mirrors the familiar habitual improvisation through which the common law has been informed and developed over centuries. Again, this chapter does not suggest that this approach is unassailable; merely, it assuages the need for novel theory in favor of an arguably more comfortable structuralist approach. Ironically, such a proposition appears to be germinating almost wholly on Australian soil, which is somewhat surprising given the extremely late recognition in Anglo-Australian law of indigenous rights and interests.[37] Any prospect for a comprehensive formulaic approach appears to be at risk because indigenous rights and interests do not have consistent incidents as evident in more familiar Australian tenures, such as freehold. While there may be a core of indigenous rights and interests generally recognized across continental Australia, this kernel may not burgeon into a fulsome analogical approach. Realistically, *profits-à-prendre* or usufructs may or may not be analogous to all indigenous rights to hunt and gather.[38]

Conclusion

The familiar bundle of common-law property rights now potentially embraces an unfamiliar universe of exotic incidents called Australian native title, previously unknown to lawyers or compensation assessors. Physical determinism[39] lies at the heart of the majority observation proficiencies utilized in assessments of compensation arising from compulsory acquisition by the state. However, such an approach is found wanting when ephemeral values such as spiritual and cultural attachment are encountered. Topographical features can be easily ascertained, but metaphysical circumstances (such as sacred sites indistinguishable from the surrounding countryside) may be invisible to even the most skilled non-indigenous observers. There is often a risk that such observers may mistakenly assume that particular spiritual or cultural features are absent, due to a lack of physical evidence.

As a result, history suggests that treaties and agreements were not sufficiently cognizant of indigenous spiritual and cultural values, revealing the historic gulf between the settlers and the indigenes in all common-law countries, including Australia and Israel. Perfunctory values are ascribed to indigenous property rights, confirming that the pre-colonial lands were regarded as economically undeveloped and hence of minimal value. This physical determinism remains embedded in current property law and practice throughout the common-law world, inhibiting the metastasis required to deal with indigenous spiritual and cultural values.

Within the common-law framework, the rights and interests asserted by the indigenous Naqab Bedouins are closely allied to those asserted by semi-nomadic and nomadic Australian indigenes. Sadly, however, the Bedouins are also in a markedly similar position to the indigenous peoples of Australia prior to the *Mabo* decision: the Bedouins suffer minimal recognition of their property rights by the State of Israel. Yet, the Bedouins can draw on groundbreaking Australian native title law to support the assertion that traditional semi-nomadic and nomadic land tenure is not illusory but a very real tenure capable of comfortable recognition.

REFERENCES

Altman, J. (2009). "No movement on the outstations." *The Sydney Morning Herald*, May 25.

Bartlett, R. (1995). "Native title: From pragmatism to equality before the law." *Melbourne University Law Review* 20(2):282–310.

Brownlie, I. (1990). *Principles of Public International Law*. 4th ed.

Duffy, M. (2005). "A good land right is a good deed." *The Sydney Morning Herald*, April 9–10.

Enright, C. (1991). *Studying Law*. 4th ed. Acton: Branxton Press.

Forman, G., and Kedar, A. (2004). "From Arab land to 'Israel lands': The legal dispossession of the Palestinians displaced by Israel in the wake of 1948." *Environment and Planning Society and Space* 22:809–930.

French, R. (2008). *Plus ca change, plus c'est la meme chose? The 2007 Amendments to the Native Title Act*. Land, Rights, Laws: Issues of Native Title Paper No. 12. Canberra: Native Title Research Unit, Australian Institute of Aboriginal and Torres Strait Islander Studies.

Gray, K., and Gray, S. F. (1998). "The idea of property in land." In S. Bright and J. Dewar (eds.), *Land Law: Themes and Perspectives* (pp. 15–51). Oxford: Oxford University Press.

Havemann, P., Thiriet, D., Marsh, H., and Jones, C. (2005). "Traditional use of marine resources agreements and dugong hunting in the Great Barrier Reef World Heritage Area." *Environmental and Planning Law Journal* 22(4):258–280.

Holland, T. (2004). *Rubicon: The Triumph and Tragedy of the Roman Republic*. London: Abacus.

Hyam, A. (2004). *The Law Affecting Valuation of Land in Australia*. Sydney: The Federation Press.

Jennings, R. Y. (1963). *The Acquisition of Territory in International Law*. Manchester: Manchester University Press.

Kedar, A. (2003). "On the legal geography of ethnocratic settler states: Notes towards a research agenda." In J. Holder and C. Harrison (eds.), *Law and Geography* (pp. 401–441). Oxford: Oxford University Press.

Leybourne, M. (1997). *La Steppe Syrienne: Degradation et Adaptations*. PhD thesis, University Lumiere Lyon II, Faculte de Geographie, Historie, Historie de l'Art et Tourisme.

———. (2006). "Rain water, governments and a dam: Changes to the nomadic pastoral system in Syria." In M. Leybourne and A.

Gaynor (eds.), *Water: Histories, Cultures, Ecologies* (pp. 28–37). Perth: University of Western Australia Press.

Lindley, M. F. (1926). *The Acquisition and Government of Backward Territory in International Law*. New York: Longroans, Green and Co.

Madanat, H. J. (2010). "Land tenure in Jordan." *Land Tenure Journal* 1(10):143–170.

Meir, A. (2009). "Contemporary state discourse and historical pastoral spatiality: Contradictions in the land conflict between the Israeli Bedouin and the State." *Ethnic and Racial Studies* 32(5):823–843.

Molebatsi, C., Griffith-Charles, C., and Kangwa, J. (2004). "Conclusions." In R. Home and H. Lim (eds.), *Demystifying the Mystery of Capital: Land Tenure and Poverty in Africa and the Caribbean* (pp. 145–156). London: The Glass House Press.

"People of Gaza discover their land." (2005). *The Sydney Morning Herald*, September 17–18.

Rigsby, B. (1998). "A survey of property theory and tenure types." In N. Peterson and B. Rigsby (eds.), *Customary Marine Tenure in Australia Oceania Monograph No. 48* (pp. 22–46). Sydney: University of Sydney.

Robertson, L. G. (2005). *Conquest by Law: How the Discovery of America Dispossessed Indigenous Peoples of their Lands*. New York: Oxford University Press.

Schoenborn, W. (1929). "La nature juridique du territoire." *Collected Courses of the Hague Academy of International Law* No. 30 1929, pp. 85–191.

Shaw, M. (1997). *International Law*. 4th ed. Cambridge: Cambridge University Press.

de Soto, H. (2000). *The Mystery of Capital*. London: Black Swan Books.

Stein, P. (1999). *Roman Law in European History*. Cambridge: Cambridge University Press.

Stephens, T. (2002). *Sir William Deane: The Things that Matter*. Sydney: Hodder.

Tamir, M. (2006). "A guide to legal research in Israel." New York: Hauser Global Law School, New York University. http://www.nyulawglobal.org/globalex/israel.htm.

Westlake, John. (1894). *Chapters on the Principles of International Law*. Cambridge: University Press.

NOTES

1. "Common law" refers to a type of legal system developed in England and passed on to other countries through British occupation, whether through colonization or other means, such as the Mandate. The common-law model differs from the Western European legal system of civil law, which is derived from Roman law. See, e.g., Stein (1999).
2. *Western Sahara* case, ICJ Reports, 1975, 12; 59 ILR, 14; *Mabo & Ors v. The State of Queensland* (No. 2) (Mabo) (1992) 66 ALJR 408.
3. Deep property describes a more comprehensive theory of property, which has great or specified extensions of the elemental conventional land property right familiar in property law.
4. For a useful discussion on a similar pluralism adopted by Australian indigenes, see Altman (2009).
5. *Milirrpum v. Nabalco Pty Ltd* ((1971) 17 FLR 141) at 264–268.
6. Positivism is described as a "school or theory of jurisprudence which defined law as rules or commands laid down or posited by the State." See, e.g., Enright (1991:3).
7. *Mabo & Ors v. The State of Queensland, supra* note 2.
8. *Western Australia v. Ward* (2002) 1901 ALR 1 per majority at 16, 25.
9. The definition of "native title" is set out in the Native Title Act 1993 (Cth), sec. 223.
10. *Western Australia v. Ward, supra* note 8, at 14.
11. Ibid. at 57–64.
12. As one Palestinian landowner reported, "the [Israeli] settlers lived here for 35 years and they were compensated when they left and it's not even their land. Our ancestors have been planting this land for hundreds of years. Who will compensate us for the houses and land that the Israelis destroyed" ("People of Gaza discover their land," 2005).
13. *El Salvador v. Honduras,* case concerning *Land, Island and Maritime Frontier,* judgment (September 11, 1992), ICJ Reports, 1992, 351, 388; 97 ILR 266, 301.
14. *Legal Consequences for States of the Continued Presence of South Africa in Namibia (South West Africa) notwithstanding Security Council Resolution 276 (1970), Advisory Opinion* (June 21, 1971), ICJ Reports, 1971, 55.
15. United Nations General Assembly, Resolution 2229, G.A.O.R., 21st Session, Supp. 16, p. 72 (1966).
16. *Western Sahara, supra* note 2, paras. 79–80.
17. Ibid., para. 87.
18. Ibid., para. 81.
19. Ibid.
20. Ibid., para. 80.
21. (1992) 66 ALJR 408, 422 per Brennan.
22. *Johnson v. M'Intosh*, 21 U.S. (8 Wheat.) 543 (1823).

23. Ibid. at 574, 592.
24. Ibid. at 591. The rejection of the application of the legal concept of conquest is significant, given that Chief Justice John Marshall, the author of the opinion, later recognized the private rights of inhabitants of conquered or ceded territories (*U.S. v. Percheman*, 8 L. Ed. 604 (1883)).
25. *Johnson v. M'Intosh, supra* note 22, at 588.
26. Ibid. at 588, 591.
27. *Worcester v. Georgia*, 31 U.S. (6 Pet.) 515 (1832); see also Robertson (2005).
28. See, e.g., *Harrington-Smith on behalf of the Wongatha People v. Western Australia* (No. 9) [2007] FCA 31.
29. Ibid. at 1135.
30. Ibid. at 1135.
31. *Solatium* is described as consolation or compensation as solace for injured feelings. See, e.g., Hyam (2004:378–383).
32. *March v. City of Frankston* (No. 1) [1969] VR 350 at 356; see, e.g., Hyam (2004:380).
33. *RK Morgan Holdings Pty Ltd v. Melbourne & Metropolitan Board of Works* (1992) 77 LGRA 102 at 115.
34. *Hackshaw v. Shaw* (1984) 155 CLR 614.
35. *Gerhardy v. Brown* (1985) 159 CLR 70.
36. For example, the compensation awarded was 3% in *RK Morgan Holdings Pty Ltd, supra* note 33, at 115.
37. The *Mabo* decision was handed down by the High Court in June 1992.
38. For a useful discussion of the protection of indigenous hunting and gathering post-*Mabo,* see Havemann et al. (2005).
39. Physical determination refers to activity-based approaches to identifying rights.

Abstract

Indigenous rights should not be equated with citizens' rights or human rights. While nation-states have engaged citizens' rights and human rights issues within national and international fora, indigenous rights have not enjoyed the same level of interest and engagement by nation-states and the international community. Rather, indigenous rights issues are marginalized in favor of perspectives on citizens' rights. This chapter presents the case of Bedouins' rights as indigenous people—mainly their rights to land and cultural continuity within the context of the Israeli state. It also places the Bedouins' situation in a comparative context by examining the experiences of other nation-states—namely, Canada and the United States—and their relations with indigenous rights issues. Bedouins of the Naqab are pursuing both the rights of citizens and the rights of indigenous peoples. Israel, as a modernizing nation-state with an absence of internal cultural consensus, does not recognize Bedouin communities as indigenous and thus does not recognize their indigenous rights. Like most other countries, Israel does not offer an institutional mechanism for acknowledging indigenous land rights or self-government. Nation-states may not achieve consensual forms of citizenship or nationality without developing participatory mechanisms for including indigenous peoples as citizens with indigenous rights.

CHAPTER 7

Indigenous, Citizens', and Human Rights: The Bedouins of the Naqab

Duane Champagne

Introduction

Every indigenous community demonstrates specific patterns of government, community, culture, and relations to land. Nation-states also have unique histories, cultures, and patterns of land ownership. Colonial relations and histories between nation-states and indigenous peoples vary, and there has been a mixture of outcomes in terms of justice, human rights, and democratic participation. It is difficult to understand the contemporary condition and history of indigenous peoples without considering their relations to nation-states. Drawing from comparative cases of indigenous peoples' experiences, this chapter analyzes the human rights, citizens' rights, and indigenous rights of the Naqab (Negev) Bedouins. While there is undoubtedly overlap between these three categories of rights, citizens' rights—those rights an individual has by virtue of citizenship in a particular nation-state—are analytically distinct from both individual human rights and collective indigenous rights.

There are several key elements to understanding issues of democratic inclusion, human rights, and indigenous rights among the Bedouins in Israel. Institutions and democracies are generally more enduring, stable, and beneficial if based on consensus—meaning agreement and shared understanding about normative, social, and cultural ground rules, and willing participation by all parties. What is the consensual basis of Bedouin citizenship within Israel? Have the Bedouins been able to establish consensual dialogue with the Israeli state, thereby addressing indigenous rights and citizens' rights issues? Does the Israeli state recognize indigenous rights and peoples? How are land rights organized, and are Bedouins able to retain indigenous territories? What patterns of self-government are expressed by the Bedouins? In investigating these questions, this chapter explores the prospects of human rights, citizens' rights, and indigenous rights among the Naqab Bedouins in Israel.

Indigenous Rights

The recent passage of the Declaration on the Rights of Indigenous Peoples[1] by the United Nations (UN) General Assembly represents a significant advancement toward the formulation and protection of collective human rights. Its framework enables ethnic groups, sub-national groups, and indigenous groups to pursue collective land and cultural rights. While the Declaration is not legally binding, it does symbolize agreement over many issues concerning indigenous peoples and collective group rights, thereby creating an international moral benchmark against which nation-states can be measured. The Declaration thus provides legal and moral tools for the protection of indigenous peoples' rights.

There is no doubt that the Declaration extends our understanding of human rights. However, despite its existence, indigenous peoples worldwide continue to struggle to protect their lands, cultures, and forms of self-government. The difficulties that indigenous peoples face, though, are not merely problems of a lack of national legal protections or weak enforcement. Indeed, some countries have honored specific articles in the Declaration, and their courts have relied on the Declaration when deciding land issues and other cases related to indigenous peoples. There have also been indications that violent abuses of indigenous peoples in many nations have declined significantly since the 1990s, in part because of the increasing recognition of the indigenous movement (United Nations Permanent Forum on Indigenous Issues, n.d.; Nettheim, 2009:135–140; Das, 2001:135–140, 234–295; United Nations Department of Economic and Social Affairs, 2009: 9, 17, 25, 35, 84–85, 192–193).

Rather, the obstacles that indigenous peoples face are of a more fundamental nature. The Declaration does not fully recognize indigenous interpretations of self-government, land, culture, and relations between indigenous peoples and nation-states. A product of much discussion and compromise over thirty years, the Declaration represents a contemporary human rights doctrine within the institutional framework of nation-states. UN member states would not accept a document that worked outside the framework of contemporary nation-state principles of property, law, government, and the consensual assumptions of democratic states, such as acceptance of constitutions or organic documents, individual voting rights, and the rights and obligations of citizenship. In fact, one of the major compromises made during the drafting process consisted of framing the Declaration in collective human rights language while at the same time avoiding discussion of the political or governance powers exercised by indigenous peoples over their own land, people, cultures, and institutions. Countries, however, can utilize the Declaration to recognize collective rights and indigenous cultures within their own legal systems and governance structures. While the Declaration represents progress, it avoids the fundamental issue of indigenous autonomy that is at the root of most relations between indigenous peoples and nation-states.

Few countries recognize indigenous communities or rights. During the negotiation of the Declaration, many states argued that indigenous peoples were already citizens of nation-states and therefore already enjoyed the protections and rights of all citizens. Indigenous rights were viewed as an appeal for special rights, and the arguments for indigenous self-government were viewed as extralegal and an infringement of state sovereignty. In the end, governments compromised on the issue of "collective" human rights—rights that are applicable to groups of people—but they declined to recognize "indigenous" rights or indigenous peoples as self-governing entities with autonomy in relation to nation-states (Anaya, 2004b:13–16, 2008; Riley, 2007:1120–1124; Henderson, 2008:22–24, 70–73, 80–89, 93).

What are indigenous rights and why are they at continuous loggerheads with nation-states? The indigenous argument holds that indigenous peoples existed before the formation of present-day countries. Most, if not all, democratic countries are less than 250 years old. Indigenous peoples and their forms of self-government, cultures, territories, and ways of life have existed for thousands of years, or from time immemorial—and in many indigenous worldviews, from the time of creation. Indigenous forms of government, community, culture, and land ownership differ profoundly from those found in market-based, democratic nation-states. There is no single form of indigenous political and cultural organization but rather thousands of unique traditions and political forms. Indigenous political arrangements often overlap with kinship, as well as cultural and economic relations and institutions, and therefore take on forms that governments refuse to recognize. While the nation-state is currently the predominant form of political organization in the international system, indigenous forms of political organization continue to persist and adapt, and have served their communities for thousands of years (see, e.g., Champagne, 2007).

Are there indigenous peoples living within the Israeli state? The Palestinian Arabs, who lived in Palestine before the establishment of Israel—and whose people represent urban communities, farming communities, and Bedouin communities—can make a strong argument for indigenous rights. The Bedouins of the Naqab have occupied the local desert for hundreds, if not thousands of years (Yiftachel,

2008:184–185). Indeed, there are biblical references to Abraham meeting and negotiating with the Bedouin peoples living around Beersheba. Bedouins had their own way of economic life and their own forms of family, kinship, tribe, and leadership. Despite many centuries of contact with a variety of civilizations, the Bedouins retained considerable political, cultural, and economic independence. By the late nineteenth and early twentieth centuries, Bedouin tribes were semi-nomadic and took up agricultural pursuits to complement their pastoral economy of herding animals. By the 1920s, the vast majority derived their livelihood from agriculture (Parizot, 2001:37–50; see Abu-Saad and Creamer, chapter 1, this volume). The Bedouins of the Naqab predated the formation of the Ottoman Empire, the British Mandate, and the Israeli state. The Ottomans and British did not force the Bedouins from their land, and they did not force Bedouins to adopt new economic modes or new forms of government. While the Bedouins conformed to the changing economic and political relations around them, much of their internal organizational structures and cultural views remained intact after the creation of the Israeli state (Yiftachel, 2008:180–181, 184–185; Balint, n.d.; Johal, 2004; Willacy, 2005; Abu-Saad, 2003; Mossawa Center, 2006:19).

Israeli Citizenship

Most democratic nation-states view their citizens as consensual participants in the political, economic, and cultural life of the national community and its institutions. This consensus is gained either through a democratic constitution or similar document, or through democratic participation in governance and legislation. In many ways, nation-states are based on the premise of a social contract. Their contemporary frameworks are inspired by Christian Protestant views of individual free will and commitment to the rules of the community or nation. In principle, nation-states are large-scale voluntary associations. In democratic countries, consensual citizenship is generally viewed as the norm, even if many governments still employ birthright criteria to grant citizenship.

Within legal and political science scholarship on citizenship, these two conceptualizations—that of ascriptive, or birthright, citizenship and that of consensual citizenship—are often juxtaposed. The ascriptive understanding grounds citizenship in the "objective circumstance" of "birth within a particular sovereign's allegiance or jurisdiction" (Schuck and Smith, 1985:4). In contrast, the consensual understanding of citizenship derives from contractarian political theorists, such as John Locke, and supports a liberal vision of political membership within the nation-state as being based on "free individual choices" (Schuck and Smith, 1985:4). Consensual citizenship as a form of membership within a political community can be established only when there is mutual agreement between the political community and the individual pursuing membership. Consent, in this Lockean view, entails an individual's expression of willingness to "submit" to a government and its institutions in exchange for certain citizenship rights, benefits, and protections.[2]

This notion of citizenship becomes problematic in the context of indigenous participation in nation-states, as many indigenous peoples and communities are not voluntary participants in the countries in which they reside. This perspective is not one of resistance, or an anti-statist position, or even a rejection of the nation-state. Rather, most indigenous peoples were simply not asked to join the state, did not participate in its formation, and when inducted into the nation-state were not asked to give their consent to citizenship or to the political government or constitution. Most countries, rather than recognizing the governments or territorial rights of indigenous peoples, have attempted to incorporate these peoples as individual citizens into the state. Generally, indigenous peoples are declared citizens through a constitutional or legislative act that does not directly request their consent. Even when declared "formal" citizens, indigenous peoples in many countries are precluded de facto from exercising the full rights of citizenship (Nettheim, 2009; Dorough, 2010; Clavero, 2009; Wessendorf, 2009).

In 1953, Israel granted mandatory citizenship to the Bedouins. The Bedouins were not involved in the formation of the Israeli state, and they did not grant their consent to become Israeli citizens, especially since it entailed the loss of land rights, self-government, and cultural identity. From 1949 until 1966, even though the Bedouins were classified as citizens, they were placed under Israeli military rule. They were not granted full citizenship rights and could exercise few, if any, civil rights (Mossawa Center, 2006:10). Under these conditions, the Bedouins continued their usual cultural, political, and economic lives to the extent possible. For instance, the Israeli government recognized or appointed nineteen existing and new sheikhs and asked Bedouin communities and individuals to ally themselves with one of the sheikhs. The sheikhs acted as intermediaries between the Israeli government and the Bedouin communities, and thus the Israeli state did not deal directly with Bedouin individuals but rather acted through their sheikhs (Jamjoum, 2009; Koeller, 2006).

By all accounts, Bedouins were citizens without full rights, and not citizens by consent (Johal, 2004). The type of citizenship granted to the Bedouins has been identified as "transparent," "invisible," "ghettoized," and even "captive citizenship" (Swirski and Hasson, 2006:2–11; see also Yiftachel, 2009). Captive citizens exercise few civil rights, often are not citizens by consent, and face costly or barred exit possibilities (Paul, 1991:41–49).

In some cases, indigenous peoples have attempted to work within the nation-state structure. For example, during the 1960s, Saami populations in Nordic countries elected members to their countries' national parliaments. However, in more recent decades, the Saami have withdrawn from these national parliaments and formed their own indigenous parliaments, which are currently negotiating with Nordic countries over land, resource rights, and powers of self-government. Thus, after trying to work within the structure of national governments, the Saami ultimately determined that they could not exercise their indigenous rights and powers within this framework—demonstrating how difficult it is for indigenous peoples to work within the nation-state structure (Josefsen, 2005; United Nations Permanent Forum on Indigenous Issues, 2007). Other countries, such as Ecuador and Taiwan, have tried forming indigenous political parties, and Brazil has incorporated protections for indigenous peoples directly into its Constitution. The efforts of working within nation-state structures have met with continued negotiation and mixed success (Poiconu, 2009; de Beldi, 2009; Ortiz, 2009).

Many indigenous peoples reject the individualization of citizen participation in nation-states, in part because it disregards indigenous powers and rights. Many indigenous individuals and communities are willing to join nation-states as citizens, but not at the price of second-class citizenship or the loss of collective protections, self-government, and territorial rights. In Canada and the United States, this debate between citizenship and indigenous rights is resolved through an informal recognition of dual citizenship of the nation-state and tribal nations (Poiconu, 2009; de Beldi, 2009; Ortiz, 2009). Most countries, however, do not recognize indigenous rights and require indigenous peoples to adhere to national norms in the same respect as all other citizens.

Consensual Ground Rules

Indigenous peoples do not share the same understandings of political culture and institutions as the nation-states within which they reside. Under these circumstances, indigenous peoples are therefore reluctant to participate wholly in nation-states at the expense of abandoning their own forms of governance (Champagne, 2005). However, indigenous peoples are often willing to participate in nation-state institutions if their participation does not mean de-indigenization and if it is consensual and respectful of their indigenous rights to land, self-government, and cultural autonomy. Yet because states are generally unwilling to recognize the special characteristics and needs of indigenous peoples, and because there is little agreement on institutional, political, and cultural ground rules, discussions between states and indigenous peoples about citizenship and indigenous rights are often fruitless (see, e.g., Ackerman, 2004:447, 455, 459; Mossawa Center, 2006:25–26). Furthermore, indigenous peoples' lack of participation in nation-state institutions and cultures tends to politically, economically, and culturally marginalize indigenous peoples. In many countries, non-participating indigenous peoples are treated like a lower caste, suffering discrimination because they dress differently, live differently, or speak different languages (Clavero, 2009).

The Israeli government and the Bedouins have not agreed on fundamental issues of culture, religion, citizens' rights, political order, or economic organization, among other things (Abu-Ras, 2006:2; Kuper, 2005:29–30; Association of Civil Rights in Israel, 2002:6–8; Parizot, 2001:104–105; Jamjoum, 2009; Mossawa Center, 2006:19, 25). Bedouin cultural and social values have not been recognized or incorporated into the organization of the Israeli state. Since the 1960s, Israel has focused on reorganizing Bedouin communities by encouraging them to abandon their home territories and take up residence in planned towns (Swirski and Hasson, 2006:4–5). The towns have been a way of removing Bedouins from their traditional land and encouraging them to enter contemporary Israeli economy as detribalized, secular, and individualized workers. Many Bedouins, despite the presence of both positive and negative incentives, have not been willing to give up their traditional lands or their traditional ways of life. Many have thus refused to move to the planned towns (Parizot, 2001:100–102). Such intense loyalties to preserving community and culture are common among indigenous peoples, who refuse to adopt wholesale a new set of cultural and social values. Instead, they emphasize finding solutions to the challenges of contemporary issues through methods informed by their own cultural and institutional viewpoints. For example, during the United States' energy crisis of the 1970s, the Northern Cheyenne were living on a small, impoverished Indian reservation in Montana. They refused lucrative coal mining and coal-gasification projects out of fear that such projects would attract non-Cheyenne to the reservation and would overwhelm and destroy the community. They favored economic development, but only those projects that did not threaten the integrity of their community and culture (Champagne, 2007).

The Israeli state is a bit more unique in terms of its dealings with indigenous communities and cultures. While the government has declared its desire to adopt a constitution, no constitution has been agreed upon yet. Importantly, indigenous issues have not been central to this inability to form a constitution. Rather, intra-Jewish cultural differences concerning the character of the Israeli state (whether it should be a religious or a secular state) and Jewish-Palestinian issues (particularly regarding the definition of the state as Jewish or for "all its citizens") have been at the root of this lack of consensus over fundamental cultural ground rules for the Israeli state (see, e.g., Yiftachel, 2002:38–42; Rouhana, 2006; Mossawa Center, 2006:16).

In its laws, in addition to being defined as democratic, Israel has been defined as a Jewish state; thus, the state has been exclusionist in some areas against non-Jewish citizens, who do not enjoy full citizenship or civil liberties.[3] This impasse has created political instabilities within the state that have negatively affected the rights and actions of non-Jewish citizens. Since there has been no strong cultural and institutional consensus at the core of the Israeli state, protections of civil rights, especially for non-Jewish citizens, have been inconsistent and unreliable. Advocates for a secular Israeli state have offered the possibilities of an engaged civil society with human rights for all Israeli

(Jewish and non-Jewish) citizens. Hence, many non-Jewish citizens have favored the vision of a secular democratic state as opposed to an ethnic Jewish state.

The lack of consensus at the core of the Israeli state has exacerbated the inability and unwillingness to extend full civil rights to Bedouin citizens. The Israeli government has usually been composed of various political parties in coalition, as no single party is able to command enough seats to maintain power. These differing coalitions, which do not include non-Jewish parties, have resulted in differing demands on the government, in turn diminishing the priority placed on the civil rights of non-Jewish, particularly indigenous, Israeli citizens (Yiftachel, 2003:22, 26–28). Bedouin communities have had little power or influence over political processes, and indigenous rights and viewpoints have rarely, if ever, been considered in policy discussions (Boteach, 2008:23–25). A similar lack of action on indigenous rights has also been seen in Canada, where numerous political parties tend to prevent consensus and action on indigenous matters, despite many reports, including a Royal Commission report, urging governmental action on a number of indigenous issues (Mitchell, 2005; Carino, 2009; Royal Commission on Aboriginal Affairs, 1996).

Without greater consensus for a more equal society, there is little likelihood of extending full rights to Bedouin and non-Jewish citizens (Yiftachel, 2002). Neither the liberal secular state model nor the ethnic Jewish state model proposed for Israel would provide consensual mechanisms for entertaining the voices, values, or interests of Bedouins or other indigenous communities.

Israeli De Facto Recognition of Indigenous Bedouins

The non-consensual character of indigenous citizenship in nation-states results in a form of coercion: indigenous peoples are forced to participate in governments, cultures, and institutions with which they do not agree. At best, indigenous peoples form a small part of the citizenry, albeit one that is both powerless and marginalized. Although the discursive premise of the Declaration on the Rights of Indigenous Peoples is the recognition of indigenous peoples, in practical terms indigenous peoples can seek redress only within the institutions of the nation-states in which they reside, while their indigenous rights are not fully recognized or realized. As described above, most nation-states do not formally recognize indigenous peoples, and there are few active national-level discussions concerning the realization of indigenous rights (Anaya, 2004a:7, 37, 42, 50–55, 137, 144–148, 267; International Labour Organization, 2009:8–34, 58–79).

Israel has not formally recognized indigenous peoples. Nevertheless, the Israeli state has sometimes undertaken practical recognition of traditional Bedouin governing structures, communities, and culture. Israel has a long historical tradition of practically recognizing Bedouin leadership. During the Ottoman period, Bedouin patterns of self-government consisted of a confederation of tribes under the leadership of sheikhs. By the early 1900s, the Turks recognized seven separate tribal groups of Bedouins living in Beersheba. During the British Mandate, the British also recognized the political leadership of the sheikhs and established a tribal court in Beersheba (Likhovski, 2006:12–42). The diverse tribal groups recognized by the British became administrative units, and the sheikhs were enlisted to collect taxes in support of the British Mandate (Marteu, 2005:271–274). This recognition and use of intermediary traditional local leadership was undertaken in large part to maintain social order and stability.

Between 1948 and 1966, the Israeli government continued the policy of traditional intermediary leadership for pragmatic reasons and recognized the leadership and tribal organization of the Bedouins through nineteen sheiks. These sheikhs were appointed by the Israeli government and subordinated to military rule, though they assumed considerable political influence within their tribes. However, this governing arrangement with the Bedouins was not established through consensual agreements; hence, there were no written contracts, agreements, or treaties (Jamjoum, 2009). Israeli policy during this time was designed largely to maintain military control over Bedouin communities.

This period of military control from 1948 to 1966 is analogous to the periods of military control over indigenous peoples in the United States and Canada during the late nineteenth and early twentieth centuries. In both cases, military authorities co-opted tribal leadership to gain greater control over indigenous peoples and their assets. In both the United States and Canada, from the 1870s until at least the 1930s, military and then civilian authorities assumed complete control over tribal communities. Indigenous peoples were moved to small reservations incapable of sustaining either traditional or Western economies. The governments assigned Indian agents to manage these reservations, where the agents, carrying out governmental policies, exercised control over many aspects of Indian life and actively sought to destroy tribal culture by transforming Indians into national citizens who would abandon tribal life. Children were exported to boarding schools and taught American or Canadian culture, and were encouraged to take up Christianity. Tribal leadership and government was generally discouraged (Williams, 1980; Evans, 2002: chs. 1–5; Miller, 1990; Cross, 1998–1999). Similarly, during that same period, the Bedouins were controlled by local military commanders (and subsequently by other civil bodies) and since the 1960s have been subjected to "modernization" and forced urbanization.

In 1966, the Israeli government changed its policy toward the Bedouins, reducing its reliance on the political leadership of Bedouin sheikhs for administering and controlling Bedouin communities. This act of withdrawing recognition of traditional Bedouin political leadership and tribal organization was not based on consensual discussions with the Bedouin peoples. Instead, the Israeli state created and implemented new policies regarding the Bedouins without their agreement or input (Yiftachel, 2003).

With the end of military rule in 1966, the administration of Bedouin affairs moved from the military to the Ministry of the Interior. The Ministry of the Interior's mandate, in accordance with governmental policy, included the relocation of Bedouins from their lands and their concentration in urban localities, thus freeing up land for governmental use, particularly new Jewish settlements (Yiftachel, 2003). This emphasis on land policy is analogous to the delegation of indigenous affairs to the Department of the Interior in the United States, where the primary purpose of the Office of Indian Affairs between 1888 and 1934 was to survey Indian land, distribute it in small plots to tribal members, and then sell surplus land to U.S. citizens. According to the U.S. government's land policy, indigenous peoples were not utilizing the land productively and therefore were to be removed from the land, placed on small reservations, and invited to join the nation-state as individual citizens (Carlson, 1981; McDonnell, 1991; Otis, 1973).

The Israeli state relied on a liberal democratic modernization argument, as well as arguments derived from the principles of the ethnic Jewish state, to justify the appropriation of Bedouin lands. The modernization argument did not recognize the continuity of Bedouin communities or their rights as indigenous peoples. According to this argument, the Bedouins were a hindrance to achieving national economic plans, and the best future for them was to urbanize, join modern Israeli society, and abandon tribal life, culture, and political organization (Abu-Ras, 2006). If the Bedouins were not willing to modernize, so the argument went, the state would enforce policies to forcibly modernize Bedouin communities without their consent. Advocates of the ethnic Jewish state saw the Naqab as new territory for Jewish settlement, and the removal of the Bedouins as a necessary means to make the land available for productive Jewish-Israeli citizens (Yiftachel, 2008:176; Abu-Ras, 2006:1–2, 7). Neither liberal democratic nor ethnic Jewish state policies recognized Bedouin rights to territory, self-government, or cultural autonomy. The Israeli state thus used coercive methods to achieve its goals of land appropriation and assimilation.

Modernization, Termination, Resettlement, and the White Paper

This policy of urbanization among the Naqab Bedouins is analogous to the Termination Policy in the United States and the White Paper plans in Canada in the early 1960s. The three policies and their timing are so similar that it is highly unlikely that they were each developed in a vacuum. The Israeli government shared similar values, at least those of the liberal democratic state, with the U.S. and Canadian governments and adopted some of the same strategies for managing internal indigenous affairs.

In the Unites States, the Termination Policy was implemented between the 1950s and the 1970s, although repercussions of this policy continued for much of the rest of the twentieth century. Ultimately, approximately 110 tribal communities were "terminated." The Termination Policy severed the government-to-government relations between American Indian governments and the U.S. federal government in an attempt to withdraw recognition of Indian governments and communities and induce indigenous peoples to adopt individual citizenship. After becoming full citizens, American Indians would presumably enjoy the benefits of modern society and a market economy. However, many tribal communities opposed the Termination Policy and mobilized against it in concert with local and state governments, which saw the policy as an unfunded mandate and a drain on their resources. They succeeded in ending most congressionally approved termination legislation by 1960. The tribal communities desired full citizenship, but not at the expense of giving up their collective rights to tribal governments, land, and cultural autonomy. Most terminated tribes re-acquired federal recognition after 1975 by petitioning Congress or winning lawsuits. This restoration of federal recognition reestablished nation-to-nation relations between the federal government and terminated tribes. The restored tribes returned to wardship status with federal trust protections and were subject to federal administration (Daly, 2009; Philp, 1999; Peroff, 1982; Fixico, 1986; Walch, 1983; Grobsmith and Ritter, 1992). The tribes defeated the forced full citizenship proposed by the Termination Policy and established de facto dual citizenship. To the present day, however, the dual citizenship model has not been formally recognized by the U.S. government.

In Canada during the late 1960s, the Trudeau administration issued the White Paper, a policy plan that similarly outlined the dismantling of tribal governments and the privatization of land in return for the promise of full citizenship and political equality for all indigenous peoples. Tribal communities countered with the Red Paper, which helped initiate a long period of indigenous activism and mobilization. The Red Paper, also known as "Citizens Plus," argued that the political equality proposed in the White Paper ignored inherent indigenous rights to self-government, territory, and cultural and political autonomy that predated the formation of the Canadian state. This mobilization eventually resulted in greater participation of indigenous leaders in the Canadian government, fuller citizenship rights for indigenous peoples, and extended negotiations with governmental officials regarding indigenous rights (Cairns, 2000; Robertson, 2008; Sherbert, 2006:384–388).

Israeli policy after 1966 was similar to that of the United States and Canada, with traditional Bedouin political structures, as well as their physical communities and lands, ignored or unrecognized. Israeli policy was designed to politically, economically, and culturally assimilate Bedouins by requiring them to vacate their land and migrate to urban towns. All three governments were willing to use coercive methods, and all three assimilation programs met with significant organized opposition from indigenous peoples. In Israel, about half of the Bedouins of the Naqab refused to comply with the government's urbanization policy. Many Bedouins preferred to remain on their land despite tremendous pressures from the Israeli state (Abu-Saad, 2009:426). In recent years, Bedouins in the unrecognized villages have continued to assert indigenous claims to land, economic development, and cultural autonomy.

The recognized towns, into which half of the Bedouin population was relocated, have not been effective platforms for economic assimilation. Like many Indian reservations in the United States and Canada, the recognized towns have lacked economic or marketable assets and contained very little economic infrastructure, making them the poorest localities in the country. Furthermore, the recognized towns have not enjoyed full powers of self-government similar to other towns in Israel, even when they have locally elected mayors and councils (as their authority has been very limited over local administrative matters). Israeli governmental bodies and officials have continued to retain many mechanisms for controlling the recognized towns (Swirski and Hasson, 2006:6–7; see also Abu-Saad and Creamer, chapter 1, this volume; Amara and Miller, chapter 2, this volume). Contemporary theory and policy in the United States and Canada suggest that tribal communities must retain powers to manage their own governments, territories, cultures, and economies (Cornell and Kalt, 1992, 1998:187; Colliou, 2005:53–57; Riley, 2007:1094–1099). However, there are few opportunities under externally managed government structures, such as that of Israel, for indigenous peoples to develop fair and efficient governments and market-based economic participation.

The Israeli government has continued its policy of assimilation and of dismantling Bedouin social, economic, and political institutions. This process has engendered cultural and social disruption among Bedouin communities and has led to considerable social distress, such as high crime, unemployment, and physical and mental health problems (Abu-Saad, 2000, 2009:425–426; Swirski and Hasson, 2006:7–11; Kuper, 2005:30; Parizot, 2001; Negev Coexistence Forum for Civil Equality, 2006:1–31). Such policy outcomes, whether intentional or unintentional, violate both indigenous and citizens' rights. Despite the relatively greater attention that Canada and the United States have paid to their respective indigenous communities' social welfare, indigenous groups in these countries still suffer disproportionately negative social and economic consequences. Hence, policy and theoretical research has continued to search for sustainable and effective alternatives that are supportive of both indigenous and citizenship rights. Ultimately, though, any such alternatives rely heavily on the political will of nation-states to implement them.

The Bedouin Advancement Authority

During the 1980s, the administration of Bedouin affairs moved from the Ministry of the Interior to the Bedouin Advancement Authority (BAA). Both the name and the exclusive administrative focus of this body represent recognition by the Israeli state that Bedouin issues cannot be managed within the agencies designed for all Israeli citizens. While the Israeli government established specific and clearly named governmental agencies to manage Bedouin affairs, these bodies were not necessarily intended for the benefit of Bedouin communities. The BAA, as part of its mandate, has seen to the task of preventing permanent settlement by Bedouins in the unrecognized villages; when permanent structures have been built, several Israeli agencies have had the power to dismantle them (Jamjoum, 2009; see also commentary on the Green Patrol in Abu-Saad and Creamer, chapter 1, this volume).

Furthermore, the Israeli government has fully controlled Bedouins' education through the Ministry of Education (for the recognized towns) and the Bedouin Education Authority (BEA) (for the unrecognized villages). Like in the United States, Canada, and elsewhere, education of indigenous children has been geared toward producing individual assimilation. Such efforts tend to challenge indigenous cultures and often leave indigenous children in a state of anomie, in which they have limited cultural anchors, especially if the nation-state does not fully welcome their entry into its society and economy (Abu-Saad, 2001). Indigenous children need to have access to the educational benefits of the nation-state, but also need to receive an education that enables them to remain intellectually tied to their own communities and cultures.

The primary activities of the BEA have emphasized the dismantling of Bedouin communities and neglected to foster Bedouin entry into the twenty-first century as a collective community that seeks consensual relations within the Israeli state. The governmental agencies assigned to manage Bedouin affairs have not actively supported Bedouin communities in the development of their land, cultural, and political resources to advance Bedouin economic and community well-being. While the Israeli state pragmatically has worked with the Bedouin communities, it has done so only from its own point of view and interests (Abu-Saad, 2001).

The Bedouin Unrecognized Villages Movement

Bedouins living in the unrecognized villages have lacked basic services, such as electricity, running water, and adequate health and educational facilities. The unrecognized villages also have lacked official local addresses, and therefore Bedouins have been unable to vote in local or municipal elections in Israel. However, Bedouins have formed a recognizable political element that has had practical visibility. The patterns of leadership in the unrecognized villages have continued the traditions of local self-rule, where sheikhs often command significant respect within their communities. In the recognized towns, Bedouin leadership has become more professionalized, with less emphasis on kinship patterns and relations to sheikhs (Marteu, 2005:278–290). Overall, while tribal identities have become more symbolic, kinship ties continue to have political and economic significance and functionality (Parizot, 2001; Willacy, 2005). Political relations between the Bedouins and Israeli authorities have been characterized by patronage, yet the Bedouins' political organization has represented indigenous interests and views on land and self-government, as well as a desire for full citizenship rights (Marteu, 2005:278–290; Negev Coexistence Forum for Civil Equality, 2006:11–12).

In May 1997, the unrecognized villages formed their own local committees within a regional council, fashioned after the language of the Israeli municipal political system. The Regional Council for the Unrecognized Villages (RCUV) sought formal recognition for the villages from the Israeli government. Since 2000, some of the unrecognized villages have been recognized and included in a new regional council, Abu Basma, headed by a Jewish appointee of the Ministry of the Interior. However, this "recognition" has required the villages to be rebuilt according to the same urban style of the previously recognized towns, which has led to overcrowding and not provided the opportunity for agricultural activity (Yiftachel, 2008:179; Swirski and Hasson, 2006:5–6; New Israeli Fund, n.d.).

Furthermore, despite officially recognizing some of these villages, the Israeli government has continued to disregard indigenous rights to self-government or territory. Instead, the newly recognized villages and the appointed regional council have been recognized as entities comprised of individual citizens within the Israeli state. The Bedouins in the newly recognized and in the unrecognized villages, represented by several non-governmental organizations, including the RCUV, have opposed urbanization and desired greater partnership and consultation in decisions that affect their communities (Abu-Ras, 2006:7; Jamjoum, 2009).

In Canada and the United States, indigenous communities have lived under a variety of traditional and Western forms of democratic governance. For example, in 1920 the Canadian government imposed "band governments," comprising an elected chief and a band council, on indigenous communities, although the administration and resources of the band governments were and have continued to be tightly controlled by the Canadian government. Over the past few decades, the Canadian government has been negotiating, but not necessarily encouraging, more autonomous assertions of self-government among Canadian bands.[4] Both U.S. and Canadian indigenous individuals have retained citizenship of their respective nation-state governments but have not forfeited indigenous membership, political government, or rights to territory.

Indigenous nations living within the boundaries of nation-states can be characterized, under certain circumstances, as "captive nations" (Snip, 1985, 1986; Paul, 1991:41–49). The imposition of nation-state policies, culture, and government places captive indigenous nations in coercive conditions that suppress expressions and realizations of culture, self-government, and community. Only consensual recognition and co-governance relations can alleviate the nation-state's imposition of power and culture over captive indigenous nations (Abu-Saad, 2009:447, 455, 459).

Indigenous Territory

Land is a critical element for indigenous peoples, one that is very often considered a gift granted to the people from the creator. While indigenous peoples may not "own" land in a Western sense of the term, they have the sacred task of preserving the land in its ecological complexity and balance. Overexploiting the land will result in disaster and a decline in future resource opportunities. Specific territories are recognized among indigenous peoples, and allocation of land and land-use rights are governed by rules that are known and respected among kinship groups and tribes. Indigenous peoples see land as a collective gift; while individuals or groups have use of the land, the land returns to the collective nation when not used by any individual member or family.

The Bedouins of the Naqab lived off the land for centuries. Their semi-nomadic lifestyle and land-use patterns existed for hundreds of years prior to the creation of the Israeli state. The Bedouins had their own customary system for land use and rights, as well as their own institutions for reconciling land-related disputes (see Kram, chapter 3, this volume). Throughout history, many empires and nations have encroached on Bedouin territory and political autonomy, and the Bedouins have engaged in diplomacy, relations, and economic trade with many of them. No empire, however, forced the Bedouins to reorganize their land-use patterns or challenged their collective right to the land. The Ottoman Empire, though, did classify the Naqab as "No Man's Land"—a term implying that there were no owners of the land where Bedouins grazed their sheep and engaged in agriculture (Swirski and Hasson, 2006:2–3; Yiftachel, 2003:21–47). Under Ottoman rule, the Bedouins were thus encouraged to register their land under the Empire's rules of land ownership. Still, few Bedouins recognized Ottoman powers over their land, and few registered their land with the Ottoman bureaucracy. Similarly, during the British Mandate, although the Bedouins became a more sedentary and agricultural-based community, most Bedouins did not register their land according to British bureaucratic methods and rules. Instead, Bedouin land rights and land use continued to be governed by their customary system, known and followed by Bedouins (Abu-Ras, 2006:2; Shamir, 1996:101–126).

After 1948, when the Israeli state assumed governmental control over the Naqab, Bedouin communities maintained their ties to the land. The 1948 War was a severe disruption, however, causing the vast majority of Bedouin individuals and families to become a diaspora.

Many Bedouin families were not allowed to return and reclaim traditional lands and livelihoods. About 11,000 Bedouins remained and were removed to the Restricted Area in the Naqab. The Israeli state treated the Naqab as state-owned land and started nationalizing and registering this land under different legal procedures (see Amara and Miller, chapter 2, this volume). One of these legal tools was the 1950 Absentee Property Law (Transfer of Property Law), which enabled Israel to confiscate the land of all Palestinian refugees, including Naqab Bedouins. Later, in 1953, the Land Acquisition (Validation of Acts and Compensation) Law validated transfers of already seized lands, as well as lands to be seized in the future, to the Israeli state (Swirski and Hasson, 2006:3). Few Bedouins won land claims against the Israeli state because the government recognized only those documents from the Ottoman Empire or the British Mandate, and not other intra-communal documents of land sale or lease. Most Bedouins did not have documents from either of the previous governments, since most held land under Bedouin rules and institutions (Abu-Ras, 2006:2–3, 6; see Amara and Miller, chapter 2, this volume). Bedouin land-use rights, like those of many other indigenous groups around the world, have been upheld in oral tradition and continuing consensual relations, and not on paper (Swirski and Hasson, 2006:3; Yiftachel, 2003:28–42; Johal, 2004; Abu-Saad, 2009:424).

In Canada and the Unites States, indigenous rights to territory have been upheld in treaties and congressional acts. While both countries have failed to recognize indigenous ownership in the Western sense of the term, they have recognized indigenous rights to use and occupy land undisturbed. Under the doctrine of discovery, both Canada and the United States have claimed ownership over land by means of the right of first discovery by a Christian sovereign. According to this doctrine, lands of non-Christians could be conquered, the people Christianized, and the land put under control of the Christian king. While the Catholic Church had abandoned the doctrine of discovery by 1690, the doctrine still became enshrined in common law in both countries.[5]

According to Canadian and U.S. law, Indians have the right to use the land and the right to sell the land, but only to the national government. In the Royal Proclamation of 1763, the King of Britain declared that Indians were subjects of the King and that the land they lived on was crown land, directly owned and managed by the King. Indians used the land and lived on the land in a usufructuary manner, but only at the pleasure of the King. Recently, Indian land in Canada has remained "Crown Land," and Indians have been unable to sell land to private parties; they have been permitted to surrender their use rights only to the Canadian state, hence putting them under the trust and protection of the sovereign state.[6] In the United States, the Supreme Court upheld the principles of British law and the doctrine of discovery in *Johnson v. M'Intosh*.[7] In its decision, the Court ruled that American Indians could not sell land to private parties; rather, they could sell only to the U.S. government, which assumed control over formerly British lands following the War of Independence. As a result, the Piankeshaw Indians were prohibited from conveying land titles to private parties.

Canadian and U.S. nation-state control over Indian land has entailed protection, or trust, over the land. As long as Indians live on the land and use the land for their purposes, these countries' governments are bound to ensure that third parties do not pillage or dispossess Indians from the land. For the Naqab Bedouins, the doctrine of "No Man's Land" that was applied to the Naqab by the Israeli government suggested that the land was empty (*terra nullius*) and therefore property of the state. This doctrine, used around the world to dispossess indigenous peoples, does not recognize indigenous land ownership or indigenous government, and does not provide protection or recognition of even usufructuary use of the land by indigenous peoples (see Sheehan, chapter 6, this volume). Under this doctrine, the

Bedouins have thus been seen by the Israeli state as squatters on land that their ancestors held from time immemorial.

Until recently, in the Canadian province of British Columbia, no indigenous rights to land use were recognized. However, over the past several decades, the indigenous tribes of British Columbia have presented their claims before provincial and national courts and have won the right to negotiate land claims and establish recognized tribal governments. The new treaties between the government and the tribes were based on *Delgamuukw v. Queen*, in which the Canadian Supreme Court, relying in part on oral history evidence gathered from tribal elders, recognized aboriginal rights to territory.[8] Most countries, including the United States, have not accepted oral evidence in support of land claims, thus undermining the validity of the customary oral land rights system of indigenous peoples. After *Delgamuukw*, the Indian nations of British Columbia and the provincial government engaged in comprehensive and wide-ranging negotiations over land claims and governmental powers. However, the provincial government's unwillingness to recognize inherent rights to self-government among the tribes has been a barrier to mutually satisfactory resolutions of land and self-government issues. Nevertheless, the *Delgamuukw* case provides an example of how the contemporary Israeli government could reconsider Bedouin land claims supported by oral evidence and thus recognize indigenous territory (see, e.g., Freedman, 1994).

Neither the vision of a liberal democratic government nor an ethnic Jewish state have provided mechanisms for mutually consensual recognition and acceptance of indigenous self-government or indigenous territory (Abu-Ras, 2006:8; Jamjoum, 2009; Amara, 2008). The liberal democratic Israeli state has insisted on individualized and documented land claims from indigenous communities that possess primarily oral and consensual relations for land use and occupation. The ethnic Jewish state has preferred to further Jewish control and domination through the removal of Bedouins from the land and through its use for Jewish settlers or other state projects (Abu-Saad, 2009:427; Mossawa Center, 2006:5). Neither of these models for national government has recognized indigenous land or autonomy, or the right of continuity of Bedouin culture. Bedouin claims to territory, along with Bedouin understandings of life and land use, have thus remained outside the ground rules of the Israeli state.

Conclusion

The Declaration on the Rights of Indigenous Peoples (as well as international human rights instruments generally) and Israeli citizenship have provided little direct value to the Bedouins of the Naqab. While international non-governmental organizations and Israeli civil society groups have been instrumental in advocating for indigenous rights and civil rights, the Israeli state has not recognized Bedouins' indigenous status, and governmental policies have not facilitated Bedouin cultural, political, or economic autonomy. Furthermore, the two primary models proposed for Israel's government, the ethnic Jewish state and the liberal democratic state, have not recognized indigenous status or provided for a protective political framework. Without recognition of the Bedouins as indigenous peoples, it is very difficult—morally, legally, and politically—to benefit from the collective human rights outlined in the Declaration on the Rights of Indigenous Peoples.

Bedouins have lived in Israel as captive citizens and a captive nation. They have been denied the rights of full citizenship and indigenous status. Israeli policies toward the Bedouins have focused on assimilation and the dismantling of Bedouin culture, government, social order, and land ownership. The cultural core of the Israeli state has inhibited recognition of civil and indigenous rights for the Bedouins. While the liberal democratic state model holds the possibility of full citizenship, it promises no mechanisms for recognition of indigenous land rights or self-government. Without recognition of indigenous rights in addition to civil rights, indigenous Bedouin communities have been denied the cultural, educational, political, territorial, and economic expression necessary to maintain their communities and identities. As indigenous peoples, they seek to participate as full citizens in the nation-state while at the same time retaining their territorial rights, institutions of self-government, and respect for their cultures (Boteach, 2008:24).

The relationship between nation-states and indigenous peoples should be based on mutual understanding. In the absence of such understanding, the collective human rights outlined in the Declaration will not be realized by many indigenous communities. The comparative examples from Canada and the United States discussed in this chapter demonstrate that other countries have adopted policies similar to those of Israel with respect to indigenous groups. But at the same time, these comparative experiences also highlight significant differences in how these nation-states have treated and interacted with indigenous peoples. There has been renegotiation and reconsideration of some relational aspects between these governments and their indigenous peoples on issues ranging from land rights, self-government, and cultural and economic autonomy. Although they do not provide ideal solutions, the Canadian and U.S. examples may help inform the Israeli state in reconsidering its own policies toward the Naqab Bedouins. If indigenous communities are not included as consensual partners in cooperative or co-governance arrangements, there will be little in the way of human rights improvements. There will also be little in the way of the complete development of democratic nation-states, for countries will not realize full democracy until they can ensure consensual participation by indigenous peoples and the recognition of indigenous rights.

REFERENCES

Abu-Ras, T. (2006). "Land disputes in Israel: The case of the Bedouin of the Naqab." *Adalah's Newsletter* 24:1–9.

Abu Saad, I. (2000). *Bedouin Towns at the Start of the 21st Century: The Negev Bedouin and the Failure of the Urban Resettlement Program.* Beersheba: Ben-Gurion University of the Negev.

———. (2001). "Education as a tool for control vs. development among indigenous peoples: The case of Bedouin Arabs in Israel." *HAGAR International Social Science Review* 2(2):241–259.

———. (2003). "The Bedouins' complaint: 'How can we be called intruders if we and our ancestors have been living in the Naqab for thousands of years?'" *Karkah* 57:31–34 (Hebrew).

———. (2009). "The Palestinian Bedouin in Israel." In K. Wessendorf (ed.), *The Indigenous World 2009* (pp. 422–429). Copenhagen: International Work Group for Indigenous Affairs.

Ackerman, J. (2004). "Co-governance for accountability: Beyond exit and voice." *World Development* 32(3):447–463.

Amara, A. (2008). "The Goldberg Committee: Legal and extra-legal means of solving the Naqab Bedouin case." *HAGAR Studies in Culture, Polity and Identities* 8(2):227–243.

Anaya, S. J. (2004a). *Indigenous Peoples in International Law.* 2nd ed. New York: Oxford University Press.

———. (2004b). "International human rights and indigenous peoples: The move toward the multicultural state." *Arizona Journal of International and Comparative Law* 21:13–61.

———. (2008). "International Indigenous Rights Situation." Presentation before the International Advisory Committee for the Native Nations Institute, Morris K. Udall Center for Studies in Public Policy. Tucson, Arizona, January 12.

———. (2009). "The rights of indigenous peoples to self-determination in the post-Declaration era." In C. Charters and R. Stavenhagen (eds.), *Making the Declaration Work: The United Nations Declaration on the Rights of Indigenous Peoples* (pp. 184–198). Copenhagen: International Work Group for Indigenous Affairs.

Association of Civil Rights in Israel. (2002). *A Status Report: Equality for Arab Citizens of Israel.* Jerusalem: Association of Civil Rights in Israel.

Balint, J. L. (n.d.). "The Bedouin in Israel: Israeli Bedouin have an ambiguous relationship with the state." http://www.myjewishlearning.com/israel/Contemporary_Life/Society_and_Religious_Issues/Arab-Israelis/The_Bedouin.shtml (accessed August 28, 2011).

de Beldi, M. L. A. (2009). "Brazil." In K. Wessendorf (ed.), *The Indigenous World 2009* (pp. 184–196). Copenhagen: International Work Group for Indigenous Affairs.

Biolsi, T. (2005). "Imagined geographies: Sovereignty, indigenous space, and American Indian struggle." *American Ethnologist* 32(2):239–259.

Borrows, J. (1994). "Constitutional law from a First Nation perspective: Self-government and the Royal Proclamation." *University of British Columbia Law Review* 28:1–48.

Boteach, E. (2008). *The Indigenous Bedouins of the Naqab-Negev Desert in Israel*. Omer, Israel: Negev Coexistence Forum for Civil Equality.

Cairns, A. (2000). *Citizen Plus: Aboriginal Peoples and the Canadian State*. Vancouver: University of British Columbia Press.

Carlson, L. A. (1981). *Indians, Bureaucrats, and Land*. Westport, CT: Greenwood Press.

Carino, J. "Poverty and well-being." In United Nations Department of Economic and Social Affairs (ed.), *State of the World's Indigenous Peoples* (pp. 13–50). New York: United Nations.

Champagne, D. (2007). *Social Change and Cultural Continuity Among Native Nations*. Lanham, MD: AltaMira Press.

———. (2010). *Notes From the Center of Turtle Island*. Lanham, MD: AltaMira Press.

———. (2005). "Rethinking native relations with contemporary nation states." In D. Champagne, K. J. Torgesen, and S. Steiner (eds.), *Indigenous Peoples and the Modern State* (pp. 2–23). Walnut Creek, CA: AltaMira Press.

———. (2009). "Contemporary education." In United Nations Department of Economic and Social Affairs (ed.), *State of the World's Indigenous Peoples* (pp. 129–154). New York: United Nations.

Clavero, B. (2009). "Cultural supremacy, domestic constitutions, and the Declaration on the Rights of Indigenous Peoples." In C. Charters and R. Stavenhagen (eds.), *Making the Declaration Work: The United Nations Declaration on the Rights of Indigenous Peoples* (pp. 344–350). Copenhagen: International Work Group for Indigenous Affairs.

Clifford, J. (2004). "Traditional futures." In M. Phillips and G. Schochet (eds.), *Questions of Tradition* (pp. 152–168).Toronto: University of Toronto Press.

Colliou, B. (2005). "The culture of leadership: North American indigenous leadership in a changing economy." In D. Champagne, K. J. Torgesen, and S. Steiner (eds.), *Indigenous Peoples and the Modern State* (pp. 53–67). Walnut Creek, CA: AltaMira Press.

Cornell, S., and K., Joseph. (1992). "Reloading the dice: Improving the chances for economic development on American Indian reservations." In S. Cornell and J. P. Kalt (eds.), *What Can Be Done? Strategies and Institutions in American Indian Economic Development* (pp. 1–59). Los Angeles: UCLA American Indian Studies Center.

———. (1998). "Sovereignty and nation building: The development challenge in Indian country today." *American Indian Culture and Research Journal* 22(3):187–214.

Cross, R. (1998–1999). "American Indian education: The terror of history and the nation's debt to the Indian peoples." *University of Arkansas at Little Rock Law Review* 21:940–978.

Daly, H. P. (2009). "Fractured relations at home." *American Indian Quarterly* 33(4):427–439.

Das, J. K. (2001). *Human Rights and Indigenous Peoples*. New Delhi: A.P.H. Publishing Corporation.

Deloria, V., Jr., and Lytle, C. M. (1984). *The Nations Within: The Past and Future of American Indian Sovereignty*. Austin: University of Texas Press.

Dorough, D. S. (2010). "Human rights." In United Nations Department of Economic and Social Affairs (ed.), *State of the World's Indigenous Peoples* (pp. 190–217). New York: United Nations.

Evans, S. (ed.). (2002). *American Indians in American History, 1870–2001*. Westport, CT: Praeger.

Fixico, D. (1986). *Termination and Relocation: Federal Indian Policy, 1945–1960*. Albuquerque: University of New Mexico Press.

Freedman, B. (1994). "The space for aboriginal self-government in British Columbia: The effect of the decision of the British Columbia Court of Appeal in Delgamuukw v. British Columbia." *University of British Columbia Law Review* 28:49–90.

Grobsmith, E. S., and Ritter, B. R. (1992). "The Ponca Tribe of Nebraska: The process of restoration of a federally terminated tribe." *Human Organization* 51(1):1–16.

Henderson, J. Y. (2008). *Indigenous Diplomacy and the Rights of Peoples: Achieving UN Recognition*. Saskatoon, Saskatchewan: Purich Publishing.

International Labour Organization. (2009). *Indigenous and Tribal Peoples' Rights in Practice: A Guide to ILO Convention No. 169*. Geneva: ILO. http://www.ilo.org/indigenous/Resources/Guidelinesandmanuals/lang--en/docName--WCMS_106474/index.htm (accessed July 14, 2011).

Jacobson, R. (2006). "Characterizing consent: Race, citizenship and the new restrictionists." *Political Research Quarterly* 59(4):645–654.

Jamjoum, H. (2009). "Ongoing displacement of Palestine's Southern Bedouin." *The Palestine Chronicle*, February 3. www.palestine-chronicle.com/view_article_details.php?id=14786 (accessed September 12, 2011).

Johal, A. (2004). "Israel's Bedouin losing ground." *Anti-War.Com*, July 29. www.antiwar.com/ips/johal.php?articleid=3205 (accessed September 12, 2011).

Josefsen, E. (2005). "The experience of the Saami 'Indigenous Parliament.'" In K. Wessendorf (ed.), *Realities and Perspectives in Russia and the Circumpolar North* (pp. 178–205). Copenhagen: International Work Group for Indigenous Affairs.

Kades, E. (2000). "The dark side of efficiency: *Johnson v. M'Intosh* and the Expropriation of American Indian Lands." *University of Pennsylvania Law Review* 148(4):1165–1190.

Koeller, K. (2006). "The Bedouin of the Negev: A forgotten minority." *Forced Migration Review* 26:38–39.

Kuper, R. (2005). "Don't say you didn't know about the Arab citizens of Israel." *Al-Aqsa* 7(2):25–30.

Likhovski, A. (2006). *Law and Identity in Mandate Palestine*. Chapel Hill: University of North Carolina Press.

Marteu, E. (2005). "Some reflection on how the Bedouin women of the Negev relate to politics: Between political marginalization and social mobilization." *Bulletin du Centre de Recherche Francais de Jerusalem* 16:271–286.

McDonnell, J. (1991). *The Dispossession of the American Indian*. Indianapolis: Indiana University Press.

Miller, J. R. (1990). "Owen Glendower, Hotspur, and Canadian Indian policy." *Ethnohistory* 37(4):386–415.

Mossawa Center. (2006). *Palestinian Arab Citizens of Israel: Status, Opportunities and Challenges for an Israel-Palestinian Peace*. Haifa, Israel: Mossawa Center.

Negev Coexistence Forum for Civil Equality. (2006). The Arab-Bedouins of the Naqab-Negev Desert in Israel: Shadow Report Submitted to the UN Committee on the Elimination of Racial Discrimination. Omer, Israel: Negev Coexistence Forum for Civil Equality.

Nettheim, G. (2009). "Human rights and indigenous peoples." *Cosmopolitan Civil Societies Journal* 1(2):129–141.

New Israeli Fund. (n.d.). "The paradox of ethnicity and citizenship." http://www.nif.org/issue-areas/israeli-arabs (accessed August 28, 2011).

Ortiz, P. (2009). "Ecuador." In K. Wessendorf (ed.), *The Indigenous World 2009* (pp. 148–160). Copenhagen: International Work Group for Indigenous Affairs.

Otis, D. S. (1973). *The Dawes Act and the Allotment of Indian Lands.* Norman: University of Oklahoma Press.

Parizot, C. (2001). "Gaza, Beersheba, Dhahriyya: Another approach to the Negev Bedouins in the Israeli-Palestinian space." *Bulletin du Centre de Rescherche Francais de Jerusalem* 9:37–50.

Paul, S. (1991). "Accountability in public services: Exit, voice and capture." World Bank Policy Research Working Paper Series No. 614.

Peroff, N. C. (1982). *Menominee Drums: Tribal Termination and Restoration, 1954–1974.* Norman: University of Oklahoma Press.

Philp, K. R. (1999). *Termination Revisited: American Indians on the Trail to Self-Determination, 1933–1953.* Lincoln, NE: University of Nebraska Press.

Poiconu, P. (2009). "Taiwan." In K. Wessendorf (ed.), *The Indigenous World 2009* (pp. 301–308). Copenhagen: International Work Group for Indigenous Affairs.

Riley, A. R. (2007). "Good (native) governance." *Columbia Law Review* 107:1049–1125.

Robertson, C. (2008). "Trickster in the press: Kainai editorial cartoonist Everett Soop's framing of Canada's 1969 White Paper events." *Media History* 14(1):73–93.

Rouhana, N. (2006). "Jewish and democratic? The price of a national self-deception." *Journal of Palestine Studies* 35(2):64–74.

Royal Commission on Aboriginal Affairs. (1996). *Report on Aboriginal Peoples.* Ottawa: Parliament of Canada.

Schuck, P. H., and Smith, R. M. (1985). *Citizenship without Consent: Illegal Aliens in the American Polity.* New Haven, CT: Yale University Press.

Schwartz, D. S. (1986). "The amorality of consent." *California Law Review* 74(6): 2143–2171.

Shamir, R. (1996). "Suspended in space: Bedouins under the law of Israel." *Law and Society Review* 30(2):101–126.

Sherbert, E. (2006). "Culture and an aboriginal charter of rights." In G. Sherbert, A. Gérin, and S. Petty (eds.), *Canadian Cultural Poesis: Essays on Canadian Culture* (pp. 381–398). Waterloo, Ont.: Cultural Studies Series.

Snipp, C. M. (1985). "Essentially, American Indians are captive nations." In R. Hummelen and K. Hummelen (eds.), *Stories of Survival: Conversations with Native North Americans* (pp. 9–11). New York: Friendship Press.

———. (1986). "The changing political and economic status of the American Indians: From captive nations to internal colonies." *American Journal of Economics and Sociology* 45:457–474.

Steinman, E. (2009). "Dual citizenship of American Indian tribal members: Newly substantive rights and social conflict." Paper presented at the annual meeting of the Law and Society Association. Chicago, May 26.

Swirski, S., and Hasson, Y. (2006). *Invisible citizens: Israel government policy toward the Negev Bedouin.* Tel-Aviv: Adva Center.

United Nations Department of Economic and Social Affairs. (2009). *State of the World's Indigenous Peoples.* New York: United Nations.

United Nations Permanent Forum on Indigenous Issues. (n.d.). "Advances in the recognition of indigenous rights since the adoption of the UN Declaration." Indigenous People Indigenous Voices fact sheet. http://www.un.org/esa/socdev/unpfii/documents/PFII8_FS1.pdf (accessed July 14, 2011).

———. (2007). "Presentation by the President of the Sami Parliament of Norway on a Nordic Sami Convention." New York, May 16.

de Vitoria, F. (1991). "On the American Indians." In A. Pagden and J. Lawrance (eds.), *Vitoria: Political Writings* (pp. 231–292). Cambridge: Cambridge University Press.

Walch, M. C. (1983). "Terminating the Indian Termination Policy." *Stanford Law Review* 35(6):1181–1215.

Wessendorf, K. (ed.). (2009). *The Indigenous World 2009.* Copenhagen: International Work Group for Indigenous Affairs.

West Bank First Nation. (2003). "Westbank First Nation and Canada sign historic self-government agreement." Turtle Island Native Networks Forum, October 3. http://www.turtleisland.org/discussion/viewtopic.php?p=2865 (accessed September 12, 2011).

Willacy, M. (2005). "Israel: Bedouin, last of the nomads." *ABC TV broadcast*, February 22.

Williams, W. L. (1980). "United States Indian policy and the debate over Philippine annexation: Implications for the origins of American imperialism." *Journal of American History* 66(4):810–831.

Yiftachel, O. (2003). "Bedouin-Arabs and the Israeli settler state: Land policies and indigenous resistance." In D. Champagne and I. Abu-Saad (eds.), *The Future of Indigenous Peoples: Strategies for Survival and Development* (pp. 21–47). Los Angeles: American Indian Studies Center, UCLA.

————. (2008). "Epilogue: Studying Naqab/Negev Bedouins; Toward a colonial paradigm?" *HAGAR Studies in Culture, Polity and Identities* 8(2):173–191.

————. (2009). "Ghetto citizenship: Palestinian Arabs in Israel." In N. Rouhana and A. Sabagh (eds.), *Israel and the Palestinians: Key Terms* (pp. 56–60). Haifa, Israel: Mada Center for Applied Research.

————. (2002). "The shrinking space of citizenship: Ethnocratic politics in Israel." *Middle East Report* 223:38–45.

NOTES

1. Declaration on the Rights of Indigenous Peoples, G.A. Res. 61/295, U.N. Doc. A/Res/61/295 (2007). In the context of examining the relationship between nation-states and indigenous communities, this chapter will refer to this Declaration as a standard-setting framework for indigenous rights. However, it will not directly address or examine the Declaration's legal provisions. See Stavenhagen and Amara (chapter 4, this volume).
2. For discussions of the theoretical and philosophical underpinnings of consensual citizenship, see, e.g., Jacobson (2006); Schuck and Smith (1985); Schwartz (1986).
3. See Basic Law: Human Dignity and Liberty (1992), art. 8; Mossawa Center (2006:17–19).
4. See, for instance, the self-government agreement between Canada and West Bank First Nation. West Bank First Nation (2003).
5. For early discussion on this point, see de Vitoria (1991:231–292).
6. The Proclamation of 7 October 1763. See also Borrows (1994).
7. *Johnson v. M'Intosh*, 21 U.S. (8 Wheat.) 543 (1823). See, e.g., Kades (2000).
8. *Delgamuukw v. British Columbia*, [1997] 3 S.C.R. 1010, para. 117. Analogous extensions of legal evidence and interpretation have occurred in the courts of New Zealand and Australia. See Clifford (2004).

CHAPTER 8

Naqab/Negev Bedouins and the (Internal) Colonial Paradigm

Oren Yiftachel

The concluding chapter to this volume charts the main approaches to the study of Bedouins in the Naqab (Negev) and argues for re-situating that study within an internal colonial scholarly paradigm. In such a paradigm, Bedouins can be defined as an indigenous community subject to a process that began as colonialism imposed from the outside and has continued as "internal colonialism" since the end of military government in the late 1960s. This chapter highlights three promising perspectives within this paradigm—settler society, indigeneity, and "gray space"—that form an initial step in redefining the field. The ideas proposed here undoubtedly need further elaboration, substantiation, and reflection, and the review presented below is not exhaustive. Neither are the ideas entirely new, as some authors—albeit very few—have already used the colonial paradigm for the Bedouin question.

Indigenous (In)Justice makes an important contribution to the field by treating the Bedouin Arabs of southern Israel/Palestine as an indigenous group, subjected in recent times to the regime of a modern settler state. To the best of the editors' knowledge, this is the first scholarly book on the Bedouins to take this approach, which is most notable

I wish to thank Ahmad Amara, Ismael Abu-Saad, Avinoam Meir, Cédric Parizot, Sandy Kedar, Safa Abu-Rabia, Yuval Karplus, Arnon Ben-Yisrael, and Batya Roded for their useful comments. An earlier and shorter version of this chapter was published in 2008 as "Epilogue: Studying Naqab/Negev Bedouins; Toward a colonial paradigm?" in *HAGAR Studies in Culture, Polity and Identities*.

in the chapters by Ismael Abu-Saad and Cosette Creamer (chapter 1), Ahmad Amara and Zinaida Miller (chapter 2), Rodolfo Stavenhagen and Ahmad Amara (chapter 4), and John Sheehan (chapter 6), but which runs as a theme in the other chapters as well.

However, the novelty of our volume further highlights the limits of existing paradigms for studying Bedouin society. These paradigms have been framed chiefly by the concepts of modernization, urbanization, politics of identity and gender, and, most recently, globalization. The settler-indigenous axis—so central in understanding the Naqab— is by and large absent (see Karplus and Meir, forthcoming).

The limitations of past studies begin with the definition of "Naqab Bedouin society." This "society" is part of a wider Arab society that lived in the region until its eviction in 1948. While the Bedouins of the Naqab share distinct cultural, geographic, and ethnic characteristics, they continue at the same time to be embedded within far wider networks in Sinai and Transjordan, the Palestinian West Bank and Gaza, and of course Israel itself (Parizot, 2004). The usage of this category should therefore be constantly problematized as reflecting a forced separation of the Naqab Bedouins from other parts of their own society. I have chosen to use the "Naqab (Negev) Bedouins" terminology in this chapter chiefly because it is the name most commonly used by this community itself, both in Arabic and Hebrew. However, I use the term with full acknowledgment of this community's existence within the larger Palestinian and Bedouin Arab societies, and not as a marker of distinct existence.

The most common scholarly approach has treated the Bedouins, previously locally known as Arab a-Sabi'a (Arabs of Beersheba), as nomads undergoing a process of sedentarization. Rich studies have traced the Bedouins' subsequent modernization, urbanization, and family, economic, political, and societal transformation (see, e.g., A.

Abu-Rabia, 2001; Al-Ham'amde, 1997; Ben-David, 2004; Dinero, 2004; Kressel, 1993; Marx, 1967, 2000; Meir, 1994, 1997; Porat, 2009). These works have dealt with issues such as immigration (Ben-David and Gonen, 2001), housing, economy, community transformations (Ben-Yisrael and Meir, 2008), and—most importantly—land (see Kressel, 2007; Kedar, 2004; Meir, 2005, 2009; Levin, Kark, and Galilee, 2010; Franzman and Kark, 2011).

Much attention has been devoted in academic and professional literature to the planning of Bedouin settlements according to the "best" modern knowledge (see Ben-Arie, 2009; Stern and Gradus, 1979; Gradus and Stern, 1979; Ben-David, 1991; Kliot and Medzini, 1985; Medzini, 2007; Soffer and Bar-Gal, 1985; Razin, 2000). More critical studies have conceptualized the Bedouins as a peripheral minority within a centralizing, ethnic state, experiencing multiple deprivations and marginalities (Abu-Bader and Gottlieb, 2008; Tarrow, 2008; A. Abu-Rabia, 2001; Fenster, 1993, 1999; Meir, 1988; Nevo, 2003; Negev Coexistence Forum for Civil Equality, 2003). These studies have focused on patterns of discrimination against the Bedouins and on their geographical, economic, and political marginalization (see, e.g., Abu-Saad and Lithwick, 2000; Swirski, 2008; Swirski and Hasson, 2006). Other studies have linked Bedouin marginality to a series of communal crises and pathologies, such as growing crime rates, communal violence, and pervasive alienation (A. Abu-Rabia, 2001; Ben-David, 2004; Meir, 1997).

Another recent approach has treated the Bedouins as part of the divided Palestinian Arab nation, embroiled in an ongoing struggle with the Israeli state. This approach focuses on land, identity, Arabness, culture, Palestinization (see, e.g., Abu-Saad, Yonah, and Kaplan, 2000; Cook, 2003; Falah, 1989; Abu-Sitta, 2001, 2010; Bar-On and Kassem, 2003; Parizot, 2004; Hameissi, 2009; Human Rights Watch,

2008), and, most recently, the Nakba and its ever-present impact on Bedouin life (S. Abu-Rabia, 2008; Abu-Mahfouz, 2008). An offshoot of this approach, but coming from an opposite political and ideological perspective, sees the rapidly growing Bedouin community as part of the Arab and Palestinian geographic and demographic threat to the supposedly embattled Jewish state. This common Israeli-Jewish discourse is led by the works of Arnon Soffer and by a variety of analysts associated with Israeli land and planning authorities (Soffer, 2007, 2009; see also Altman, 2009; Zandberg, 2009; Krakover, 1999; for empirical analyses, see *Statistical Yearbook of the Negev Bedouin*, 1999, 2011).

Bedouin society has also been studied in recent years through the lenses of gender and globalization. The former places gender relations, especially the plight of Bedouin women, at the center of inquiry, showing the prevalence of deep patriarchy and observing increasing signs of mobilization and resistance among Bedouin women (Al-Krenawi and Graham, 1999; Abu-Bader and Gottlieb, 2008; Fenster, 2002; Abu-Rabia-Queder, 2008). The latter lens, the globalization perspective, explains the effect of worldwide economic and cultural trends on Bedouin life, linking them to an accelerating pace of social transformation, a marked decline in community cohesion, and growing Islamism, among other things (Gradus, 2008; Meir, 2006).

The Need for a New Perspective

The existing approaches, sketched above only very briefly, explore and explain key aspects of Bedouin life and grievance in the Naqab. Yet, they appear to largely skirt around a fundamental factor: Bedouins' existence as a colonized indigenous people residing within a settler state. This factor underlies much of the Bedouin experience since 1948 and has affected every aspect of Bedouins' lives. Colonialism, I argue, critically informs the modernization, dislocation, discrimination, and gender inequality experienced by the Bedouins.

Most Israeli scholarship considers the state's democratic, modern, and Western character as a given. This assumption is based on Israel's European origins, the self-perceptions of the state-founding elites, and the existence of formal and partial democratic and liberal "features" that have glossed over an ethnocratic state structure (see Yiftachel, 2006). To buttress this position, Israeli scholarship has used a set of erasure practices, including the near total dismissal of the Palestinian Nakba (the 1948 "disaster" during which two-thirds of Arabs in Palestine were driven out of Israel). Most historical and social science accounts skip over the events of the 1948 war and discussion of ethnic cleansing and destruction of Arab society in Palestine.

The routine treatment of Israel as Western and democratic also "necessitates" the bracketing out of the Palestinian refugee issue from analyses of Israeli society. In Israel, the post-1967 occupation was treated as temporary while awaiting resolution as part of a "peace process." In this vein, many studies have presented the Bedouins as "only" a peripheral community struggling to adjust to life in a modern Western society. An extension of this analysis has disconnected Bedouins from the history of the Nakba and daily reality of the occupation—both critical foundations of the Judaization policy, which also directly affects Bedouin life in the Naqab.

Hence, as already noted, the treatment of Bedouin society as a marginalized modernizing minority, important as it is, ignores a central factor in Bedouin existence since 1948—namely, Israel's ethnic internal colonialism in the Naqab. This colonialism has led directly to dispossession, displacement, and constant struggles with Israeli authorities for land, development, and housing rights. Bedouins' concentration into planned "development towns" has been marked by poverty and social degradation (see Abu-Saad, 2001; Yiftachel, 2003). Under the Israeli regime, Bedouins have become "invaders" of their ancestors' land and "obstacles" to development. Past scholarship has been unable to answer a simple question: why are the Bedouins discriminated against more than other minorities in Israel/Palestine?

The answer lies in two critical goals pursued by Zionist settler society: land and demography. Bedouins present acute impediments to Israel's ethnocratic regime (Law-Yone, 2003; Yiftachel, 2006) and its consistent push to Judaize (and hence de-Arabize) the territories under its control, both in Israel and the Occupied Palestinian Territories. Prior to 1948, Bedouins in the Naqab held vast expanses of lands, estimated at three to five million dunams in varying types of possession (Kedar, 2004). This helps explain the particular severity of what some scholars call the ethnic cleansing in this region, whereby some 80%–85% of Arabs were driven outside state boundaries during and after the 1948 war.

This enabled Israel to "legally" appropriate most of the Bedouins' land and allocate it for Jewish use. The Bedouins who remained in Israel were strictly controlled and their traditional land ownership system disregarded (see Kedar, 2004; Livnat-Raanan, 2010; Shamir, 1996), allowing the state to claim total territorial control. Demographically, the Bedouins are commonly accused of having "dangerously" high fertility rates that threaten the modern and enlightened way of life sought by the architects of Israeli society. In this respect, an overtly racist discourse has often existed, essentializing the Bedouins as different and inferior.

The above observation must be qualified, because the colonization of the Bedouins has not been the only face of Israeli policies, which display other characteristics, at times progressive and enabling. Moreover, Israeli policies have not been homogeneous, embodying competing approaches toward the management of Bedouins. Yet, it is imperative to understand that the Judaization approach has offered a hegemonic meta-narrative for most policy directions and has provided relatively clear limits for policy makers for over six decades.

Looking Again through a Colonial Lens: Settler Society, Indigeneity, and "Gray Space"

I suggest that scholars reexamine their approaches to the study of Bedouin Arabs under the Israeli regime. Credible research should no longer sidestep the issue of the Israeli ethnocratic regime, particularly Jewish colonization of Israel/Palestine. Analysts and policy makers should use the most comprehensive and robust analytical frameworks that can best interpret community dynamics (for some beginnings in this direction, see Abu-Saad, 2003, 2009; S. Abu-Rabia, 2008; Yiftachel, 2003, 2009b; Livnat-Raanan, 2010).

This does not mean, of course, that studies taken from other angles are of lesser value—rather, such studies would benefit from dealing seriously with the internal colonial dynamic. Further, the credibility of studies using the colonial angle would be tested by their engagement with other scholarly perspectives that highlight the complexity of societal processes beyond the colonizing-indigenous binarism.

Scholarly accuracy, however, is not the only aspect here; adopting a colonial framework is also an act of mobilization that unveils vitally important forces in a critical and possibly liberating manner. The use of the colonial "angle" also exposes the previous scholarly "politics of depoliticization," as it shows how overlooking the colonial setting conceals state and ethnic oppressions. Hence, my call is for a scholarship that would not only be accurate but also amend the distortions of the power-knowledge nexus of previous studies—that is, open up the scholarly discussions to approaches removed from state power, agenda, and vocabulary.

Let us move to some necessary definitions. Colonialism is, of course, a much-discussed and debated term. Space does not allow us to enter these debates here (see Fredrickson, 1988; Kipfer, 2007; Stasiulis and Yuval-Davis, 1995; Gregory, 2006: ch. 3). For this chapter, and based on the definitions provided by these scholars, suffice it to define colonialism as an external group's systematic project of seizing, appropriating, and expanding control over contested regions, lands, people, and resources. In colonial relations, the incoming group is placed "above" the land's previous inhabitants. Colonialism is not limited to the European form prevalent during "the colonial era." Throughout human history, other colonial systems have developed—most notably territorially contiguous systems of expansion, appropriation, and domination over neighboring groups and regions.

Colonialism can be both "external" (and hence often imperial), expanding beyond the boundaries of sovereignty, and "internal," affecting internal frontier areas. Internal colonialism is particularly important for this chapter. It implies the adoption of development, land, and planning policies that discriminate, exploit, and displace minority populations in frontier areas within the sovereign state. As developed by the works of Michael Hechter (1975), Elia Zureik (1979), Pablo Gonzalez Casanova (1965), and David Walls (2008), the relationship between settlers and an area's native population is similar to a colonial relationship between nations. The formal citizenship of the indigenous group, if such citizenship exists, is emptied of much of its content through a series of discriminatory laws and regulations. The internal colony produces resources and power for those ethnically or economically close to the government and generally alienates the indigenous population, which is different in its ethnic, religious, or racial identity.

With regard to studying the Bedouins, I suggest that important aspects of Bedouin life—such as modernization, urbanization, patriarchy, domination, education, tribalism, human rights, gender, and globalization—cannot be separated from this "meta" colonial point of reference. Consequently, I propose three main scholarly perspectives through which the colonized experience of the Bedouins should be studied: settler society, indigeneity, and "gray space." This is not an exhaustive list by any means but rather a suggestion for a preliminary research agenda that can tease out the profound impact of colonized subordination. As noted, these directions are not entirely new: previous studies have followed Zureik's pioneering study (1979) and framed Zionism within the colonial framework (see Kimmerling, 2004; Shafir, 1996; Yiftachel, 1992; Yuval-Davis and Abdo, 1995). Several studies have even analyzed practices of "internal colonialism" toward Israel's Palestinian citizens (see Falah, 1989; Yiftachel, 1996). However, as noted, apart from a few exceptions (see Abu-Saad, 2003; Yiftachel, 2003; Stavenhagen and Amara, chapter 4, this volume; Sheehan, chapter 6, this volume), very few scholars have used these colonial perspectives to explain the plight of Bedouins of the Naqab.

Settler Society

The settler society approach has long informed the study of the New World and has developed concepts critical to understanding the process of societal construction through "frontierism," immigration, settlement, new nationalism, and rapid development. Several important studies have started to analyze Israeli society within this framework, most notably headed by Baruch Kimmerling (1982, 2004), Gershon Shafir (1989), and Nira Yuval-Davis and Abdo (1995), who have focused mainly on the sociology and political economy of the immigration-settlement process, while largely neglecting the geography and planning aspects.

But geography, needless to say, is highly relevant for the interaction between Bedouins and the institutions, practices, legalities, and discourses of a Jewish settler society. The suggested research angle could focus on these interactions and interfaces, where lofty ideas of development and progress meet the naked internal colonialism project that typifies settler societies. In Israel, as is well known, the state has promoted long-standing goals of "conquering the wasteland," "making the desert bloom," and "Judaizing the frontier." Although settling the southern frontier has declined in recent years as a societal value, Judaizing the region has remained high on the Israeli government's agenda. New policy efforts have thus focused on increasing state land control, the allocating of land to Jewish settlements, and attempts to restrict Bedouin construction and cultivation (see Yiftachel, 2006: ch. 8).

The most visible and painful interaction between Bedouins and the Israeli state has been the practice of land dispossession. This has involved a denial of ancestral land rights, massive forced relocation, and persistent segmentation. Since 1948, Israel has conducted a concerted policy to Judaize the Land of Israel, or historic Palestine, building close to 1,100 Jewish settlements between Jordan and the Mediterranean Sea. At the same time, it destroyed over 400 Arab villages and forbade Arabs to build new localities anywhere in this territory. The only exception was the (coerced) concentrating of the Bedouins in the Jaleel/Galeel[1] and Naqab, for which the state has built twenty-eight Bedouin towns and villages to date. These localities offer urbanizing Bedouins a path of modernization and access to many urban services lacking in traditional Bedouin settlements. Despite this, however, the planned Bedouin localities have remained isolated and impoverished. As a result, most Bedouin landowners (claimers) have remained on their ancestral lands rather than move to the planned localities. The Bedouin experience must therefore be studied within these highly relevant geopolitics. This is particularly relevant to the Naqab region, where the state has worked to minimize Bedouin land control, block the return of refugees, and marginalize Bedouins in terms of planning, development, education, and local government status (see Abu-Saad, 2003).

Importantly, however, all settler societies are not identical, and a credible use of this perspective necessitates engaging with the specific nature of Zionist colonialism. This begins with the troubled history of persecution and genocide that drove Jews to Palestine, making Zionism in effect a "colonialism of refugees" (Yiftachel, 1997), with Israel being a recognized and sovereign Jewish state. Yet, an attitude of insecurity still prevails among many Jews and Israeli policy makers, despite massive augmentation in Israeli and Jewish power since the early Zionist days. This constitutes the basis of the enormous importance attached to "security" within the Israeli regime and its governing apparatus.

Scholars should also note the variety within Zionist groups and over time with regard to the colonization of Israel/Palestine. Several Zionist groups, such as Brit Shalom and the Communist Party, actively opposed the movement's colonialist attitudes and programs, while others, such as Etzel (the Irgun), promoted for decades not only the Judaization of Israel/Palestine but also Jewish control and settlement on the East Bank of the Jordan River. The variety of historical periods is also meaningful—Zionism's early stages were marked by legally legitimate methods of immigration and colonization, centering around land purchase and development programs coordinated with the colonial British regime. During these early periods, relatively little contact existed between Jews and Bedouins, and when it occurred it was generally amicable (Meir, 2009). The later stages of the Zionist project, on the other hand, were increasingly violent and outwardly colonial, peaking with the hotly contested occupation and illegal settlement of the West Bank.

Another important feature of Israeli settler society is the strong sense of Jews belonging to the land. Zionism not only aimed to find a safe haven for Jews but carefully chose the ancient Hebrew homeland (believed to be the cradle of Judaism) as its target territory. It mobilized to liberate Jews from their subaltern diasporic existence, thereby creating a strong sense of indigeneity among the settlers. In that respect, one may conclude that in terms of self-perception, *both Bedouins and Jews in the Naqab see themselves as indigenous.*

An additional factor is the intensifying diversity of Jewish society, which has deepened in recent years with the large-scale migration of ethnic Jews from the former Soviet Union and Ethiopia and with Israel's growing economic liberalization and the associated socio-economic gaps. These aspects—mentioned here only briefly—should be explored seriously as scholars ask questions about the interaction between Bedouins and the Israeli society and economy.

To complicate matters, the Naqab Bedouins were also formally included in the Jewish state, receiving formal citizenship in 1949–1950, which came into effect (at least formally) with the lifting of military government in the late 1960s. Citizenship has allowed Bedouins to campaign for rights and equality and to organize politically in a way not possible for Bedouins under other regimes. In some important ways, the Naqab Bedouins have used the spaces for mobilization offered by the Israeli system, most notably in the local politics of recognized towns, which have created a process of gradual democratization, built local autonomy, and hence mobilized the population.

Yet, outside their small enclaves, Bedouin citizenship remains largely formal—a method of registration, organization, and surveillance, offering negligible political clout. It has not allowed for genuine participation in state or regional affairs, nor has it served as a platform for receiving a fair share of public resources. The Bedouins have remained, as noted by Swirski (2008), "transparent citizens," observing the settler state mobilizing massive resources for Jewish seizure of their ancestors' lands (see also Noach, 2009; Livnat-Raanan, 2010; Tzfadia and Katz, 2010). The meaning of minority citizenship in such a settler society still awaits serious exploration. It is noteworthy that most Israeli scholars who study Bedouin land and resources have adopted the state's interpretation—that the indigenous population possesses no land ownership rights. They have written this explicitly (see Ben-David, 2004; Levin, Kark, and Galilee, 2009; Franzman and Kark, 2011; Kressel, 2007) or, more typically, have remained silent on the issue.

Characteristic of colonial engagements, Bedouins' interaction with the Israeli settler state has made them subject to policies of division and identity manipulation. In order to minimize their resistance, the state has attempted to emphasize their "Israeliness," divide them from other Palestinian communities in Israel/Palestine, and consequently de-Palestinianize and even de-Arabize their identity (see Yonah, Abu-Saad, and Kaplan, 2004). Bedouins have been frequently constructed as culturally "unique": an exotic people whose loyalty belongs to the desert and not to any particular culture or nation. While the Naqab Bedouins do possess their own cultural and ethnic features, they have always been part of the general Arab world and undoubtedly belong to the Arabs of Palestine. Their natural inclusion as "Palestinians of Bedouin origins" within Palestinian societies in exilic locations attests to this orientation, as clearly shown by Mazin Abu-Mahfouz (2008).

Scholars have also explored how Israel's divisive strategy has been accompanied by a system of partial co-optation whereby the state has attempted to incorporate the Bedouins while keeping them on the margins. In the Naqab, this strategy received support from some local Arab leaders who enshrined their leadership over towns and tribes with the aid of the state's colonizing apparatus. But state support came at a price: the state severed Bedouin ties with Palestinian and other Arab and Muslim groups, pressured Bedouins to serve in the Israeli army, and effectively obligated Bedouins to condone Judaization of the region outside its Arab enclaves (see Livnat-Raanan, 2010).

This identity regime has also attempted to segregate Bedouin society internally by supporting the traditional patriarchal tribal system and by condoning practices such as the marriage of close relatives and minors, pervasive and increasing polygamy (Al-Krenawi and Graham, 1999), and internal racism. The Israeli state even quietly condoned, until the late 1980s, the activities of the highly conservative Islamic movement, which was seen as providing a "softer" locus of identity than the national Palestinian movements' identity, which highlighted Palestinian national identity. Here lies a paradox: settler societies, including Israel, commonly represent themselves as modern and Western, yet they take actions to prolong and deepen reactionary practices among the local populations. These aspects have rarely been studied, and their exploration is critical to the interaction of the settling state with the indigenous population.

Finally, another important interaction worth studying is the rise of civil society. Specifically, Arab-Jewish organizations have begun to articulate a joint struggle on behalf of the Naqab's various ethnic communities. This has surfaced in joint regional struggles around environmental hazards, investment incentives, and tax concessions. While this is still a minor phenomenon, it is gradually influencing regional discourses and policies. Recently, several key civil society organizations with considerable funding have begun to construct a common Arab-Jewish space and struggle, in which the democratization of a (post)colonial settler society can be imagined, debated, and planned (see Negev Coexistence Forum for Civil Equality, 2011).

Indigeneity

An important field of study, highly relevant to the Bedouin experience, has recently developed around the experience of indigenous peoples and the concept of indigeneity. A range of theoretical, historical, and empirical studies have accumulated into a burgeoning body of knowledge about people residing in colonized regions and states who have subsequently become or been labeled "indigenous." This field illuminates the plight of minorities commonly ignored by previous state-centric approaches of knowledge generation. It has politicized the traditional anthropological and Orientalist approaches of studying these people as exotic phenomena to be "documented" prior to their likely disappearance through modernist assimilation. This politicization views "the indigenous" as an agent of history and a perpetrator of development and struggle—and no longer a passive recipient of colonial policies.

While there is no one definition of "indigenous," most studies and legal approaches emphasize the following features:

- prior occupation and use of colonized homeland regions
- maintenance of customs, laws, language, and cultures different from those of the colonizing group
- unbroken residence in the colonized region (save forced evictions)
- dispossession and economic marginalization
- loss of pre-existing self-rule

Indigenous status under the post-colonial approaches has become a claim for power, self determination, culture, and place (Smith, 1999; Tsosie, 2002; Howitt, 2006; Johnson et al., 2007). It combines scholarly approaches with an anticolonial surge, equipping colonized people not only with a critique of the powers ruling over their lives but with substantive knowledge about their history, struggles, and resistances. This body of knowledge has found its way to a wide range of fora in which indigenous peoples have developed strategies for turning their subordination into more equal coexistence with other groups now residing in their territory, while rebuilding their culture and sovereignty (see Abu-Saad and Champagne, 2006).

A particularly rich area of inquiry has revolved around different forms of indigenous legalities, customary laws, and regulatory systems, as well as the ability to imagine and design "multiple sovereignties" between indigenous groups and the modern nation-states established on their territories (see Burrows, 2005; Daes, 1999; Kedar, 2004). In addition, indigeneity has inspired new epistemologies drawing on native "ways of knowing" and traditional methods of managing indigenous lives (see Malone, 2007; Louis, 2007) and on new perceptions of politics, culture, and identities (see Riseth, 2007). The political climax of this genuinely global campaign was the 2007 adoption of the United Nations Declaration on the Rights of Indigenous Peoples,[2] which identifies a range of protections for the culture, land, and sovereignty of indigenous peoples.

This surge has led to a variety of political, legal, and cultural struggles in which indigenous peoples have begun to rally around their history, identity, and resources. One of the major achievements was the Australian High Court's famous 1992 *Mabo* decision,[3] which recognized for the first time the existence of native title in Australia and hence repealed the *terra nullius* doctrine used for over a century to annul aboriginal land rights (see Howitt, 2006). *Mabo* has had a major influence on indigenous peoples' land struggles worldwide, including the Bedouins in the Naqab, who have used the example of this Australian breakthrough in their dealings with Israeli authorities and courts (see Meir, 2009).

The relevance of the *Mabo* decision to the Naqab Bedouins is clear. Like Eddie Mabo's community, the Bedouins are a group that resided on ancestral land for centuries prior to Zionist European settlement, while subsequently facing dispossession and marginalization. Prior to Israeli rule, the Bedouins had a system of tribal governance and a set of well-established traditions and customary laws, which operated largely uninterrupted under the Ottoman and British colonial regimes (see Bailey, 1980, 2009; Luz, 2008; Avci, 2009; Meir, 2009; Falah, 1983, 1989; Abu-Sitta, 2003, 2010).

The history of every group is of course unique, but Bedouin history—particularly the manner in which Bedouins interact with the new rulers of their land—resembles in important ways that of other indigenous peoples, such as the Maori in New Zealand, Aborigines in Australia, and Zapatistas in Mexico; all lost their self-determination but have continued to struggle to regain land control and cultural autonomy (see Abu-Saad, 2008; Stavenhagen and Amara, chapter 4, this volume; Sheehan, chapter 6, this volume).

The indigeneity angle can develop these comparisons and interrogate fascinating questions regarding the impact of indigenous consciousness on the Bedouins' struggle, the rise of indigenous globalism, the intertwining of indigenous awareness, and Islam. In addition, research can explore the sensitive relations between the various segments of Bedouin society itself, in which stratification is often based on an internal "indigeneity order" whereby Arab immigrants and farmers (*fellaheen*), who came to the region mainly during the nineteenth century, enjoy a lower social status than those perceived as original land owners (*asliyeen*). Another sensitive issue is the relationship between the general Palestinian and specific Bedouin senses of indigeneity, as the two coexist in the struggle for a post-colonial future for Israel/Palestine.

"Gray Space"

Another angle in which to study Bedouin existence is the recent developments in political geography, globalization research, and urban studies, which explore the growing phenomenon of urban informality. This refers to enclaves, populations, and economies only partially incorporated into their "host" society. I have termed this phenomenon "gray space"—positioned between the "whiteness" of legality/approval/safety and the "blackness" of eviction/destruction/death. Gray spaces are neither integrated nor eliminated, forming pseudo-permanent margins around today's urban regions that exist partially outside the gaze of state authorities and city plans (see Yiftachel, 2009b).

In the urban policy sphere, including planning, gray spaces are usually quietly tolerated, while subject to derogatory discourses such as "contaminating," "criminal," and being a "public danger" to the desired "order of things." Typically, the concrete emergence of "stubborn" informalities is "handled" not through corrective or equalizing policy but through a range of delegitimizing and criminalizing discourses. This creates boundaries that divide urban groups according to their status—a process of "separating incorporation" and "creeping apartheid." This double-edged move tends to preserve gray spaces in a state of permanent temporariness—concurrently tolerated and condemned, perpetually waiting to be "corrected." A multitude of informalities has come to characterize a vast number of metropolitan regimes. While this phenomenon is deeply rooted in colonial times and urban planning (Perera, 2009), its recent manifestation in cities of the global South has amplified to the extent that more than half the population can be classified as "informal" (see Davis, 2006; Neuwirth, 2005; Roy, 2005, 2009; Yiftachel, 2009b).

The relevance to Bedouin society is obvious. Around the city of Beersheba, gray spaces have rapidly grown into sprawling expanses of Bedouin Arab shanty towns and villages, constructed of wooden and tin shacks (Yiftachel and Yacobi, 2004). This is a clear byproduct of Israeli policies, which have refused to recognize Bedouin ancestral land ownership, effectively turning the Bedouins into "invaders." Gray space is also evident in the planned Arab development towns around Beersheba, where squatters are increasingly occupying public open spaces. There is also a growing number of "temporary" Arab residents in the metropolis of Beersheba, who reside mainly in the dilapidated Ottoman Arab city center and the adjacent impoverished neighborhoods. While around one thousand professional Arabs are permanent residents of the city, a few thousand others constitute an "urban shadow." These people are usually not registered as city residents, nor are they represented in the city's local government; subsequently, they are denied basic communal services, such as Arab education facilities, places of worship, and political representation (see Abu-Saad, 2009; Yiftachel, 2009a).

The Bedouin experience around Beersheba could thus be more thoroughly studied and compared to the plight of indigenous urbanizing populations in vast regions of the global South. Studies have shown that in such regions, new types of ethno-class relations have been formed in today's cities, based on new spatial configurations of residence, power, and capital resources. This emerging urban order may be conceptualized as "inverse colonialism," which constitutes a de facto form of metropolitan governance, facilitating the dominant interests through limited minority mobility, alongside exploitation, denial, and segregation, within growing neoliberal metropolitan regions (see Mbembe and Nuttall, 2004; Roy, 2007).

In this sense, Naqab Bedouins' existence within globalizing Beersheba exposes them simultaneously to old and new types of colonial relations. The first alludes to the ethno-national expansion "from above," described earlier, whereby the dominant population seizes control over indigenous groups and their resources. The latter points to a new phase of centripetal colonialism, during which marginalized populations create gray spaces "from below." In this way, they become subject to exploitation and segregation, and are unevenly incorporated into the latest product of capitalist globalization (Mbembe and Nuttall, 2004; Davis, 2006). It is time to explore this aspect of Bedouins' existence and this additional layer of exclusion—namely, the economic relations forged under the current neoliberal age.

Sumood

Importantly, processes of colonization—both old and new—are never unilateral. In most cases, including that of the Naqab Bedouins, these processes meet resistance and change. Recent international studies have shown that in a wide variety of cases, colonized populations find resourceful ways to challenge, penetrate, and even prevail over oppressive power relations. Asef Bayat (2007), for example, notes the "quiet encroachment of the ordinary"; that is, the gradual, un-heroic movement of residents, traders, and workers who continue to pour into urban space as sites of opportunity. Further, Nihal Perera (2000) notes a process of inverse "indigenization" of colonial infrastructure. Arjun Appadurrai (2001), Ananya Roy (2007), and Tom Angotti (2006) show how local politics are organized in today's slums and how they are creating new hubs of globalizing civil society networks, often with a surprising effect on tempering centralized power.

The Bedouin Arabs, like most indigenous groups, have not been passive recipients of colonial and globalizing forces. A notable process of self-empowerment and politicization has taken place during the last few decades, with a stubborn struggle of *sumood*—the Palestinian Arab term for "hanging on" and surviving against persistent crises and difficulties. In the Bedouins' case, *sumood* has meant the daily and non-heroic effort to hold on to their ancestral land communities after several rounds of evictions and dispossessions (see Abu-Frich, 2010; Noach, 2009; Yiftachel, 2009a). This has been promoted through the formation of several civil bodies and institutions, most notably the voluntary Regional Council for the Unrecognized Villages, which has assumed a leadership role in guiding the Bedouin struggle.

Like most indigenous politics, which operate under the coercive, fragmenting, and luring attraction of colonial power, Bedouin politics have been highly volatile. They have waxed and waned between the need to present a united front against a dispossessing government and the deeply rooted tribalism, chauvinism, cynicism, and tensions emanating from differing agendas and personalities. Another source of tension exists vis-à-vis Northern Palestinians in Israel and the Palestinian national cause, both steeped in profound uncertainties and divisions, but framed within a common struggle and a post-colonial vision. For indigenous Bedouin communities, there are powerful and confusing forces at work daily as Bedouins negotiate their position within their traditional and colonized homeland.

Finally, resistance and survival under a colonizing regime also involve positive elements, such as the nurturing of cultural traditions and community spirit. As Barbara Ehrenreich (2007) and Raewyn Connell (2007) remind us, celebration and joy have always been a central part of native and minority life and survival, not least among the Palestinians (Serhan, 2008). Somewhat removed from the direct political arena, communal events such as weddings, holidays, youth activities, women's groups, art, poetry, and music sustain Bedouin communities and display their ability to enjoy and celebrate survival under harsh circumstances. This, too, can be a promising line for future cultural-political research.

Indigenous (In)Justice is indeed a major step in generating knowledge about the dynamics of settler-indigenous relations through the lens of the Bedouin Arab communities of southern Israel/Palestine. Yet, as this chapter illustrates, more is needed in order to unpack, understand, and challenge the (internal) colonial relations currently existing in the Naqab and, equally important, to construct ways to transform Naqab society into a post-colonial stage of indigenous injustice. This is a major challenge for future research and policy development.

REFERENCES

Abu-Bader, S., and Gottlieb, D. (2008). "Education, employment and poverty among Bedouin Arabs in southern Israel." *HAGAR Studies in Culture, Polity and Identities* 8(2):121–136.

Abu-Frich, A. (2010). "'Aleyhom' (attack) against the Bedouins." *Hevra* 46:22–23 (Hebrew).

Abu-Mahfouz, M. (2008). "The odyssey of the Abu-Mahfouz Tribe: From Al-Naqab to exile." *HAGAR Studies in Culture, Polity and Identities* 8(2):221–226.

Abu-Rabia, A. (2001). *A Bedouin Century: Education and Development among the Negev Tribes in the 20th Century.* New York: Berghahn Books.

Abu-Rabia, S. (2008). "Between memory and resistance, and identity shaped by space: The case of the Arab Bedouins." *HAGAR Studies in Culture, Polity and Identities* 8(2):93–120.

Abu-Rabia-Queder, S. (2008). *Excluded and Loved: Educated Arab Women in the Naqab.* Jerusalem: Eshkolot (Hebrew).

Abu-Saad, I. (2001). "Education as a tool for control vs. development among indigenous peoples: The case of Bedouin Arabs in Israel." *HAGAR International Social Science Review* 2(2):241–259.

———. (2003). "Israeli 'development' and education policies and their impact on the Negev Palestinian Bedouin." *Holy Land Studies* 2(1):5–32.

———. (2008). "Spatial transformation and indigenous resistance: The urbanization of the Palestinian Bedouin in southern Israel." *American Behavioral Scientist* 51:1713–1754.

———. (2009). "The indigenous Palestinian Bedouin in southern Israel." In K. Wessendorf (ed.), *The Indigenous World 2009.* Copenhagen: International Work Group for Indigenous Affairs.

Abu-Saad, I., and Champagne, D. (eds.). (2006). *Indigenous Education and Empowerment: International Perspectives.* Walnut Creek, CA: AltaMira Press.

Abu-Saad, I., and Lithwick, H. (2000). *A Way Ahead: A Development Plan for the Bedouin Towns in the Negev.* Beersheba: The Center for Bedouin Studies and Development and the Negev Center for Regional Development, Ben-Gurion University of the Negev.

Abu-Saad, I., Yonah, Y., and Kaplan, A. (2000). "Identity and political stability in an ethnically diverse state: A study of Bedouin Arab youth in Israel." *Social Identities* 6(1):49–61.

Abu-Sitta, S. (2001). *The End of the Palestinian-Israeli Conflict: From Refugees to Citizens at Home*. London: Palestine Land Society and Palestinian Return Centre.

———. (2003). "Beer Sheba: The forgotten half of Palestine." *Al Majdal* 18:32–37.

———. (2010). *The Denied Inheritance: Palestinian Land Ownership in Beer Sheba*. London: Palestine Land Society.

Al-Ham'amde, F. S. (1997). *Turâth Waqadâ' 'Ashâ'ir `Arab An-naqab*. Unpublished manuscript (Arabic).

Al-Krenawi, A. (ed.). (2004). *Psycho-Social Challenges of Indigenous Societies: The Bedouin Perspective*. Beersheba: The Center for Bedouin Studies and Development, Ben-Gurion University of the Negev.

Al-Krenawi, A., and Graham, J. R. (1999). "The story of Bedouin-Arab women in a polygamous marriage." *Women's Studies International Forum* 22(5):497–509.

Altman, G. (2009). "The young Bedouin generation learns the advantage of violating the law and is brought up to disrespect and disregard the state's requirements." *Karkah* 66:42–49 (Hebrew).

Angotti, T. (2006). "Apocalyptic anti-urbanism: Mike Davis and the planet of slums." *International Urban and Regional Research* 30(4):456–467.

Appadurai, A. (2001). "Deep democracy: Urban governmentality and the horizon of politics." *Environment and Urbanization* 13(2):23–43.

Avci, Y. (2009). "The application of Tanzimat in the desert: The Bedouins and the creation of a new town in southern Palestine, 1860–1914." *Middle Eastern Studies* 45(6):969–983.

Bailey, C. (1980). "The Negev in the nineteenth century: Reconstructing history from Bedouin oral traditions." *Asian and African Studies* 14(1):35–80.

———. (2009). *Bedouin Law from Sinai and the Negev: Justice without Government*. New Haven, CT: Yale University Press.

Bar-On, D., and Kassem, F. (2004). "Storytelling as a way to work through intractable conflicts: The German-Jewish experience and its relevance to the Palestinian-Israeli context." *Journal of Social Issues* 60(2):289–306.

Bayat, A. (2007). "The quiet encroachment of the ordinary." *Chimurenga* 11:8–15.

Ben-Arie, R. (2009). "Alternative spatial planning: Between the professional and the political." *Teorya Uvikoret* 34:93–122 (Hebrew).

Ben-David, J. (1991). *The Condition of the Negev Bedouin*. Jerusalem: Jerusalem Institute for Israel Studies.

———. (2004). *The Bedouins in Israel: Land Conflicts and Social Issues*. Jerusalem: Jerusalem Institute for Israel Studies (Hebrew).

Ben-David, J., and Gonen, A. (2001). *The Urbanization of the Bedouin and Bedouin-Fallakhin in the Negev*. Jerusalem: Floersheimer Institute for Policy Studies (Hebrew).

Ben-Yisrael, A., and Meir, A. (2008). "Renaming space and reshaping identities: The case of the Bedouin town of Hura in Israel." *HAGAR Studies in Culture, Polity and Identities* 8(2):65–92.

Burrows, J. (2005). *Recovering Canada: the Resurgence of Indigenous Law*. Ottawa: Native Press (electronic version).

Connell, R. (2007). *Southern Theory: The Global Dynamics of Knowledge in Social Sciences*. Melbourne: Allen and Unwin.

Cook, J. (2003). "Bedouin in the Negev face new 'transfer.'" The Middle East Research and Information Project (MERIP). http://www.merip.org (accessed November 17, 2011).

Daes, E.-I. A. (1999). "Human rights of indigenous peoples: Indigenous people and their relationship to land." U.N. Doc. E/CN.4/Sub.2/1999/18.

Davis, M. (2006). *Planet of Slums*. London: Verso.

Ehrenreich, B. (2007). *Dancing in the Streets: A History of Collective Joy*. London: Granta Publications.

Falah, G. (1983). "The development of the 'planned Bedouin settlement' in Israel 1964–1982: Evaluation and characteristics." *Geoforum* 14(3):311–323.

———. (1989). "Israel state policy towards Bedouin sedentarization in the Negev." *Journal of Palestine Studies* 18(2):71–90.

Fenster, T. (1993). "Settlement planning and participation under principles of pluralism." *Progress in Planning* 39(3):169–242.

———. (1999). "Space for gender: Cultural roles of the forbidden and the permitted." *Environment and Planning D: Society and Space* 17:227–246.

———. (2002). "Planning as control: Cultural and gendered manipulation and mis-use of knowledge." *HAGAR International Social Science Review* 3(1):67–86.

Franzman, S., and Kark, R. (2011). "Bedouin settlement in the late Ottoman and British mandatory Palestine: Influence on the cultural and environmental landscape, 1870–1948." *New Middle Eastern Studies* 1:1–22.

Fredrickson, G. (1988). "Colonialism and racism: United States and South Africa in comparative perspective." In G. Fredrickson (ed.), *The Arrogance of Racism* (pp. 112–131). Middletown: Wesleyan University Press.

Gonzalez Casanova, P. (1965). "Internal Colonialism and National Development." *Studies in Comparative International Development* 1(4):27–37.

Gradus, Y. (2008) "The Beer Sheva metropolis: Polarized multicultural urban space in the era of globalization." In Y. Gradus and E. Meir-Glitzenstein (eds.), *Beer Sheva: Metropolis in the Making.* Beer Sheva: Negev Center for Regional Development, Ben-Gurion University of the Negev (Hebrew).

Gradus, Y., and Stern, E. (eds.). (1979). *Beer Sheva.* Jerusalem: Keter Press Ltd. (Hebrew).

Gradus, Y., and Stern, E. (1985). "From preconceived to responsive planning: Cases of settlement design in arid environments." In Y. Gradus (ed.), *Desert Development: Man and Technology in Sparselands* (pp. 41–59). Dordrecht, Netherlands: Reidel.

Gregory, D. (2006). *The Colonial Present: Afghanistan – Palestine – Iraq.* Oxfrod: Blackwell Publishers.

Hameissi, R. (2009). "To exit the black box." *Karkah* 66:69–85 (Hebrew).

Hechter, M. (1975). *Internal Colonialism: The Celtic Fringe in British National Development.* Berkeley: University of California Press.

Howitt, R. (2006). *Rethinking Resource Management: Justice, Sustainability and Indigenous People.* London: Routledge.

Human Rights Watch. (2008). *Off the Map: Land and Housing Rights Violations in Israel's Unrecognized Bedouin Villages.* New York: Human Rights Watch.

Johnson, J., Cant, G., Howitt, R., and Peters, E. (2007). "Creating anti-colonial geographies: Embracing indigenous peoples' knowledges and rights." *Geographical Research* 45(2):3–17.

Karplus, Y., and Meir, A. (forthcoming). "Past and present in the discourse of Negev Bedouin geography: A critical review." In S. Abu-Rabia-Queder et al. (eds.), *Rethinking the Paradigms: Negev Bedouin Research 2000+.* London: Routledge.

Kedar, A. (2004). "Land settlement in the Negev in international law perspective." *Adalah's Newsletter* 8:1–7.

Kimmerling, B. (1982). "Settlers without frontiers." *The Jerusalem Quarterly* 24:114–128.

———. (2004). *Immigrants, Settlers and Natives: The Israeli State and Society Between Cultural Pluralism and Cultural Wars.* Tel-Aviv: Am Oved Press (Hebrew).

Kipfer, S. (2007). "Fanon and space: Colonization, urbanization, and liberation from the colonial to the global city." *Environment and Planning, D: Society and Space* 25: 701–726.

Kliot, N., and Medzini, A. (1985). "Bedouin settlement policy in Israel: Another perspective." *Geoforum* 16:428–439.

Krakover, S. (1999), "Urban settlement program and land dispute resolution: The State of Israel versus the Negev Bedouin." *GeoJournal* 47:551–561.

Kressel, G. M. (1993). "Nomadic pastoralists, agriculturalists and the state: Self-sufficiency and the state in the Middle East." *Journal of Rural Cooperation* 21:33–49.

———. (2007). "The availability of agricultural land in the Negev for the public and members of it: Bedouin and Jewish. *Mifne* (December):24–28 (Hebrew).

Law-Yone, H. (2003). "From sedentarization to urbanization: State policy towards Bedouin society in Israel." In D. Champagne and I. Abu-Saad (eds.), *The Future of Indigenous Peoples: Strategies for Survival and Development* (pp. 175–183). Los Angeles: American Indian Studies Center, UCLA.

Levin, N., Kark, R., and Galilee, A. (2010). "Maps and the settlement of southern Palestine, 1799–1948: An historical/GIS analysis." *Journal of Historical Geography* 36(1):1–18 (Hebrew).

Livnat-Raanan, Y. (2010). "Colonial governing of citizens: The case of the residents of the unrecognized Bedouin villages in the Negev." In C. Katz and E. Tzfadia (eds.), *Abandoning State: Surveillancing State: Social Policy in Israel, 1985–2008* (pp. 291–308). Tel Aviv: Resling (Hebrew).

Louis, R. P. (2007) "Can you hear us now? Voices from the margin: Using indigenous methodologies in geographic research." *Geographical Research* 45(2):130–139.

Luz, N. (2008). "The creation of Modernist Beer-Sheva: An Imperial(ist) Ottoman project." In Y. Gradus and E. Meir-Glitzenstien (eds.), *Beer-Sheva: Metropolis in the making* (pp. 163–178). Beersheba: Negev Center for Regional Development, Ben-Gurion University of the Negev (Hebrew).

Malone, G. (2007). "Ways of belonging: Reconciliation and Adelaide's public space indigenous cultural markers." *Geographical Research* 45(2):164–175.

Marx, E. (1967). *Bedouin of the Negev*. Manchester: Manchester University Press.

———. (2000). "Land and work: Negev Bedouin struggle with Israel bureaucracies." *Nomadic Peoples* 4(2):106–120.

Mbembe, A., and Nuttall, S. (2004). "Writing the world from an African metropolis." *Public Culture* 16:347–372.

Medzini, A. (2007). "Planning policy towards the Bedouins: Success or failure?" *Ofakim Begeographia* 67–68:237–251 (Hebrew).

Meir, A. (1988). "Nomads and the state: The spatial dynamics of centrifugal and centripetal forces among the Israeli Negev Bedouin." *Political Geography Quarterly* 6:251–270.

———. (1994). "Territoriality among Negev Bedouin in transition: From nomadism to sedentarism." In U. Fabietti and P. Zalzman (eds.), *The Anthropology of Pastoral Societies* (pp. 159–181). Como, Italy: Ibis.

———. (1997). *As Nomadism Ends: The Israeli Bedouin of the Negev.* Boulder, CO: Westview Press.

———. (2005). "Bedouins, the Israeli state and insurgent planning: Globalization, localization or glocalization?" *Cities* 22(3):201–235.

———. (2006). *Economy and Land Among the Negev Bedouin: New Processes, New Insights.* Beersheba: Negev Center for Regional Development (Hebrew).

———. (2009). "Contemporary state discourse and historical pastoral spatiality: contradictions in the land conflict between the Israeli Bedouin and the state." *Ethnic and Racial Studies* 32(5):823–843 (Hebrew).

Negev Coexistence Forum for Civil Equality. (2003). "The unrecognized villages in the Negev update: 2003." Submission to the United Nations Committee on Economic, Social and Cultural Rights, 30th Session: Israel.

———. (2011). "Negev Coexistence Forum for Civil Equality." http://www.dukium.org (accessed November 16, 2011).

Neuwirth, R. (2005). *Shadow Cities: A Billion Squatters, a New Urban World.* London: Routledge.

Nevo, Y. (2003). "The politics of un-recognition: Bedouin villages in the Israeli Negev." *HAGAR International Social Science Review* 4(1–2):203–213.

Noach, H. (2009). *The Villages that Were, and Are: The Unrecognized Bedouin Villages in the Negev.* Tel-Aviv: Pardes Books.

Parizot, C. (2004). "Crossing and constructing borders within daily contact: Social and economic relations between the Bedouin in the Negev and their networks in Gaza, the West Bank and Jordan." Centre d'Economie Regionale, de L'emploi et des Firmes Internationales, http://halshs.archives-ouvertes.fr/halshs-00080661/en/ (accessed September 4, 2011).

Perera, N. (2009). "People's spaces: Familiarization, subject formation and emergent spaces in Colombo." *Planning Theory* 8(1):51–75.

Porat, H. (2009). *The Negev Bedouins: Between Nomadism and Urban-ization*. Beersheba: Negev Center for Regional Development (Hebrew).

Razin, E. (2000). *The Fiscal Capacity of the Bedouin Local Authorities in the Negev*. Beersheba: The Center for Bedouin Studies and Development and the Negev Center for Regional Development, Ben-Gurion University of the Negev.

Riseth, J. A. (2007). "An Indigenous perspective on national parks and Saami reindeer management in Norway." *Geographical Research* 45(2):204–211.

Roy, A. (2005). "Urban informality: Toward an epistemology of planning." *Journal of the American Planning Association* 71(2):147–158.

———. (2007). "The 21st century metropolis: New geographies of theory." *Regional Studies* 41:1–12.

———. (2009). "Strangely familiar: Planning and the worlds of insurgence and informality." *Planning Theory* 8(1):7–11.

Serhan, R. (2008). "Palestinian weddings: Inventing Palestine in New Jersey." *Journal of Palestine Studies* 37(4):21–37.

Shafir, G. (1989). *Land Labor and the Origins of the Israeli-Palestinian Conflict, 1882–1914*. Cambridge: Cambridge University Press.

———. (1996). "Zionism and colonialism: A comparative approach." In M. Barnett (ed.), *Israel in Comparative Perspective: Challenging the Conventional Wisdom* (pp. 227–244). Albany: SUNY Press.

Shamir, R. (1996). "Suspended in space: Bedouins under the law of Israel." *Law and Society Review* 30(2):231–257.

Smith, L. T. (1999). *Decolonizing Methodologies: Research and Indigenous Peoples*. London: Zed Books.

Soffer, A. (2007). "The Bedouins in Israel: Geographic aspects." *Ofakim Begeographia* 67–68:224–236 (Hebrew).

———. (2009). "The Negev and its strategic facilities will become neglected: Israel will withdraw to 'Tel-Aviv state.'" *Karkah* 66:17–23 (Hebrew).

Soffer, A., and Bar-Gal., Y. (1985). "Planned Bedouin settlement in Israel: A critique." *Geoforum* 16:423–451.

Stasiulis, D., and Yuval-Davis, N. (eds.). (1995). *Unsettling Settler Societies: Articulations of Gender, Race, Ethnicity and Class*. London: Sage.

Statistical Yearbook of the Negev Bedouin. (1999, 2011). Beersheba: The Center for Bedouin Studies and Development and the Negev Center for Regional Development, Ben-Gurion University of the Negev.

Stern, E., and Gradus, Y. (1979). "Socio cultural considerations in planning towns for nomads." *Ekistics* 277:224–230.

Swirski, S. (2008). "Transparent citizens: Israel government policy toward the Negev Bedouins." *HAGAR Studies in Culture, Polity and Identities* 8(2):25–45.

Swirski, S., and Hasson, Y. (2006). *Invisible Citizens: Israel Government Policy Toward the Negev Bedouin.* Tel Aviv: Adva Center.

Tarrow, N. (2008). "Human rights and education: The case of the Negev Bedouins." *HAGAR Studies in Culture, Polity and Identities* 8(2):137–158.

Tzfadia, E., and Katz, C. (eds.). (2010). *Abandoning State—Surveillancing State: Social Policy in Israel, 1985-2008.* Tel Aviv: Resling (Hebrew).

Walls, D. (2008). "Central Appalachia: Internal colony or internal periphery?" http://www.sonoma.edu/users/w/wallsd/internal-colony.shtml (accessed September 6, 2011).

Yiftachel, O. (1992). *Planning a Mixed Region: The Political Geography of Arab-Jewish Relations in the Galilee.* Aldershot: Ashgate.

———. (1996) "The internal frontier: The territorial control of ethnic minorities." *Regional Studies* 30(5):493–508.

———. (1997). "Nation-building or social fragmentation? Internal frontiers and group identities in Israel." *Space and Polity* 1(2):114–132.

———. (1999). "'Ethnocracy': The politics of Judaizing Israel/Palestine." *Constellation: An International Journal of Critical and Democratic Theory* 6:364–390.

———. (2003). "Bedouin-Arabs and the Israeli settler state: Land policies and indigenous resistance." In D. Champagne and I. Abu-Saad (eds.), *The Future of Indigenous Peoples: Strategies for Survival and Development* (pp. 21–47). Los Angeles: American Indian Studies Center, UCLA.

———. (2006). *Ethnocracy: Land and Identity Politics in Israel/Palestine.* Philadelphia: University of Pennsylvania Press.

———. (2008). "Epilogue: Studying Naqab/Negev Bedouins; Toward a colonial paradigm?" *HAGAR Studies in Culture, Polity and Identities* 8(2):83–108.

———. (2009a). "Critical theory and 'gray space': Mobilization of the colonized." *City* 13(2–3):240–256.

———. (2009b). "Theoretical notes on 'gray cities: The coming of urban apartheid?" *Planning Theory* 8(1):88–100.

Yiftachel, O., and Yacobi, H. (2004). "Control, resistance and informality: Jews and Bedouin-Arabs in the Beer-Sheva region." In N. Al-Sayyad and A. Roy (eds.), *Urban Informality in the Era of Globalization: A Transnational Perspective* (pp. 118–136). Boulder: Lexington Books.

Yonah, Y., Abu-Saad, I., and Kaplan, A. (2004). "De-Arabization of the Bedouin: A study of an inevitable failure." In A. Kemp, D. Newman, U. Ram, and O. Yiftachel (eds.), *Israelis in Conflict: Hegemonies, Identities, and Challenges* (pp. 65–80). Brighton, England: Sussex Academic Press.

Yuval-Davis, N., and Abdo, N. (1995). "Palestine, Israel and the Zionist settler project." In M. Stasiulis and N. Yuval-Davis (eds.), *Unsettling Settler Societies: Articulations of Gender, Race, Ethnicity and Class* (pp. 291–323). London: Sage.

Zandberg, H. (2009). "The conflict over the land ownership is not the main issue of the Bedouin in the Negev." *Karkah* 66:94–105 (Hebrew).

Zureik, E. (1979). *The Palestinians in Israel: A Study in Internal Colonialism.* London: Routledge.

NOTES

1. "Galilee" in English.
2. Declaration on the Rights of Indigenous Peoples, G.A. Res. 61/295, U.N. Doc. A/Res/61/295 (2007).
3. *Mabo & Ors. v. The State of Queensland* (No. 2) (Mabo) (1992) 66 AJLR 408.

AFTERWORD

A number of critical developments have occurred in the Naqab (Negev) Bedouin Arabs' struggle for land, housing, and recognition since the manuscript of this volume entered the production phase. Academic research and writing, by their very nature, cannot keep abreast of all ongoing developments. Therefore, we highlight in this afterword some of the major developments that have taken place between the completion of the chapters and going to press.

The most significant recent event was the Israeli government's adoption, on September 11, 2011, of the so-called Prawer-Amidror Plan, which is another attempt to establish a permanent land and settlement solution for the Bedouins. If fully implemented, the Prawer-Amidror Plan would lead to the partial or full dislocation of thirty-five unrecognized villages and their inhabitants, estimated at 70,000.[1] Further, a new Israeli police force is being established for the purpose of implementing the plan.[2] The Prawer-Amidror Plan has already triggered a strong public and legal struggle against its implementation. The Prawer-Amidror Plan has been strongly rejected by Bedouin Arab communities and their supporters, as they view the Plan's recommendations as unjust and unrealistic and as denying Bedouin history and land rights.

In contrast to the Prawer-Amidror Plan, the Regional Council for the Unrecognized Villages has recently prepared, with a coalition of organizations, a comprehensive alternative master zoning plan that demonstrates the possibility of legalizing the status of the unrecognized villages while limiting Bedouins' displacement and relocation to extreme cases only. This alternative plan has offered a path for the recognition and development of all Bedouin localities. It was prepared with the participation of the local community and has contributed to significant debate both within the community and between the Bedouins and the government.

In another important development, in March 2012, the Beersheba District Court dismissed the case of the Al-Ukbi tribe, which had attempted to register its lands in Al-Araqib; in its decision, the Court deemed the claimed land as state property. The Court's decision conforms to Israeli judicial precedents on *mawat* (dead) land, discussed in chapter 2 of this volume. While the Court's rejection of the case was nothing new—it was but one of many such rejections during the last decade—the *Al-Ukbi* case involved, for the first time in Bedouin history, a unique litigation team and strategy. The litigation team presented the most thorough and comprehensive legal, historical, and geographical account supporting the Naqab Bedouin Arabs' land rights. The submissions included new evidence, never before presented to Israeli courts on land disputes in the Naqab.

One of the editors of this book, Professor Oren Yiftachel, submitted an expert opinion supporting Al-Ukbi claims. Yiftachel presented comprehensive research that included the historical geography of the Naqab, the patterns of land cultivation and habitation, and the substantial autonomy that the Bedouins had enjoyed under the Ottoman and British governments, including the development of an autonomous indigenous property system. He also demonstrated that despite Israel's claim to legal continuity, the Israeli government has been distorting Ottoman and British legislation and its intent and implementation. He showed how the two previous regimes had respected Bedouin land rights, allowing Bedouins to sell and register their land at will.

On the state's side, Professor Ruth Kark, an expert who has frequently supported the government's position in courts, argued that the Bedouin Arabs were nomads until recently. She claimed that they did not cultivate the land and that neither the Ottoman nor British regimes had recognized their customary land rights.

The District Court's judgment ignored most of the new evidence on Bedouin history and the Bedouins' land system, preferring to rely on earlier Israeli precedents. It hence adopted Kark's expert opinion and reinforced the state's position that the Bedouins have been considered a nomadic group until only recently and that they previously had no intensive cultivation habits—and thus no land rights.

The Court's decision, though unsurprising, caused widespread disappointment because it was the first time that the Court heard the Bedouin position supported by new historical research and evidence. The *Al-Ukbi* decision has been appealed to the Supreme Court, where it currently awaits a decision.[3]

Outside the courtroom, several researchers began to question the notion of Bedouin indigeneity. Notable among these efforts were two articles published in 2012 co-authored by Professor Kark; Havatzelet Yahel, the head of the land unit in the Attorney General's Office in the Southern District, and responsible for leading the land claims against the Naqab Bedouins; and Dr. Seth Frantzman, a recent U.S. immigrant to Israel. Their articles vociferously challenge Bedouin claims of indigeneity and attempts to gain land, planning, and cultural rights.

Let us elaborate a bit on these claims: in their "Contested Indigeneity"[4] article, the authors attempt to study the emergence of the "sudden discourse" (and by implication "invented") of the Bedouins as indigenous to the Naqab, while in their "Fabricating Palestinian History"[5] article, the authors argue that the Naqab Bedouins are not an indigenous group. The authors advance several arguments to deny the Bedouins' indigenous status. They begin by shrinking Bedouin history in the region, claiming that most Bedouins arrived during the eighteenth century to an already existing legal regime and authority—namely, the Ottoman Empire—whose sovereignty they accepted.

Further, they argue that the Bedouins have changed their culture and lifestyle, and as such do not meet a central condition of indigeneity. Most importantly in their eyes is the Bedouins' demand for private (or family) land ownership, which differs from the claims of most indigenous groups, who typically aspire for collective land rights. The three authors also use a comparative lens to contend that the Bedouins' claim to indigeneity appears questionable, as no other Bedouin groups in neighboring Arab states demand such a status.

This is not the place to engage thoroughly with these claims, except to comment briefly on their questionable nature. First, indigenous status is dependent not on length of time but rather on occupation and establishment of complete society prior to the current regime. Furthermore, historical evidence shows that the Bedouins began to live in the Naqab hundreds of years before the eighteenth century. Second, indigenous peoples, like all societies, change their culture over time, including their land system. It is true that most indigenous groups around the world seek collective ownership of land and resources, but there are also several key cases of freehold title among indigenous groups, such as in Guatemala, Paraguay, and Australia. Indigeneity—that is, existence of a self-governing society prior to the current regime—does not require collective ownership under any accepted definition. Finally, the lack of indigenous claims in the Arab world chiefly derives from the fact that Bedouins in Arab states do not view the regime as colonial or foreign to them, and hence they do not utilize claims of indigeneity.

The chapters in this volume, as well as a growing body of convincing research, show that the Bedouin Arabs of the Naqab constitute a rather typical case of an indigenous group that has maintained a full self-governing society in the area for many generations prior to its oppression by modern regimes. Bedouin laws and traditions (including land ownership) reigned supreme in the area, with negligible external intervention for centuries, before the 1948 conflict and the subsequent Israeli policies of colonization, displacement, and resettlement fundamentally changed the space and society in the Naqab. It is noteworthy that both the Ottomans and British allowed traditional law to function in the region by sanctioning tribal courts and that the few attempts, mainly by the Ottomans, to subject the Bedouins to their rule encountered persistent resistance.

Kark, Yahel, and Frantzman's claims against the Bedouins' indigenous status appear to be related more to their active role in denying the Bedouins' land rights than to accurate historical research. At a broader level, however, the indigeneity argument touches on other dimensions of the Zionist-Palestinian conflict. The priority-of-time element in the indigeneity claim poses a challenge to the Zionist ideology of the exclusive Jewish historical right to Palestine (Land of Israel). In their conclusion to "Fabricating Palestinian History," the authors note that "[i]f anything, the Bedouin have more in common with the European settlers who migrated to other lands, coming into contact with existing populations with often unfortunate results for the latter [referring to alleged Bedouin attacks on *Fallahin*]."[6] Later in the article, their argument becomes even clearer when the authors describe self-claimed Jewish diaspora rights as superior to the rights of local residents, and as necessitating the denial of Bedouins' indigeneity:

> The Jews have always considered the Land of Israel their national homeland. . . . This spiritual relationship is also expressed in both Jewish daily prayers and Israel's Declaration of Independence. . . . [S]urely Jews can also raise a claim to be the indigenous people in Israel, a land which they called home thousands of years before the Negev Bedouin.[7]

The contestation over indigeneity has also moved beyond the courtroom and academic journals to the public and international arenas. A notable exchange recently took place between the Israeli government and the United Nations Special Rapporteur on the Rights of Indigenous Peoples, Professor James Anaya.

On February 1, 2011, the Special Rapporteur sent a communication to the Israeli government that included his own observations on the situation of the Naqab Bedouin Arabs, drawing the government's attention to the fact that its land rights denial and home demolitions violate international law. The Special Rapporteur received a response from the Israeli government in August 2011, which used claims similar to those of Kark, Yahel, and Frantzman to reject the classification of the Bedouin Arabs as indigenous peoples.

The government also argued that while the Bedouins have no legal rights to the land, the state is willing to go beyond the letter of the law and offer them compensation.[8] The following paragraphs from the Special Rapporteur's response to Israel are telling:

> 25. [T]he Special Rapporteur acknowledges the position of the State of Israel that it does not accept the classification of its Bedouin citizens as an indigenous people. . . . The Special Rapporteur notes, however, the longstanding presence of Bedouin people throughout a geographic region that includes Israel, and observes that in many respects, the Bedouin people share in the characteristics of indigenous peoples worldwide, including a connection to lands and the maintenance of cultural traditions that are distinct from those of majority populations. Further, the grievances of the Bedouin, stemming from their distinct cultural identities and their connection to their traditional lands, can be identified as representing the types of problems to which the international human rights regime related to indigenous peoples has been designed to respond.
> . . .
> 27. [T]he Special Rapporteur would like to respond to Israel's position that Bedouin people do not have customary rights to lands in the Negev given that the land laws of the State of Israel, as developed from the Ottoman and British laws that preceded them, do not recognize Bedouin custom as a source of private land rights. In the view of

the Special Rapporteur, such a position, which is based in colonial era laws and policies, should be reviewed. Far from providing a justification for the current failure to recognize indigenous peoples' land rights based on their customs, the historical denial of these rights and the dispossession of indigenous peoples from their traditional lands are acts that are now understood to be inconsistent with international human rights standards.[9]

It should also be noted that the use of indigeneity has also been contested, to a much lesser degree, by Arabs as well. Adopting the indigeneity approach, Dr. Mansour Nasasra has recently responded, in part, to Kark, Yahel, and Frantzman's argument against indigeneity, but he has also noted that some Bedouin leaders have expressed unease with the indigeneity approach.[10] In addition, interviews conducted by the team of the Harvard International Human Rights Clinic in 2007 stressed the Arab-Palestinian national identity and voiced reservations about the term "indigenous." Some interviewees pointed to the vulnerable and primitive characteristics associated with the term, with which they are reluctant to identify.

Further, in light of the exotic nature of scholarship and discourse around the Bedouins, it is easier to think of them alone—and not the rest of Palestinians—as indigenous, and thus reinforce the ethnic fragmentation of Palestinian society (Muslim, Christian, Bedouin, Druz, and Carcasians).[11] This exposes the danger of further de-nationalizing the Bedouins or de-indigenizing the Palestinians. In our view, these concerns are valid, but relate more to Israel's attempt to fragment the Palestinians, as well as internal socio-political tensions within the Palestinian society, than to the status of the Bedouins (as well as all other Palestinians) as an indigenous people overtaken and oppressed by a modern settler state.

Without a doubt, the recent development of the indigeneity discourse, its utilization in advocacy, and its contestation deserve a far more profound discussion. Yet, we contend that the different identities at play (e.g., Palestinian, Bedouin, Arab, and indigenous) should be seen not as mutually exclusive but rather as complementary and overlapping.

Another notable recent scholarly development has been the publication of a major research article by two editors of this book—Oren Yiftachel and Ahmad Amara—with Dr. Sandy Kedar. The article is the first of its kind to present a comprehensive challenge to the state's legal "Dead Negev Doctrine," which has classified Bedouin lands as *mawat* (i.e., "dead" land with no owners). The authors conducted a thorough interdisciplinary research and concluded that the historical geography and legal history of the Naqab do not justify the classification of large segments of land as *mawat*.[12]

The above are small snippets of the recent developments regarding Bedouin land, resources, settlement, and development. The growing body of research on these matters indeed illuminates the settler-indigenous nature of the conflict, which has revolved around issues similar to those of other settler-indigenous conflicts.

Together with these updates, our aim in this volume is to provide, for the first time, rich and systematic research on the struggles of the Naqab Bedouin Arabs through the lens of international indigenous peoples' struggles. We further wish to remind the readers that the reason for the development of an indigenous discourse and research has been the constant quest for indigenous justice—to which we hope this volume makes a worthy contribution.

Ahmad Amara, Ismael Abu-Saad, and Oren Yiftachel
New York and the Naqab

NOTES

1. Adalah. (n.d.). "The Prawer Plan." http://adalah.org/eng/?mod=articles&ID=1589 (accessed September 11, 2012).
2. Ibid.
3. Civil Appeal 7161/06, *Suleiman Al-Ukbi et al. v. The State of Israel*, March 15, 2012, Beersheba District Court. Full text available at http://www.law-pubshop.co.il/?CategoryID=266&ArticleID=6662 (in Hebrew).
4. Frantzman, S., Havatzelet, Y., and Kark, R. (2012). "Contested indigeneity: The development of an indigenous discourse on the Bedouin of the Negev." *Israeli Studies* 17(1):78–104.
5. Havatzelet, Y., Kark, R., and Frantzman, S. (2012). "Fabricating Palestinian history: Are the Negev Bedouin an indigenous people?" *Middle East Quarterly* 3–14.
6. Ibid. at 13–14.
7. Ibid. at 14.
8. Anaya, J. (2011). "Report of the Special Rapporteur on the rights of indigenous peoples." U.N. Doc. A/HRC/18/35/Add.1, annex VI; see para. 23 for a summary of the Israeli government's response.
9. Ibid., paras. 25, 27.
10. Nasasra, M. (2012). "The ongoing Judaisation of the Naqab and the struggle for recognising the indigenous rights of the Arab Bedouin people." *Settler Colonial Studies* 2(1):81–107, at 87, 88.
11. Jakubowska, L. (1992). "Resisting ethnicity: The Israeli state and Bedouin identity." In C.
Nordstrom and J. Martin (eds.), *The Path to Domination, Resistance and Terror* (pp. 85–105). Berkeley: University of California Press.
12. Yiftachel, O., Kedar, A., and Amara, A. (2012). "Re-examining the 'Dead Negev Doctrine': Property rights in the Bedouin- Arab space." *Mishpat Umimshal* 1(2):7–147 (Hebrew).

CONTRIBUTORS

ISMAEL ABU-SAAD is a professor of educational policy and administration in the Department of Education, founding director of the Center for Bedouin Studies and Development, and the holder of the Abraham Cutler Chair in Education at Ben-Gurion University of the Negev in Beersheba. His research interests include educational policy and development among indigenous peoples, Palestinian Arab education and higher education, social identity in heterogeneous societies, the impact of urbanization on the Naqab Bedouin Arabs, and organizational behavior in multicultural contexts. He has authored and edited over one hundred publications, including the books (co-edited with D. Champagne) *Indigenous Education and Empowerment: International Perspectives* (2006) and *The Future of Indigenous Peoples: Strategies for Survival and Development* (2003); and (co-authored with K. Abu-Saad and T. Horowitz) *Weaving Tradition and Modernity: Bedouin Women in Higher Education* (2011).

AHMAD AMARA is a PhD candidate in history and Hebrew and Judaic studies at New York University. Before pursuing his PhD degree, Amara served for three years as a clinical instructor and global advocacy fellow with Harvard Law School's Human Rights Program. His work at Harvard focused on social, cultural, and economic rights in the Middle East and on the Law of Occupation, and he has published a number of reports and articles in this area. Amara holds an LLB and LLM from Tel-Aviv University, where he also served as a teaching assistant and a coordinator of the Street Law Clinic Program at the Faculty of Law. He is a member of the Israeli Bar. In 2005, he completed a second master's degree in international human rights law at Essex University in the United Kingdom. In 2005, he co-founded a human rights organization, *Karama* (Arabic for "dignity"), in Nazareth, where he served as a senior staff attorney. Amara's current research focuses on the legal history of property law in Palestine, including Ottoman, British, and Israeli legislation.

DUANE CHAMPAGNE is a member of the Turtle Mountain Band of Chippewa from North Dakota. He is a professor of sociology and American Indian studies at UCLA and a member of the Faculty Advisory Committee for the UCLA Native Nations Law and Policy Center. He is also contributor of the education chapter for the United Nations Permanent Forum on Indigenous Issues' *State of the World's Indigenous Peoples Report*. Previously, Champagne was director of the UCLA American Indian Studies Center and editor of the *American Indian Culture and Research Journal*. He has written and edited numerous publications, including *Social Change and Cultural Continuity Among Native Nations* (2007); *Notes From the Center of Turtle Island* (2010); and *Captured Justice: Native Nations and Public Law 280* (2012). Champagne's research and writings focus on issues of social and cultural change in both historical and contemporary Native American communities; the study of justice institutions in contemporary American Indian reservations, including policing, courts, and incarceration; and policy analysis of cultural, economic, and political issues in contemporary Indian country.

COSETTE CREAMER is a PhD candidate in the Department of Government at Harvard University. She also holds a JD from Harvard Law School and is a member of the Massachusetts Bar Association. Her research and teaching interests include methods of human rights research, the politics of international law and institutional design, comparative criminal law and procedure, comparative judicial politics, and police practices.

NOA KRAM is a PhD candidate in the Social and Cultural Anthropology program at the California Institute of Integral Studies (CIIS). The program combines critical social thought with advocacy, while prioritizing education for social justice. Her research employs post-colonial and feminist theories in the context of nationalism and indigenous peoples' rights in Israel. In her dissertation research, she uses the lenses of law, history, advocacy, and anthropology to examine the Naqab Bedouins' struggles for land rights based on their customary practices of land ownership. Kram holds an MA in cultural anthropology and social transformation from CIIS and a law degree from the Hebrew University of Jerusalem. She has worked as a criminal attorney in Israel and as a lecturer and coordinator of the preparatory academic program for Bedouin students at an Arab community college in Beersheba.

RASHIDA MANJOO is a part-time professor in the Department of Public Law in the University of Cape Town and is the United Nations Special Rapporteur on Violence against Women. Formerly, she was parliamentary commissioner of the Commission on Gender Equality (CGE) in South Africa, a constitutional body mandated to oversee the promotion and protection of gender equality. Prior to being appointed to the CGE, she was involved in social-context training for judges and lawyers, designing both content and methodology during her time at the Law, Race, and Gender Research Unit, University of Cape Town, and at the University of Natal, Durban. Manjoo has held numerous visiting professorships, including most recently at the University of Virginia. She served as the Des Lee Distinguished Visiting Professor at

Webster University, where she taught courses in human rights, with a particular focus on women's human rights and transitional justice. She was the Eleanor Roosevelt Fellow with the Human Rights Program at Harvard Law School (2006–2007) and also a clinical instructor in the program (2005–2006).

ZINAIDA MILLER is currently a PhD candidate in international relations at the Fletcher School, Tufts University. She holds a JD from Harvard Law School. Previously, she was a visiting fellow in international studies at the Watson Institute at Brown University and recipient of a Harvard University Sheldon Fellowship to support research in Israel and the Occupied Palestinian Territories. She has served as a consultant to the International Human Rights Clinic of Harvard Law School and has published in journals, including the *International Journal of Transitional Justice* and *Harvard Human Rights Journal*. Her research interests include critical examinations of human rights, transitional justice, political transition and democratization, and the politics of humanitarian aid.

JOHN SHEEHAN is a leading Australian property theorist and expert on compensation assessment arising from compulsory acquisition of native title in Australia. He is deputy director of the Asia Pacific Centre for Complex Real Property Rights, and adjunct professor at the University of Technology, Sydney. He is a former acting commissioner with the Land and Environment Court of New South Wales, and previously a member of the Aboriginal and Torres Strait Islander Land Tribunal of Queensland. He is also a life fellow of the Australian Property Institute. In November 2010, Sheehan was one of the invited members of the expert meeting "Land Tenure Issues and Requirements for Implementing Climate Change Mitigation Policies in the Forestry and Agriculture Sectors" convened in Rome by the Food and Agriculture

Organization of the United Nations. The report of the meeting, which focused on traditional and customary tenures, was submitted to inform the subsequent Cancun Conference.

RODOLFO STAVENHAGEN is professor emeritus of sociology at El Colegio de México and former United Nations Special Rapporteur on the Rights of Indigenous Peoples. Previously, he was assistant director general for social sciences and their applications at UNESCO. In Mexico, he founded the Mexican Academy of Human Rights. In 1997, the Mexican government awarded Stavenhagen the National Prize of Sciences and Arts. He has been a visiting professor at the universities of Chicago, Harvard, and Stanford. His research interests include social development, agrarian problems, ethnic conflicts, indigenous peoples, and human rights. His books in English include *Making the Declaration Work: The United Nations Declaration on the Rights of Indigenous Peoples* (2010); *Ethnic Conflicts and the Nation-State* (1996); *The Ethnic Question: Development, Conflict and Human Rights* (1990); and *Between Underdevelopment and Revolution: Essays on Latin America* (1980).

OREN YIFTACHEL teaches urban studies and political geography at Ben-Gurion University (BGU) of the Negev in Beersheba. His research focuses on critical understandings of the relations between space, power, and conflict, with particular attention to ethnic, social, and urban aspects of these relations. He has published numerous articles and books, including *Planning as Control: Policy and Resistance in Divided Societies* (1995) and *Ethnocracy: Land and Identity Politics in Israel/Palestine* (2006). At BGU, Yiftachel has held a range of positions, including head of department (1999–2003), head of faculty research committee (2003–2005), and head of senate conference committee (2005–2007). He founded and has chaired the new master's program in urban and regional planning in the Geography Department. Yiftachel was also the founding editor of BGU's journal *HAGAR Studies in Culture, Polity and Identities*. He has taught as a guest professor at a number of universities, including Melbourne, Curtin, Columbia, Penn, Berkeley, Venezia, Calcutta, and Cape Town. Yiftachel has worked as an urban planner and activist for a range of human rights and social organizations, including the Regional Council for the Unrecognized Villages and B'Tselem.